Sword of Rome
The Complete Campaigns

Omnibus of the Best-selling Historical Series

Richard Foreman

First published 2013 by Endeavour Press Ltd.

This edition published 2014 by Endeavour Press Ltd.

Sword of Rome: The Standard Bearer

1.

The boats drew closer to the white cliffs. Sunlight glinted off a myriad of swords, breastplates and helmets. Spray from the turquoise channel blew up into his face, but sweat more than seawater moistened Lucius Oppius' palms as he gripped the Tenth Legion's eagle. His eyes were as blue and cold as the Mediterranean. His friend Roscius had commented, half jokingly and half in earnest, how Oppius would have been considered handsome – if he ever bothered to smile. A grim expression again carved itself into the soldier's face as he gazed up at the jeering barbarians, their bodies smeared with woad, upon the cliff tops. Even the most cowardly of tribes in Gaul would fancy its chances from such advantageous ground, Oppius mused. The sound of their jeers was occasionally accompanied by the high pitched swish of an arrow, as the odd archer tried his luck. Invariably the missile would zip harmlessly into the sea, or at best a thud could be heard as it struck a Roman scutum or the hull of a ship.

Oppius turned his gaze towards the lead trireme where his general, Caesar, stood at the prow. Did the standard bearer notice the hint of a wry smile on his commander's face? Caesar had encountered such defiance before. Many had rolled the dice against Caesar and the Tenth, but in the end the Venus throw always came up and Rome was victorious. His red cloak blew in the wind.

Caesar was still handsome, whether he smiled or not. His hairline had been retreating of late more than the armies of Gaul but his body was still taut with muscle, his face clean-shaven. His eyes took in everything, yet often remained unreadable. Although brave, Caesar was not foolhardy, Oppius thought. Should he choose to attack now then the legions – the Seventh and Tenth – would be slain from a barrage of missiles before the boats could even reach the beach.

"If their blood lust is anything like their lust for alcohol then we could be in trouble," the standard bearer heard a legionary mutter behind him, only partly as a joke.

"The one often fuels the other." The knowing reply came from a man that the legion nicknamed Teucer, for his skill with a bow. The wiry, pale-faced soldier was a Briton, who had left his homeland and travelled to Gaul. Most Britons were recruited by Rome's enemies on the continent but Teucer had chosen to fight for the Republic. Caesar himself had witnessed his abilities with a bow and bent the rules to promote him to the Tenth. Oppius liked the Briton – and not just because he had saved his life in battle on more than one occasion. He was amiable and intelligent, picking up Latin as quickly as he picked up the legionary's black sense of humour. Oppius briefly wondered how his comrade was now feeling, as he journeyed towards invading his homeland. What was it like, to view your countryman as your enemy? Oppius hoped that he would never have to find out.

The standard bearer was far from the only Roman to focus his attention upon the figure of Caesar as the trireme's captain approached his commander. Many of the newer recruits thought, hoped, that Caesar would point to the captain to sail back to Gaul. Yet Oppius had faith in his General that he would give the order for the fleet to sail onwards, along the coast, and discover another landing site. Indeed Oppius had more faith in Caesar than he did the Gods – and sure enough he observed his commander nod his head in the direction of Britain rather than Gaul. Onwards.

Not even the gods could stop Caesar when he set his mind towards something.

2.

The previous night.

Through the flames and smoke of the campfire, through the blackest of evenings, through a sea of bobbing heads, Oppius could still see the precious, gleaming head of the legion's silver eagle. The eagle nested in the sacellum, a sacred shrine dedicated to the standard. Even in the safety of the Roman encampment the standard bearer tried to keep an eye on the semi-divine totem. Oppius was one of the youngest ever legionaries to be awarded the honour of serving as an aquilifer – a standard bearer. Lucius sometimes missed being in the thick of the fighting however, owing his duty to protecting the standard rather than fighting alongside his friends and comrades. Although the eagle had tasted blood a couple of times recently when an enemy had been a glory-hunter, or just plain mad. Gore had smeared the eagle's beak and talons as the aquilifer had fought off the barbarians. Oppius was honour bound to sacrifice his life rather than the standard.

His attention was taken away from the shrine when Teucer handed him a plate, with a charred piece of venison on it. Oppius drained half his cup of wine and poured the remainder over his plate, to soften and moisten the meat. At the same time however he watched Roscius down his cup in one and quickly refill it.

"You should pace yourself Roscius. We have a long day ahead tomorrow. You don't want to spend the voyage forever emptying your guts over the side of the boat," Teucer remarked, full-knowing how his warning would probably fall on deaf ears. As their general often exclaimed that "Caesar must be Caesar", so too Roscius was Roscius, a drinking and killing machine.

"If I am ill tomorrow or go weak at the knees, it'll be due to sea sickness rather than any hangover," the hulking legionary replied, wine dribbling down his stubbled chin. "If man was meant for the sea, the gods would have given us gills."

"I remember the last time when you went weak at the knees, when you fell for that whore in Massilia," the Briton remarked, smiling and taking a swig of watered down acetum from his own cup.

"Aye, I nearly lost my heart to that girl. I also nearly lost a more important part of my body, due to the itch she gave me," Roscius replied, laughing at his own joke.

"So what is Britain like Teucer?" Marcus Fabius asked, when the laughter had died down. Marcus Fabius was a teenager, a new recruit. He was the son of a merchant who had once been Oppius' centurion, when the standard bearer was a raw recruit himself. The elder Fabius had asked Oppius to keep an eye on his son. The youth's ambition was to be a poet but the father had entered the son into military service. "I want to put some steel into his soul. I just don't want some Gaul putting some steel between his ribs." Combat had yet to scar his body or war ravage his features and innocence. "The enemy won't know whether to fuck you or fight you lad," Roscius had commented on first being introduced to the sensitive looking adolescent.

"There are parts of my homeland that are green and lush but that's mainly because it rains so much. The people can be friendly, especially when they've had a drink or two. Yet my people can also be violent, especially when they've drunk too much. The tribes are forever squabbling between themselves, although our imminent invasion might just unite the usually fractious tribal leaders. Caesar must aim to divide and conquer. He also needs to avoid a pitched battle on open ground, as the enemy archers and charioteers might pick us off in a piecemeal fashion," Teucer posited, picking at his venison in an equally piecemeal fashion.

"And what of your people? What are they like?" Fabius asked, his eyes filled with curiosity, although his heart was somewhat filled with fear in regards to the strange barbarian race.

"My people can be proud, rapacious, ignorant, brave and noble – in short, they are much like everyone else Marcus."

"But will you consider them just like everyone else when you pull back your bowstring tomorrow and they're in your line of sight?" Roscius gruffly asked.

"No, but I'll still know which side I'm on, don't worry about that Roscius. A Briton will still receive an arrow in his front, as opposed to a Roman receiving one in his back. In fighting for Rome though, I believe I will also be fighting for my homeland and its people still. I have little doubt that Rome will subdue

Britain eventually – and unfortunately that subjugation may well be bloody, as our experiences in Gaul have proved. But it also may be a price worth paying. Rome will tax Britain and mine it for its tin and take a share of the harvest, but in return we will receive laws, security, increased commerce and advances in the arts and sciences. Tin and corn are a fair trade for a more civilised society."

His voice was clear and confident but Oppius couldn't help but notice how the Briton appeared troubled, or pained, as he spoke.

3.

It was Caesar's turn to look troubled and pained as he stood at the prow of his trireme again and assessed the situation. The bulk of the barbarian force, led by its cavalry, had tracked his fleet along the coast and was marshalling itself around the beach where he was intending to land his own army. Caesar had given the orders for his ships containing his archers and artillery to anchor at both ends of the beach, in order to flank the enemy and provide covering fire. Word was passed around that the legions should ready themselves for the attack. Yet whereas on land the soldiers would have commenced to snarl, jeer and thump their shields Caesar witnessed a sea of hesitant faces. He was worried too, about the depth of the water and the strength of his enemy. He could lose as many men to drowning as he could to British spears. Yet the time to attack was now. Caesar would not be Caesar if he suffered defeat or a retreat, the proconsul judged.

Oppius winced slightly at the brightness of the searing blue sky. Perhaps the Gods had dispelled the clouds in order to get a better view of the imminent, bloody spectacle he fancied. The legionaries looked at each other, with blank rather than eager expressions. Even Fabius' glowing olive skin had lost a little of its colour. The boats had still to brush against the seabed beneath them. Enemy archers had assembled towards the rear of the beach. The shields of the soldiers in the transport vessels nearest to them began to look like pin cushions. The sea breeze whistled around their ears. Although the sun blazed down over them the wailing sound still sent chills down spines. Even Roscius appeared apprehensive.

Caesar had crossed the channel. The die was cast. He could not go back. His pride would not allow him to. Caesar could not suffer the ignominy of failure. Even in victory Cato and other backward-looking members of the Senate had criticised him. Yet he could not move forward without his legions. If he was on land he could give a rousing speech and direct his officers and troops with purpose. Battles often rage like fires but every fire needs a spark, Caesar thought. He drew his sword, hoping that the action would somehow serve as an inspiration or signal.

The light reflected off the commander's sword, into the standard bearer's eyes. Lucius Oppius was the son of a soldier. His father had intended to work out his service in the army and gain a plot of land that he could call his own. The veteran legionary ultimately craved peace. Yet the son craved promotion over peace. Perhaps it was the voice of his dead father, Gnaeus Oppius, whispering in his ear now. Lucius had heard stories from veterans about how his father would lead from the front when he had served under Marius, Caesar's uncle. Or were the gods now whispering in his ears? As when a barbarian would look to capture a Roman eagle, were madness and vain-glory taking possession of his soul?

"Once we're on that beach, we'll soon bring peace to this barbarous land," Roscius exclaimed, trying to convince himself of his argument as much as others.

"If you want peace, prepare for war," Fabius replied, almost in a whisper, quoting one of the writers that the would-be poet was so fond of.

Yet Oppius barely heard the youth's words, as he prepared to make his leap of faith.

4.

Brine rather than sweat drenched his entire body as Oppius rose up from out of the sea, having leapt over the rail of the transport vessel. The silver eagle of the standard broke forth first from out of the foaming water, the sunlight glinting off its head and reflecting into the eyes of Caesar.

Before he had jumped into the water Oppius had offered up the legionary's prayer,

"Jupiter Greatest and Best, protect this legion, soldiers every one. May my act bring good fortune to us all."

Witnessing the act of a madman - and eyeing the prize - a brace of enemy cavalry broke off and charged towards the isolated standard bearer. The first horseman screamed wildly and raised his axe, ready to bring its flesh-stained head down upon the Roman's shoulder and chest – yet instinct and timing kicked in as Oppius drove the standard upwards and into the torso of his enemy, knocking him off his coal-black mare. But where was the second horseman? Spray misted up in front of Oppius and stung his eyes. The second Briton was less obliging in offering up a war cry up to reveal his position, as he came at the Roman from the side. His sword edge was a foot or so from his enemy's head – but it travelled no further as a Roman pilum sang through the air and skewered his stomach. Blood turned the blue dye purple.

"And there you were thinking that you could defeat the bastards all by yourself," Roscius shouted and grinned. The brutal looking legionary had jumped into the water shortly after the standard bearer. He would have followed his friend into Hades, for he knew Oppius would do the same for him. Teucer and – more hesitantly – Marcus Fabius followed their comrades into the sea. The legion was shocked and irate at witnessing such a suicidal act. But as they witnessed another dozen or so horsemen ride towards the eagle they scrambled into the sea too and rallied around the valiant, or unhinged, standard bearer. The loss of the eagle would mean a loss of honour for all and the stain could never be washed away. Far more than Rome, the Tenth Legion fought for the Tenth Legion.

At first Caesar cursed his aquilifer for such a rash act but his mouth, twisted in rage, soon formed itself into a smile. He had his spark. Now he needed to fuel the flames. Caesar immediately gave the order for his archers and artillery to provide covering fire. He also called for the captain of his own ship to close in on the beach. Caesar was keen to wash his sword in the blood of the irksome barbarians too.

Individual splashes swiftly turned into one long whooshing tumult as the Seventh, not wishing for the Tenth to shame them or take all the glory, disembarked from their transports too. The legions formed themselves into make-shift shield walls and moved forward, some chest deep in the sea, their pilums held aloft to defend against the enemy's cavalry. For all of their bravery and numbers the barbarian army could not prevent the Romans from driving forward and making it onto the beach.

Rome had landed upon Britain.

5.

The tang of blood and brine filled the air. The turquoise sea was streaked with gore. The clash of arms and blood-curdling screams drowned out the sound of the sea breeze. The Tenth had landed on the beach, but it had not captured it.

"Teucer, climb on top of that rock there and start loosening some arrows into some of these bastards," Oppius exclaimed whilst surveying the field of battle. The Tenth had landed upon the right side of the beach and across to the left the Seventh were taking casualties, but advancing nevertheless. Their enemy was fighting ferociously but they were ill disciplined. Their light armour and weaponry made them agile but the legions were used to fighting against similar foes in Gaul (albeit the Britons seemed to have more spirit, perhaps fuelled by more wine). The standard bearer noticed an island of resistance forming at the back of the beach - centred around a giant Briton who appeared to be wielding a huge hammer. He was swotting away legionaries like flies, with shields buckling under the weight of his heavy blows.

"Roscius, bring down that fat bastard with the hammer. He's boring me."

Roscius made his way towards the heart of the fighting, whilst Oppius was heartened to see how a group of Roman infantry had formed a square at the other end of the beach. A line of shields surrounded a group of legionaries, who were unleashing their pilums into a mass of enemy cavalry.

"What would you like me to do sir?" Fabius asked, trying to dispel the fear from his voice and features.

"Just stay close to me lad and try not to get yourself killed."

Roscius assessed his enemy as he marched purposefully towards him. The savage brute was strong, but overweight and predictable. A half a dozen men from the Seventh formed a semi-circle around the barbarian, but they were wary of closing in having witnessed their comrades fail to bring the giant down.

"Hey, shithead, why don't you pick on somebody your own size?" Roscius announced, whilst throwing down his shield. The scutum would be an encumbrance for what the legionary had planned.

The wild-eyed Briton stood even taller and wider than Roscius, a mix of flab and muscle. Blood – that of his foes rather than his own – flecked his face. He growled and ran towards the Roman, lifting the fearsome hammer above his head. Roscius moved just in time however and the large iron head of the mallet thudded into the sand, at which point the legionary swiftly lifted his foot up and brought it down upon the shaft of the weapon, splitting it in two. The Briton, his face twisted in even greater rage, swung what was left of the shaft at Roscius' head but the Roman swung his sword in return and the gladius truncated the oak shaft even further. The blade of the sword met the barbarian's fist too when he then swung a punch. His blood flecked the legionary's face and he howled in pain – before the savage fell to his knees and Roscius buried the gladius in his chest.

"Never send the Seventh in to do a job that only the Tenth can do," Roscius declared with relish at the end.

Oppius glanced across the beach and nodded in approval at Rocius having defeated the troublesome barbarian. He was also pleased to see that his friend had come through the fight uninjured. The standard bearer again surveyed the battlefield. The tide was turning Rome's way. The Britons were retreating as reinforcements now landed on the beach without opposition. Caesar himself was leading a cohort from the front and spurring his men on. The standard bearer ordered Teucer to try to bring down a couple of the cavalry horses who were escaping up a narrow track that led up to the top of the cliffs. Should he fell the animals then they would hinder the retreat of the rest of the cavalry and infantry retreating up the path. A number of enemy archers and peltists still lined the tops of the cliffs and covered the retreating forces however.

One such archer drew back his bow, with the standard bearer in his sights. The Briton had watched both his courageous leap into the water and his marshalling of legionaries as they arrived on the beach. Both had been crucial to the imminent victory. At least he would stop the standard bearer invading Briton. His arms bulged with muscle as he drew the bow back, yet despite the tension in the string his body remained calm, composed. He took a deep breath and then released the arrow. His skill and technique as an archer were not dissimilar to Teucer's.

Oppius remained blindsided and did not notice the missile whistling down from above, aiming straight for his chest. The force of the arrow was such that it would pierce through his breast plate – but yet it only went so far as to pierce through Marcus Fabius' shield. The youth had seen the arrow and, positioned just next to Oppius, had reacted with speed and bravery to move his scutum aloft and across in time.

Both Oppius and Fabius looked up at the cliffs to see where the arrow had come from. The would-be assassin wore a scowl across his face and pointed down at the standard bearer – and then drew a line along his neck. The Briton also wore a number of bronze bangles and an elaborate necklace to signify his importance. Before Oppius could scrutinize the savage more he spat out an indecipherable curse, turned away and disappeared.

"It seems that that you've made an enemy already. At least it's unlikely that you slept with his wife. But he was keen on killing you it seemed," Roscius exclaimed, walking towards his friend.

"If that's the case then the bastard can get in the queue. Now I suppose I better thank you lad for saving my life. I owe you one. Let this be a lesson to you though. The shield is mightier than the pen. I for one am glad your father wants you to be a soldier rather than poet."

Marcus Fabius smiled, but blushed too. He was pleased that he had earned the standard bearer's respect.

"I'm wondering if I should join that queue," a stern voice issued from behind the standard bearer. Oppius turned to see Caesar standing before him, his face unreadable. Lucius had hoped that Caesar would have witnessed his bravery earlier, but his actions in putting the eagle at risk could as easily meet with punishment as opposed to a reward. The legionary stood to attention before his general, unable to look him in the eye, awaiting his fate.

"After your actions today I cannot now have you serve as a standard bearer to the legion."

Oppius' heart sank, in unison with his face dropping. He felt too sorrowful, ashamed, to feel anger.

"No, your actions today have left me with no other choice but to promote you to the rank of centurion," Caesar exclaimed, his marble features breaking out into a smile. Caesar then approached Oppius and warmly clasped him on the shoulder.

"Now stand at ease. I should be saluting you. I'm still undecided as to whether you're mad, or just lucky, but I'd like you to join me for dinner this evening so I can finally make up my mind."

6.

Oppius dressed himself, to the sound in the background of the legions felling trees and constructing the walls of the army's camp. Caesar had defeated the enemy but due to the absence of cavalry he could not rout them after forcing them off the beach. The legions would need to fortify themselves against a counter-attack. The newly promoted officer had ordered Fabius to wash his best tunic – and he permitted himself a smile after thinking that it was the first order he had ever given to someone as a centurion. Oppius had also shaved and polished every piece of metal he had on display. He was perhaps more nervous about meeting Caesar for dinner than he had been before any battle.

"I knew his father Joseph," Caesar remarked to his manservant, a wizened Jew who had been part of the Julii household since before his birth. Although Joseph spent most of his time in Rome, Caesar would occasionally have the cynical and dry-witted servant attend him on campaign. "Gneaus Oppius. I remember Marius once saying that he was worth two cohorts."

Joseph, who was just finishing up from shaving his master and rubbing oils into his skin, thought to himself how it was unlikely that Marius paid him the wages of two cohorts.

"Sulla once said about Caesar that he saw many a Marius in me. I am hoping that similarly there is many a Gneaus Oppius within his son. I could use a man like that Joseph. But I fear I may be boring you with military matters my old friend. Tell me, what do you think of Britain?"

"I'm not sure I'm the best person to ask. All I've seen of it so far is a beach full of corpses and a forest at night. I'm hopeful the sights will improve though. I confess that I prefer Rome. For one thing it rains less. From what I'm told, everywhere rains less than here. I also miss my wife - although I'm sure that I'll be cured of any fondness I'm feeling for her once I see her again."

Caesar smiled. He always enjoyed his conversations with his manservant. From an early age Joseph had used humour to temper his master's seriousness, or he would become serious whenever Caesar grew too flippant.

"I was confident that you'd somehow find a way to contain your excitement about the campaign Joseph. But we are close to the edge of the map here, writing a new chapter in the history of Rome," Caesar remarked whilst checking his hair and how his tunic hung in the large silver mirror his manservant placed before him.

"Just make sure that your obituary's not a footnote in that history," the Jew replied, unable to hide the worry and affection he carried for his master. He had neither been blind to his flaws nor greatness since an early age.

"Would you miss me then Joseph, as much as your wife?" Caesar replied, touched and amused slightly by the sage old man's rare show of emotion.

"There are times when I miss my bouts of indigestion more than my wife sir, if that's anything to go by. No, I'm more concerned about being too old to break in a new master," Joseph replied, allowing himself a flicker of a smile as he packed away his jars of aromatic oils.

Caesar let out a laugh.

"Some people might say I give you too much licence Joseph."

"Ignore such people sir. Clemency is a fine virtue, especially when displayed towards someone who holds a razor to your throat each day."

"You are as wise as your people's Solomon Joseph."

"But not as rich, unfortunately."

"You wouldn't know how to spend such wealth if you had it."

"No, but my wife would."

Again Caesar laughed and again a flicker of a smile could be seen on the wrinkled, good-natured face of his old servant. Partly, he was pleased to have cheered his master up. When he had first entered his quarters that evening Joseph had witnessed Caesar anxiously reading and replying to correspondence. Caesar had looked like he was about to fall off the edge of the map.

7.

Lucius Oppius' nerves increased when he realised that he would be dining with Caesar alone. The soldier was far more comfortable holding a gladius than a conversation. He awkwardly stood before his commander. Rain splattered down upon the roof of the tent. Numerous lamps gave the room – for all intents and purposes a triclinium, given its furnishings – a homely glow. Some hours ago Caesar had looked every inch a general. Now, clad in a gleaming white tunic bordered with purple, Caesar appeared every inch an aristocrat. Fine wines and exotic foods adorned the table. Oppius also recalled once seeing Caesar in Rome at the Forum, every inch the statesman, dressed in a white toga, also bordered with purple. Despite his age, Caesar looked as fit and virile as any young officer. Oppius could smell a woman's perfume lingering in the air and he thought about his commander's reputation as a lover. Many a woman would just lie back, close her eyes and think of Rome when with most statesmen, but not with Caesar. He acted as if he were still in his prime – and perhaps he was, Oppius mused.

Caesar welcomed the centurion and clasped his forearm in a Roman handshake.

"Firstly – and most importantly perhaps – let's get you a drink. I'm going to insist that you try the Falernian. You'll thank me for it," Caesar remarked, nodding to an attendant to pour a cup of the vintage.

The wine and Caesar's gregarious manner soon helped Oppius relax and the centurion was flattered to be asked his opinion about various matters of soldiering. Caesar again thanked his newly promoted officer for his actions that day too.

"You captured my respect and loyalty today Oppius, as well as that beach. You have earned my gratitude – and a promotion. Your father was a standard bearer too, no? He would be proud of you."

Oppius was shocked and intrigued to hear Caesar mention his father. It seemed that it was only after his death that Oppius had started to get to know him, from stories from other legionaries. His father had spent little time at home when Oppius was young. He had resented back then how his father had devoted more time to the legion than to his own wife and son. Yet now he understood just how much the legion was its own family too, often full of orphans.

"I met and knew your father a little. I was even there, with my uncle, on the day that he died in the arena. He fought bravely, like a lion. Unfortunately his combatant was a snake."

Gneaus Oppius had died during a gladiatorial contest with a soldier from the Ninth Legion. The duel was meant merely to be a display of arms between two champions, to fight for the honour of their legions. Yet rumour had it that Gneaus' opponent had baited his sword with poison. What seemed like a minor flesh wound at the time ultimately proved fatal.

"If you are just half the soldier that your father was Lucius, then you'll be twice as great a soldier as most."

Oppius was at a loss as to how to respond. Should he feel like he should live in the shadow of his father, or have him serve as an example of the kind of soldier he should be? Perhaps witnessing his guest's awkwardness Caesar changed the subject.

"There has been plenty of conjecture, both back in Rome and among the men too I warrant, as to why I have come to this island. It's certainly not for the women. I did acquaint myself with one of them however whilst in Gaul. She only spoke her native language but I considered that a blessing. Most women, like children, should be seen and not heard. But back to the matter. Some have judged that I have travelled to Britain in order to mine its tin and assess the rest of its natural wealth. Or – and in Cato's eyes especially I dare say – I have invaded this land merely to satisfy my vanity and a lust for glory. Or I am here because of my love of pearls. Some have said that this is all a propaganda exercise, to furnish me with some colourful anecdotes for after dinner speaking. There is a grain or two of truth to all of these theories Lucius, but what I'd like to talk to you about is another reason why I have landed on this sodden isle."

Caesar here leaned forward a little whist couched on a sofa, as Oppius involuntary did so too - drawn in by his commander's magnetism.

8.

"Several months ago I received intelligence that one of our very own countrymen had landed on these shores, charged with the task to recruit warriors to aid Gaul in the fight against our forces. Someone in Rome is conspiring against me. I do not lack enemies, nor am I averse to making more of them if needs be. The report went on to say that the agent possessed a knowledge of the language and a chest filled with gold. As you may have realised the number of Britons fighting in Gaul has increased over the past six months Lucius. This man is proving to be a thorn in our side."

The charm and warmth went out of Caesar's aspect as he spoke about the agent. His eyes were narrowed in scorn, his voice cold. Oppius could not help but despise the treacherous agent too, in sympathy.

"The latest intelligence from my own agents suggests that he is recruiting among the tribes and villages in Kent, a region not far from here. You are familiar with the British archer in our ranks?"

"Yes," Oppius replied, with a part of him now wishing that he didn't know the man. For the centurion could sense what lay on the horizon.

"And he is familiar with this area and that of Kent I believe. Do you trust him?"

"Yes," Oppius again replied, cursing his own honesty and Teucer's trustworthiness. Every "yes" was like a nail in his own coffin, he fleetingly thought.

The rain thrummed over the roof of the tent even louder and thunder rumbled in the distance. Bowls of squid, mushrooms, quail eggs and honey-glazed slices of pork lay before him but Oppius no longer felt hungry.

"Britain is far too hostile at present for me to send a cohort out to track down this recruiting officer. No, less will prove more. Two men will prove far more efficient than two hundred for the job ahead. I mentioned earlier Lucius how I couldn't quite figure out if you were mad or lucky. Well I am now asking you to be mad and lucky. Mad enough to accept this mission, not that you have much choice in the matter unfortunately. And I also want you to be lucky enough to complete it," Caesar remarked, popping an olive into his mouth and smiling, as if amused by the shock that he had just inspired in his centurion.

"And should I locate the agent," Oppius remarked.

"Ideally I would like you to capture the rogue and bring him back to me, but failing that – kill him," Caesar replied, whilst grinning in an altogether different manner. "You have my blessing to torture him too, in order to extract the names of his employers out of him."

Oppius finished the remainder of his blood-red wine. The falernian was a world away from the watered-down acetum he was used to drinking. Perhaps Caesar had opened the vintage as he suspected that it would be the soldier's last good meal. Oppius thought how his father was considered a legend within the legion. He would now be making history too, Lucius grimly joked to himself, as the shortest ever serving officer with the legion. Promoted one day, killed the next.

9.

After listening to Caesar run through some finer points of the mission the centurion was finally dismissed, with the general insisting that he take the remaining food and wine from the table and distribute it among his unit. The rain abated not as Oppius made his way from Caesar's tent back to his own. Yet getting wet was the least of the soldier's problems. Never mind the rain, life was shitting upon him, he judged. He recalled one of Caesar's last comments. Either he should return having completed his mission – or not bother returning at all. Caesar could display both warmth and a steely coldness within the space of a sentence.

Rather than try to soften the blow for Teucer by giving him a measure or two of Falernian first Oppius recounted his meeting – and disclosed their imminent mission – as soon as he returned.

"With friends like you, who needs enemies?" the archer exclaimed, filling the air with curses – in Latin and his native tongue. "It's a suicide mission, at best. Can we not somehow get out of it?"

"Caesar's not one to take no for an answer," Oppius replied, shaking his head. The centurion recalled how his co-consul, Bibulus, once tried to defy Caesar during their term in office. Caesar bullied and humiliated his colleague to such an extent - at one point even stooping to dump excrement over his fellow consul

- that Bibulus remained in his house for the rest of the year. The people had called it "the consulship of Julius and Caesar", such was his dominance and will at getting his own way.

"And he wants just the two of you to head into enemy territory and find this agent?" Roscius asked. Part of him felt relief at being excluded, but part of him felt uneasy at not being able to be there for Oppius.

"I was all for volunteering you to join us but Caesar repeated that less is more. He said that we needed to be a blade, which cut through the land, rather than a hammer, trying to bludgeon our way to success."

"Caesar is a bastard for ordering you to go on such a mission," Roscius replied, whilst also silently offering him thanks for providing the unit with a veritable banquet of food, to be washed down with plenty of wine.

"Caesar is Caesar," Oppius responded, shrugging his shoulders.

Within the hour however, after several cups of wine, the four men were toasting their commander – and raising their cups also to Oppius and Teucer. Roscius joked to the Briton that he could have his gladius if he didn't come back, rather than inherit his bad luck. Fabius alone was quiet during the drinking session and banter. Oppius took him aside later that evening and said, "You're not to start mourning me yet lad," offering him a smile and the last quail's egg. Oppius also took Roscius aside however and asked him to keep an eye on the youth - and make him practice his

32

archery - until he returned. The Roman handshake the two friends gave each was firmer than usual that night.

10.

Oppius adjusted his trousers again in the muggy heat, feeling ill at ease in his woollen barbarian clothes. Trousers were unnatural he considered. The skirt of a tunic felt more natural, manly. The centurion also felt uncomfortable wearing bits of barbarian jewellery. A man was not supposed to jangle as he walked along. He missed the feeling of his gladius hanging from his belt too. He was duly armed with a dagger and bow however.

"You look like a Briton," Fabius had remarked, whilst nodding in approval earlier that morning.

"I look like a complete c-"

"Convincing mercenary," Teucer remarked, cutting Oppius off.

Teucer naturally looked and felt more comfortable as he walked alongside his friend – and he permitted himself an ironic smile that morning when he changed into the garb of his native land.

Thankfully it had stopped raining. The two men walked, trying their best not to march, through a half-formed track in a wood and came out to look over a lush valley. Lucius had to admit that Britain was an attractive and fertile island – or "a sometimes green and pleasant land," Teucer said.

"This is Kent. The garden of Britain," the archer remarked, not without a little pride, as he gazed across the valley.

"You're still clearly fond of this land."

"It's my home, for better or for worse."

"Why did you leave?"

"It's a long story."

"It's a long walk."

Teucer, whose real name was Adiminus, was born into relative privilege in his tribe, being the youngest son of the region's chieftain.

"I was not the hardiest of children and my father took little notice of me, preferring to spend his energies on my elder brother, Caradog. They often hunted together. I was either too young or ill to join them. My mother doted on her eldest son too. He was athletic and charismatic, although personally I grew to find him dull and often cruel. I was largely left to grow up by myself, although I possessed a curious mind and I would often spend time with visiting traders and craftsmen. Once I developed physically I also went off on my own and practised my archery. The harder you practise the luckier you get... Shortly after I came of age my father had a hunting accident, which left him crippled and bed-ridden. I began to spend a lot of time with him. Partly I felt sorry for my father and partly he grew to enjoy my company. He often asked me about the foreign ideas and stories that I had picked up from people who had visited the tribe over the years. I expressed to him how I wanted to one day leave the village and venture further afield, beyond Britain and Gaul even. He who knows only of the village knows nothing of the village, I somewhat conceitedly remarked to him. Trade and exchange, in the form of goods, skills and culture

35

should be encouraged, I argued. Ideas should have sex with one another, to create new ideas. I dare say I sometimes bored myself with my zeal but my father I think was influenced by my arguments. He confided that he wanted me to succeed him as chieftain. "Don't be the chieftain I was," he confessed one time to me... Recognising how close father and I had become – and seeing that my father was perhaps positioning me to succeed him – my brother became envious and resentful towards me. I suspect that Caradog hated me even more because I was neither envious nor resentful of him at this time... My father died and Caradog accused me of poisoning him. His death was sudden and suspicious; there was no real evidence against me though. Yet my brother swiftly poisoned the tribe's minds against me and I was banished. My mother and a number of the tribal elders interceded to stop me being condemned to death... I think about it nigh on every day, whether my brother planned to have my father killed and to implicate me – but at the end of each day I'm no closer to discovering the truth."

"Do you want revenge?" Oppius asked, thinking as much about his own father's death as Teucer's. He would sharpen, rather than bait, his sword if ever he encountered the man who had murdered him. And then challenge him in single combat.

"I would much rather just have my father back," the archer replied, with a gentle but mournful expression on his face.

36

11.

The embers of dusk glowed akin to the embers of the ensuing camp fire that evening. Teucer trapped and cooked a couple of rabbits. Over supper the Briton schooled the Roman in a few choice words and phrases in his language that might get him out of trouble. Oppius would be attacked and executed instantly if he revealed himself to be a Roman, even if he pretended to be a deserter. In terms of deserting Oppius remarked how he would not blame Teucer if he had thoughts of returning home.

"I do not want the garden of Britain to serve as your grave."

"The legion is my home now. This mission may not be such a lost cause too. If there's one thing a recruiting officer will do, it's make himself available for a couple of mercenaries looking for employment," the Briton replied, his tone conveying twice the confidence that he felt inside.

The two men set off early the next morning and soon came to a large settlement. From the intelligence provided by Caesar, Teucer thought it was as good a place as any to locate the Roman agent. Oppius was far from overwhelmed by the village of Gowdhust. The houses were rickety, at best. Hope and prayers, far more than building materials and architectural skills, kept most of the dwellings upright. Wild-eyed children scampered about, ankle deep in mud and grime. The entire settlement smelled like a sewer,

Oppius thought to himself, scrunching up his face in disgust on first being assaulted by the stench.

The only cheer emanated from the hut which housed and served alcohol.

"Well if I were recruiting for the army I'd head for the nearest place which served alcohol. If you wait here, I'll see if I can find some answers," Teucer remarked and headed off to the hut where a bunch of Britons were either roaring with laughter or asleep in a corner. Oppius tried not to look conspicuous whilst wearing a scowl across his face, to help dissuade anyone from approaching him. The unwelcoming expression was little different to the one he normally wore. The inhabitants of the settlement seemed little interested in the stranger however. They had seen plenty of mercenaries in their time and raised not their pale, drawn faces to the large archer as they walked by him.

Thankfully Teucer returned relatively quickly. He bought a couple of loose-tongued barbarians a drink (although Caesar did not furnish the centurion with a cohort for the mission, he did furnish him with plenty of gold) and then came back after downing his drink.

"The bad news is it seems we missed our quarry by a day or so. But the good news is I know where he's heading."

"The worst news is that the agent is travelling with a bodyguard of three picts," the Briton remarked as the two men walked toward the next major settlement.

"Picts?" Oppius replied, only half concentrating on his friend as he shook his head in disapproval again at the quality of the road that they were travelling on. Numerous wagon tracks scarred the ground and the path seemed to meander more than the Tiber. Britain would not be built in a day, but Rome would build it up, the centurion thought to himself.

"They're from the north. They've got a language, dress sense and cuisine all of their own – which you'd want them to keep for themselves. With their red hair, pale skin and rasping war cry they'll be some of the scariest foes you've ever encountered. And their women are even scarier. Indeed this trio are probably down from their home to get away from their wives," Teucer expressed, half in jest. "But these picts could prove formidable. They fight hard and dirty. Think of this agent as being protected by Roscius, times three. Caesar and Rome would do well not to poke the hornet's nest of the tribes in the far north."

Oppius and Teucer had little time to worry about barbarians from the north however, as they were soon attacked by local brigands.

12.

Rain began to spit down again from a slate coloured sky. Leaves rustled and then bracken snapped.

They appeared quickly, in two pairs, from either side of the dense woodland that the road ran through. All four of the young men had their bows drawn. Oppius briefly wondered to himself whether the youths had camouflaged themselves, or if they were naturally grimy and feral. Both Oppius and Teucer knew that they were at a disadvantage and resisted reaching for their weapons.

The apparent leader of the brigands stepped forward and occupied the middle of the road. The youth had a sinewy body, harelip and sadistic aspect, which shone as brightly as the dagger he held up, after slinging his bow back over his shoulder.

"This here is our road – and you need to pay a toll."

Teucer fancied that he would gladly have paid the toll if he thought that it would have gone to the upkeep of the road.

Oppius assessed the situation. The youths would be easy to best, just as soon as they lowered their bows. With the three youths still training their bows on the two of them it was likely that at least one of them would not escape falling to the brigands. Already the centurion noticed how the youth's arms were tiring though, whilst they grinned inanely as they thought about what they would spend their booty on. They would also soon switch to holding their daggers too, as greed overtook them and they searched their victims for any valuables they possessed. The two brigands to his right, nearest to him, looked strong but unskilled. He would allow Teucer to deal with their leader in front of him and the pock-marked barbarian to his left.

"Let's not fuck about. What have you got on you?"

Both soldiers, thinking the same thing, merely raised their arms – willing to be searched – rather than retrieving their valuables themselves. The lead brigand paused however, just as he was about to search Teucer.

"Do I know you?" he asked, squinting suspiciously at the archer.

"Doubtful. I probably would have killed you if we had met before."

"No, I do know you. You're Adiminus. This, lads, is the brother of our chieftain. Caradog should reward us if we bring him back with us," the youth remarked, his harelip curling even more, in a smirk.

"How is my brother?"

"He's doing a lot better than you, by the looks of it," he replied, with a snigger. His companions grinned at his joke too. Two of them slung their bows over their shoulders and removed their hunting knives.

"And how is my mother?"

"She's dead. She crossed over a year ago."

"Give her my regards, when you see her."

"What? You should be worried about the kind of regards your brother is going to show you. He'll welcome you with a campfire – and then cook you on it," the brigand replied, letting out a laugh.

They all looked at each other and laughed. It was the distraction that the professional soldiers had been waiting for. In one swift, smooth movement Teucer gripped the brigand by the throat in one hand and plucked an arrow from the quiver on his back with the other – plunging it into his enemy's right eye. The blood curdling scream cut through the air, as all matter of creatures retreated further into the woods, frightened by the unnatural noise. Reacting at the same time – and with the same swiftness - Oppius pulled out his dagger and threw it into the barrel-chest of the youth who still had an arrow nocked on his bow. Shortly afterwards he was attacked by the other brigand to his right. Oppius caught his knife-hand though as he was about to slash – and slammed his forearm into his opponent's face, crunching and crushing the cartilage in his nose. Oppius then twisted his hand back so the brigand relinquished his dagger to him. The blood gushing from his face soon ran into that coming from his throat, as the centurion sliced open his neck. Oppius looked up to check where the remaining brigand was, readying himself to fend him off – but all he could see was a figure racing through the forest. The wood was too dense for Teucer to take him down with a shot from his bow.

"How far is the nearest village?" Oppius asked, concerned that the remaining brigand could quickly raise a larger force.

"Far enough, but we should get moving," the Briton replied, seemingly unmoved by the news about his mother and older brother.

13.

Evening fell.

Caesar finally dismissed his legates and high-ranking centurions. On his own, he sighed and buried his head in his hands, his elbows resting upon a make-shift map unfurled on the table. He closed his eyes and massaged his temples. Not even Servilia was this exhausting, he joked to himself. The encampment was fortified though and supplies sufficient, for now. Yet a prospective shortage of food and the absence of his cavalry meant that he could not make further inroads into Britain and satisfy his ambitions. He sighed again and screwed up his face in disdain as he thought about how he would have to court and win over some of the local tribal chieftains. It should have been that they needed to court and win him over. Perhaps he should make an example of one of the tribes – and the rest might fall into line. Such an action could galvanise them against him. Yet they already seemed to have allied themselves against him. Original intelligence had suggested that factional in-fighting would prevent a grand alliance. Was it the case that the Roman agent on these shores was not just recruiting soldiers for Gaul, but conspiring with the tribes here to defeat him?

Caesar briefly turned his thoughts to his new centurion and wondered how he was progressing. He had fought well in the shallows upon the beach; Caesar envisioned that he would fare equally well upon being thrown in at the deep end. One of the legates had approached him that day, saying that one of Oppius' comrades, Roscius, said that he would be willing to be sent out to help the centurion with his mission. Caesar admired the centurion for the loyalty and friendship he had inspired but he refused the request. At the very least he hoped that Oppius would be able to kill the traitor. Joseph had asked him the other evening that if the centurion returned and said that he had completed his mission and murdered the agent how would he know if he was telling the truth?

"Soldiers are honest souls Joseph - it's a politician who you need to distrust when he promises you something."

Caesar next turned his attention to some of the correspondence on his table. Letters from Brutus, Pompey and Balbus all needed responding to. Yet the first letters he replied to were that of Julia, his daughter, and Octavius, his young nephew. He smiled at reading Julia's letter when she mentioned overhearing Cicero at a party.

"Do you know any man, even if he has concentrated on the art of oratory to the exclusion of all else, who can speak better than Caesar? Or anyone who makes so many witty remarks? Or whose vocabulary is so varied and yet so exact?"

He smiled, partly because Cicero was the sole person who Caesar would have said the above in relation to as well. Although he did not always share his politics, Caesar was constant in his admiration for the former consul. He thought of how he would try to introduce

Octavius to the great writer and statesman when he was next in Rome.

Caesar heard someone approach and he wiped the expression of fatigue off his face, as if he were wiping away a film of sweat. As it was Joseph, however, who entered Caesar soon wore tiredness – and warmth – in his features. He could not help but yawn though.

"You should get some sleep," the old Jewish servant remarked, in a spirit of both fussiness and concern.

"I've got too much on my mind. I'm finding it difficult to sleep."

"Perhaps I could make boring you to sleep part of my official duties."

"And how would you go about fulfilling such a duty?"

"Hmm, I could either recite some of Cato's speeches or tell you about the most interesting dish British cuisine has to offer."

14.

The coals on the brazier burned as intensely as the heated look in the chieftain's eyes. Caradog flared his nostrils and stared at the breathless pock-marked youth who had just delivered the news, that not only had three of his warriors been slain but that his brother had returned. Had he come back to take his revenge? Caradog creased his brow in thought – and worry. If Adiminus had returned to take his revenge however, why was he travelling in the opposite direction to his village? Caradog angrily dismissed his attendants – and even the woman he intended to take tonight. She could have the pleasure of his company and favour another time.

The jewellery-laden chieftain poured himself a large measure of wine. His mind was filled with a hundred thoughts, breeding like rats. He could not ultimately find out his brother's intentions until he encountered him. He could not ultimately live in peace until his brother was dead. First the Romans arrived, unsettling the region – and now his brother had returned to cause him personal disquiet. Yet were the two things related? Caradog recalled how one of his archers had reported seeing his brother fighting alongside the Romans on the beach. The chieftain had laughed at the idea at the time, but now it made sense. Should Adiminus now be serving in the Roman army – and rather than being a deserter Caradog judged that he was gathering intelligence for the enemy - then he would need to make his way back to their camp upon the south coast. His plan of action would be to send a small force to pursue his brother, but Caradog would also lead a small force of his own to lie in wait for him when he returned to camp. He believed he knew the route his brother would take. Wine stained his teeth as he grinned, wolfishly, thinking of how Adiminus always fancied himself as an archer and trapper. Caradog would now show his brother that he was superior to him in both of those trades.

15.

Midday.

Oppius waited just inside the tree line at the edge of the settlement, sharpening his knife, as Teucer returned from his reconnaissance mission.

"He's here. He's pouring lies into their ears and drinks down their throat in that large hut closest to us. The three picts are with him. They've been drinking, but they can hold their drink as well as hold their own fighting anyone. They're well armed, carrying shields as well as swords and axes. I overheard which settlement they'll be heading to next – and they'll be heading along the track leading this way into the forest."

"We'll lie in wait for them here. We shouldn't allow them to get into the forest, as our bows will be redundant there. At the same time we should wait until they're away from the hut. We don't want his new recruits entering the fray. Do you see that tree stump by the track? We'll hit them there. There's no cover. We'll both take out one of the bodyguards with our bows. The third will prove more difficult as his shield will be up. I'll race over to take him out at close quarters whilst you wing the agent, to prevent him escaping. Shoot him in the arse or leg."

"Are you looking to capture rather than kill him then? And bring him back with us?" the archer asked, his tone laced with a warning at how difficult the task could prove.

"Yes. Those are our orders. To quote one of Fabius' poems, ours not to reason why, ours but to do and die. What's that though?" Oppius asked, nodding his head towards an item Teucer had brought back with him, wrapped in cloth.

"A present," the Briton replied, handing over the bundle.

The centurion unfolded the cloth and held up the gladius, the polished steel glinting as brightly as the soldier's aspect.

"Someone was selling it as a spoil of war. I thought you might like it."

"It's the gift that keeps on giving," Oppius remarked.

The two men did not have long to wait before the picts, forming a triangle around the agent, appeared. Teucer had not been exaggerating about the size and strange fearsomeness of the northern Britons. They all seemed as large and powerful as Roscius. All were crowned with shaggy locks of long red hair. Oppius thought they might be brothers, such was their similar appearance, although Teucer had remarked how incest was as popular as drinking in some parts of the country. In contrast to the picts surrounding him the agent was slight, spindly. He was dressed like a barbarian but pick off that scab and Oppius would recognise the kind of haughty Roman who could tax both your patience and income. The centurion recalled Caesar's comment the other evening, how he distrusted men with a lean and hungry look.

It seems he was right in this instance. The agent carried a dagger, but had the look of a politician rather than a soldier. He was more likely to stab himself with the weapon than anyone else, Oppius fancied.

Both men took a breath and nooked an arrow.

"You take out the one in front of the agent. I'll deal with the one on his left," the centurion ordered, his tone devoid of emotion. Soldiers killed people. Lucius Oppius was a soldier. Therefore Lucius Oppius killed people. The syllogism appeared as straight and true to the centurion as Teucer's aim.

16.

Teucer breathed out in time to the sound of the arrow sighing as it left his bow. The arrowhead pierced through the Pict's long red beard and into his throat – his life extinguished in a half-formed gurgle. The intake of breath from his cousin was taken in both shock and pain as Oppius' arrow buried itself easily and deeply into his stomach. This time a scream and then a groan caused the air to shudder. Mourning his comrades not, however, the third bodyguard raised his large shield up in a defensive position and ordered the agent to stand behind him. The agent barely heard the Briton though, as he raced away in the opposite direction to the attack. He caught the sight and sound of an arrow whistle past him as Teucer tried to shoot him in the leg and bring him down.

Oppius covered the ground between the tree line and his enemy quickly, drawing his gladius as he did so. The remaining Pict unsheathed a large Roman cavalry sword, a spartha, in reply – another spoil of war. The centurion took in his opponent. He was equal, if not superior, in size and strength to the Roman. As the barbarian snarled Oppius noticed that there were plenty of gaps where teeth once resided. Few Britons seemed to have good teeth. His nose was as crooked as a Roman tax collector. A long red welt of a scar, in the shape of a lightning bolt, ran across his chest.

Swords clanged against each other. The barbarian roared wildly, but there was still method in his madness. He was agile for his size and his power made up for any deficiencies in technique. The centurion tried to get inside but the large sword and shield kept him at bay. Oppius believed that he could perhaps ultimately defeat his opponent if he kept chipping away at him and picked his moments – but as he caught the agent escaping out of the corner of his eye he realised that time was of the essence in nullifying the bodyguard.

Oppius soon formed a plan. He tried to keep his distance from the Pict, parrying any attack, and used his footwork to circle his enemy. The barbarian smirked, sensing that he had the beating of his now defensive minded opponent. He grinned at his ambusher – but one of the last sights the barbarian would see was that of his enemy smiling back at him, as an arrow from Teucer struck him in the spine. The Pict arched his back in pain, his arms were spread-eagled. Oppius wasted little time in stepping in and slashing his gladius across his opponent's unprotected chest. Lightning can strike twice in the same place.

As much as Oppius would grant a portion of respect to his opponent for his skill and courage as a fighter, he stood over his defeated enemy not – but rather set off in pursuit of the agent immediately. Confusion and fear had driven the Roman to head off in the opposite direction to the settlement. His fear and confusion increased when his pursuer caught up with him, zigzagging between the trees, and called out to halt, in his native language.

Where words slowed the agent not, Oppius' knife did – as he threw the blade into the back of his prey's thigh during a clearing in the woods.

Both men panted as they attempted to catch their breath whilst the agent winced in pain on the ground.

"Who are you working for?" the agent scornfully exclaimed, offering his enemy a look that was as sharp as the dagger in his leg.

"It's customary for the captor to ask the questions. Now, who are you working for? Tell me, or I'll cut everything out of you, except your tongue," the centurion replied, drawing his sword and smiling sadistically. Should somehow he be unable to bring the agent back to Caesar for interrogation, Oppius thought it prudent to try and extract some information now.

"I refuse to talk to you," the agent spat back with disdain. "You're just a soldier, a dog. You're no better than my barbarian bodyguards."

"I'd rather be a dog than a snake in the grass. And if I'm no better than your bodyguard, at least I can say that I've got more life in me than them. Now tell me who you're working for."

"Never. I am armed with my philosophy. My stoicism will act as a shield against any of your bribes or threats," the agent announced, his intended boldness not quite being mirrored in his reedy, quivering voice.

"Your shield didn't perform too well deflecting my dagger. It's doubtful it'll be able to blunt the point of my sword. Everybody talks – and sooner rather than later," Oppius replied, slightly distracted by the appearance of Teucer.

"I see you caught up with the bastard. Has he talked yet? I'd be happy to loosen his tongue, in either language."

"He'll talk. Caesar will make him scream more than any woman he's been with. But how are things out there?"

"We've started to cause a stir. A few people have just seen the bodies. We should leave, now."

"I will take my leave of you too. My death is the final duty I owe to my master. A plague be on the tyrant, Caesar," the agent exclaimed as he clutched his dagger and, though his features were twisted in fear and hesitation, he closed his eyes and rammed the point of the knife into his neck. Oppius was too far away to prevent the agent's sudden and dramatic action. Blood gushed from the mortal wound and his face quickly became ashen.

"At least now we won't have to carry the bastard back with us and listen to his yammering," Teucer remarked, after a pause.

"Let's return to the camp. I've seen enough of the garden of Britain not to want to see any more of it," the centurion replied, disappointed that he would not be able to bring the agent before Caesar and unmask the traitor in Rome.

17.

Evening.

The canopy of the trees sheltered the two soldiers from the rain as they sat close to their small fire and finished sucking the bones dry of the two wood pigeons that the archer had brought down.

"Some argue that the channel provides your greatest, natural defence against invasion. Instead I think it's your weather. No one will want to conquer a land in which it rains so much," Oppius remarked, whilst tossing another piece of wood onto the fire.

"Never mind the rain. Which way do you think the wind will blow, in regards to what Caesar will do next? Did he give you any indication at your dinner?"

"Caesar wishes to re-draw the maps and frontiers of the world, but ultimately Rome is his home. Also securing peace in Gaul is more important than making war in Britain. I warrant that we'll be sailing back soon."

"Do you consider Rome to be your home too? Do you have anyone waiting for you? Who wants to see you?"

"My mother still lives in a village outside of Rome. There's also my ex-wife. Whether she wants to see me or not, the channel and climate will thankfully help keep her at bay," the centurion remarked, breaking off another leg of his wood pigeon as he did so.

"Did you not love her once? Is there still a spark?"

"It was lust more than love, attraction more than affection," Oppius replied, looking wistful for once.

"What happened?"

"The usual. Life gets in the way of love. I didn't spend enough time with her – and she spent too much of my money. What about you? Is there a particular flower in the garden of Britain that you pine for?"

"There used to be too many – I was the chieftain's son after all – which is why there was never just one. Sometimes I feel I missed out. I'm not sure how much of our love lives could serve as an inspiration for Fabius' poetry."

"My job is to teach him how to kill rather than kiss."

"I'm sure Fabius prefers that scenario too."

18.

Late morning.

Just as Oppius and Teucer came out upon a field from leaving the forest the sun similarly came out from behind a flock of pink clouds. They were almost home.

"It looks like that we may just make it back alive. Things went more smoothly than I thought," the Briton remarked, squinting a little in the sunlight.

"Don't tell Caesar that. It may encourage him to send us out again behind enemy lines," the centurion replied, half thinking about how Caesar would react to his success, or lack of, in regards to the mission.

"Aye, it's a shame we don't have any war wounds to show him to prove how much we've been to Hades and back."

No sooner had the Briton finished speaking than he let out a cry, as an arrow slammed into his thigh, cutting through skin, sinew and muscle. He fell to one knee and nearly passed out. Oppius looked up to see a brace of arrows flying towards him. He quickly dove to his left to avoid the missiles, which plunged into the ground just behind where the centurion had been standing. When Oppius looked up he saw half a dozen barbarians, armed with bows, rushing towards him from out of the trees. The ground shook beneath him as another barbarian galloped towards Teucer upon a horse. Oppius would be struck by at least three arrows before he would have the time to draw his bow and unleash just one in return.

"Adiminus, put the bow down. I meant to shoot you in the leg. I can as easily arrange to shoot you in the head," Caradog called out whilst riding towards his brother.

Blood seeped out from Teucer's wound, as did any feelings of hope or revenge it seemed. He placed his bow on the ground. He glanced at Oppius, who was being surrounded by a trio of savage but skilled warriors, their bodies smeared with sweat and woad. Caradog glanced at the centurion too – with a look of recognition, his expression twisted in contempt.

"It's you. Roman bastard," the cruel-faced Briton exclaimed – and then spat at the centurion. "Tell your foreign friend that I missed him on the beach, but I won't miss him again."

It dawned on Oppius who the barbarian was. He recognised the same jewellery. The same hatred. Although he could not understand what he was saying, Oppius sensed that he was not inviting him to share his lunch. When Teucer finished translating the centurion met the barbarian's vicious glare and replied.

"Tell your brother that I'll only require one shot. I won't need a second."

Before Teucer was able to reply however Caradog spoke.

"Why did you come back?"

"I missed the weather."

"You have a joke for everything brother, but I'll have the last laugh. Now, unless you know them yourself, ask your friend what Caesar's plans are?"

"He doesn't know anything."

"Burning him alive might help him cook up some thoughts."

Teucer translated the question for Oppius, although the centurion gazed off into the distance somewhat, seemingly distracted. Perhaps he was collecting his final thoughts, or praying. Oppius thought about the question for a moment or two and then replied.

"What are Caesar's plans for Britain? To encourage Britons to start dyeing their clothes instead of their bodies."

19.

The chieftain manoeuvred his horse over towards the foreigner and kicked him in the face, in reply to his insolence.

"Your brother is as hospitable as the climate," Oppius remarked to Teucer. He smiled, in defiance. The smile was also due to the fact that half of his captors had now slung their bows back over their shoulders.

"The Roman will eventually reveal what he knows of Caesar's plans. Everybody talks. I'll be more open and reveal my plans to you. I'm going to take you both back to the village. I'll take as much pleasure in keeping him alive – and torturing him just for the fun of it – as killing our unwanted visitor to these shores. And as for you brother, I'll be having you for dinner. You'll be your own last meal," the chieftain remarked and laughed, inspiring mirth in his warriors too. As his brother grinned Teucer noticed his filed, sharpened, teeth. His brother was a cannibal.

"And did you put poison in father's last meal?"

"This question has probably been eating away at you for years little brother, no? I am nothing if not a merciful leader though and I will put you out of your misery. I poisoned him. But you, through your grab for power in trying to usurp me, killed him."

Sadness and anger swelled up in his stomach and Teucer's fingers crept closer to the knife hanging from his belt. Despite his wound he would attempt to stand and kill his brother. Oppius witnessed the look in Teucer's eye and saw him slowly reaching for his dagger. The centurion knew however that he would be cut down by an archer before he had a chance to attack his brother. Oppius decided that it was time.

"Caradog," the Roman exclaimed, attracting the attention of the chieftain. Oppius met his enemy's baleful stare and then drew his finger across his throat as a sign.

The chieftain looked somewhat confused and amused, yet an expression of alarm soon clouded his face as he heard the sound of two arrows thud into the backs of two of his archers. As soon as the arrows struck, Oppius drew his knife and threw it into the remaining warrior who had an arrow upon his bow. Roscius and another legionary, unknown to the centurion, appeared from out of the trees and ran towards the enemy, roaring to distract the Britons from their prisoners. Two of the barbarians retrieved arrows from their quivers. Yet just as they nocked their arrows they were both struck in the chests by pilums, launched with deadly accuracy and power by the advancing legionaries.

Sensing defeat Caradog turned his horse around and abandoned the fight, riding in the opposite direction to his enemy. The remaining barbarian drew his large hunting knife and ran towards Teucer, who still remained on the ground from his wound. He would at least kill one of the bastards, before fleeing too. He stood over the helpless, weakened Adiminus. But rather than his blade meeting the neck of his enemy it clanged against Oppius' sword.

The warrior attacked the Roman but, after parrying the Briton's offensive, Oppius stepped inside and butted his opponent in the face, disorientating him enough to then slash the barbarian's face, twice.

Teucer's heart raced in unison with the tamp of his brother's horse upon the turf. As heavy as his eyelids felt the biting pain in his thigh kept him conscious. Teucer propped himself up as best as he could on the ground. The grass felt cold, or perhaps it was his body growing colder, dimmer. He took a breath and nocked an arrow. Teucer grimaced as he pulled back the bow, aiming out of the corner of his eye. He followed the course of the arrow as it arced in the air and lodged itself into the back of his brother's throat.

20.

Oppius wiped his sword on his trousers, which he hoped he would never have to wear again, and looked up to see Fabius appearing from out of the trees, along with another young recruit, clutching a bow too.

"We were in the area, for archery practise of all things," Roscius exclaimed, grinning.

"Well as Teucer says, the harder you practice the luckier you get," Oppius replied whilst the two men gave each other a firm, meaningful handshake. As ever, much remained unsaid between the two friends and soldiers. "Fabius, I could get used to you helping to save my life. I may have to write a poem in your honour," the centurion called out to the recruit. "Now attend to Teucer, before I have to give you another compliment."

The youth smiled sheepishly and attended to his comrade.

"I must thank you too, legionary," Oppius remarked to the soldier who had rushed out of the forest with Roscius.

The soldier turned around, after pulling his javelin out of the barbarian. He was older than Oppius, a veteran. His build was compact, his body marked with scars.

"Thank me with a drink, or four, and we'll be even," the veteran replied, grinning as he found a couple of silver coins on the dead

Briton. As he smiled Oppius noticed that one of his front teeth was missing and the other one was chipped.

"Lucius, meet Tiro Casca," Roscius remarked.

"I served a little with your father. He was a good man, tough as leather. It seems you can handle yourself in a fight too. I also saw you on the beach. You're your father's son," Tiro Casca announced, nodding in approval and respect.

21.

When they returned to camp Caesar assigned his own personal physician and surgeon to attend to the wounded archer. He also instructed his cook to muster up anything that the returning heroes wanted. Such were the appetites of Tiro Casca and Roscius that the cook was as verily exhausted as Oppius by the end of the feast. Before he could eat, however, the centurion delivered his report to his commander on the success of his mission.

"I am indebted to you Lucius. You have served Caesar and Rome in a way that is above and beyond the call of duty. In the past few days you have completed a mission that not even an entire cohort could have managed. It's only fair then that I reward you and the Briton with the equivalent wage of a cohort for the past few days. Please do not insult me by thinking of refusing my offer. Leave the curse of pride to Caesar," the General announced, finishing off a piece of correspondence whilst talking.

"Can I accept on behalf of my mother and arrange to send any payment back home? The money will make her comfortable in her remaining years."

After the debriefing Caesar ordered the centurion to eat, rest and return that evening for a light supper.

Before returning to his tent, however, Oppius visited Teucer, who was resting in bed after his surgery. Despite all they had shared over the past few days – or because of it – the conversation between the two comrades was a little stilted. Finally, after one of many pauses, Oppius announced,

"If you like I can petition Caesar for you should you wish to remain here. Your tribe needs a chieftain."

But the Briton shook his head, in a mixture of sadness and relief.

"I'm afraid you're going to have to suffer my company some more. There's nothing left for me here, not even an embittered ex-wife."

"Britain's loss is Rome's gain. Now get some rest," Oppius replied, fraternally squeezing the archer on the shoulder.

"You should give yourself the same order. You look tired, as though you've been out all night with Roscius, drinking."

"I will. I'm so fucking exhausted that I won't even need to read some of Fabius' poetry to send me off to sleep."

Rain began to drum on the roof of the tent again. Both men briefly looked up, rolled their eyes and smiled wistfully.

22.

Outside the tent a bulbous moon and a treasure trove of stars lit up the night sky, majestically and coldly imperious towards the squalid world beneath.

Inside braziers flanked the general. Servants continued to bring in all manner of dishes for the "light supper." He would definitely need Roscius by his side should his next mission be to clear the table of food, the centurion thought to himself.

"Marius once said to me that, rather than a great centurion, give me a lucky one. It seems that you may be both Oppius," Caesar exclaimed, popping another salted olive in his mouth and washing it down with diluted wine. "Firstly, how is Teucer?"

"He'll live. I am sorry again that I could not keep the agent alive. We learned nothing."

"There's no need to apologise. We learned more than you might think, too. The manner of his death and his zealous devotion to stoicism has given me food for thought as to the identity of his employer. We also confirmed the existence of a conspiracy – and doused the flames of the treachery. It will be some time before news of his death will reach his master back in Rome. Recruitment will dry up during that time. Similarly it will take a while for someone to take the place of the agent. During that respite I will look to defeat our enemies across the channel – be they Gauls, Britons or Romans."

"So are we returning to Gaul?"

"Not all of us, all at once. But you will be returning with me. You've proved yourself to be of far too much use. You've become a victim of your own success. Although I have promoted you to centurion Lucius, you're still my standard bearer. But rather than a silver eagle, I want you with a sword in your hand – bloodied with the enemies of Rome and Caesar. There is a storm on the horizon. Gaul has only been half-tamed, civilised. There are still weeds in our garden there to pull up. The business of Britain and Rome can wait."

Oppius observed the good-humoured glint in his commander's eye go out again, clouded over with a furrowed brow and expression of icy determination.

Later that evening, after the centurion had been dismissed, Joseph looked in on his master. The braziers were still glowing, but barely. Caesar was finishing off some correspondence, a letter to Brutus. Caesar's relationship with his young friend's mother had been long and intense. He looked on Brutus as being like a son. He had encouraged him in his studies, taught him soldiering. As he wrote to Brutus though Caesar could not help but sneer as he thought about the other father-figure in his life, his uncle – Cato.

"Would you like anything before I go to bed?"

"No thank you Joseph. Get some rest. Try to get some for me too," Caesar replied, wearily.

As he stood by his master the old servant couldn't fail to notice how the map of Britain on the table had been replaced by one of Gaul. He squinted in the half-light, attempting to read the name of the town Caesar had recently circled.

Alesia.

Sword of Rome: Alesia

1.

The campfire and wine warmed their hearts in the winter chill. A scarlet darkness was swelling on the horizon, encircling them like their enemies were about to.

"How do you castrate a Gaul? Kick his sister in the jaw," Roscius exclaimed and then boomed with laughter at his own joke - to the point of drowning out the laughter of his comrades. The tough looking but good-humoured soldier drunk from the jug of wine and then passed it on to Teucer (an archer from Britain who now served as a legionary), indicating that it was his turn to tell a joke.

The centurion Lucius Oppius sat a little away from the group. Thankfully there was just enough light for him to go through the quartermaster's accounts for the month. He was more of an administrator than a soldier nowadays - more likely to be wounded by a stylus than spear, the officer thought to himself. He watched Teucer take a large mouthful of wine out of the corner of his eye. He could not help but notice how his drinking had increased, ever since their mission behind enemy lines in Britain a few years ago. During the mission the archer had been told about his mother's death. So too Teucer had killed his own brother, after finding out how his brother had murdered their father. Yet as long as the Briton carried out his duties and could shoot straight then Oppius was as happy for Teucer to drink as much as Bacchus, or Roscius even.

"What do you call ten thousand Gauls with their hands up? An army," Teucer remarked, the dancing flames of the campfire gleaming in his eyes.

Again the men laughed, as much from the drink as from the joke. Oppius mused how the enemy was no longer a laughing matter though. While many battles had been won at little cost, with the Gallic forces either surrendering or retreating, they had now formed an army which some argued outnumbered Caesar's forces by four to one. As well as possessing formidable numbers the Gauls now possessed an intelligent and inspiring leader in the form of Vercingetorix. He had united the tribes.

Teucer passed the wine jug to Marcus Fabius. Fabius was no longer a raw recruit, but he had still yet to lose his air of innocence and youthfulness. The would-be poet sipped from the jug - knowing that he could not hold his drink as well as his fellow legionaries - and thought of a suitable joke.

"What's the shortest book ever written? The war heroes of Gaul."

"Good one lad, but I thought that the shortest book ever written was the list of all the women you've slept with," Roscius jested.

"Or perhaps it's the list of all the books you've read," the youth swiftly replied in good humour.

Roscius grinned and nodded in approval – in that Fabius was finally finding his voice and some balls.

"Not bad lad. Now pass the jug around before you get drunk or, worse, start reciting poetry."

Fabius was about to get up and pass the jug over to Oppius when it was taken out of his hand. Upon realising who the thief was they all stood – including Oppius – to attention.

2.

"What can a Gaul do in five minutes? Surrender – twice!" Mark Antony exclaimed, with an infectious laugh and grin. Oppius liked and admired Caesar's new lieutenant. He was an intelligent and courageous soldier. Such was his bronzed skin and taut, muscular figure that, should Mark Antony stand still, one might have mistaken him for a Greek sculpture. Teucer had joked that he made even Fabius appear old and ugly in comparison.

"At ease men," the charismatic officer announced, shaking Oppius' hand and then warmly embracing him. Unlike many other legates and centurions Mark Antony did not look down on Oppius at having been promoted from the ranks. He cared more that a man could fight, as opposed to whether he came from the right patrician family or not. Oppius had recently spent some time with the famous, or infamous, officer. Although he was possessed of charm, courage, a generous nature and ambition he would still forever live in the shadow of his mentor, Caesar, Oppius judged. He lacked his commander's sense of duty, pride and greatness. Yet Antony was great company, the centurion would concede.

"How are you Roscius? Are you still drinking your own body weight every week?" the officer asked, taking a large swig from the jar of wine and handing it to the merry legionary.

"No, Sir. Every weekend."

"Glad to hear it. If ever the legions run out of acetum we can just siphon off your blood. And Teucer, are you still the best shot in the army when it comes to the tournaments?"

"It depends on how much money I've bet on myself," the Briton replied, wryly smiling.

"And Fabius, you're still with us I see. If you can survive the first five engagements, you can go on to survive the next fifty. Give my regards to your father when you next write to him. I still owe him money but tell him I owe my service to Caesar and Rome first. Please forgive me for disturbing you all gentlemen. I know how hard you have been working on the ramparts and defences these past days and you deserve your down time. But, Oppius, Caesar has requested that you attend a meeting with the senior officers."

Oppius rose. He was flattered that Caesar had invited him into his inner circle, albeit he was also wary that the meeting would not be about him receiving a pension and retirement home in Puteoli for good service. Their backs were up against the wall – or rather it would soon be two walls. They would soon be fighting, simultaneously, the large relief force, as well as the army inside Alesia. The besiegers would become the besieged.

"Enjoy the rest of the evening gentlemen. Hopefully you'll wake in the morning not knowing if the hammering is from a hangover or the engineering works," Mark Antony remarked, and then led Oppius off.

The two men walked through the camp, the smell of sweat and wine filling their nostrils. Many a man called out to Antony or offered him a drink. He had a smile, wave or ribald comment for everyone - in contrast to the taciturn centurion.

"So how are you Lucius? You look a little tired. But we're all tired in some way. I'm certainly growing tired of Caesar routinely speaking well of you," Antony joked, grinning and striding onwards, his hand clasped over the pommel of his large cavalry sword. Without pausing for a reply Antony put an arm around his friend.

"I'd like to make you an offer you can't refuse. I would like you to serve on my personal staff. You fight well – and I also need someone to stay the course with me during my endless campaigns of drinking and whoring. Are you married by the way Lucius? I've never asked."

"I'm divorced."

"Marriage and divorce are two sides of the same coin, as far as I'm concerned. My advice to you my friend is to marry into money, so as to be able to afford a better class of mistress. But back to the matter. Would you be interested in serving as my adjutant?"

"It'll be Caesar's decision," Oppius replied, with neither enthusiasm nor resistance to the idea in his voice. The centurion's loyalty was towards Caesar, but his debts were beginning to mount up - especially in regards to looking after his mother. Antony believed that his new friend would leap at the opportunity he was giving him – and felt slighted at his lacklustre response. For a fleeting moment Oppius witnessed the gregarious light in the charming aristocrat's eyes go out, to be replaced by derision.

"No matter what Caesar decides, however, I'm up for sword practice tomorrow morning should you still want a work out."

"We'll see. I have just purchased a slave girl from Decimus Brutus and I'll need to go through her new duties with her this evening. I'm hoping that she'll provide me with a sufficient work out in another way."

3.

Caesar finished off his letter to Cicero, again thanking him for a previous missive in which the statesman had expressed his condolences at Caesar having lost his beloved mother and his daughter, Julia, in quick succession.

"Rome too should mourn, for you have lost two great advisers and virtuous influences in your life. Yet you must also continue to consult the guides of your reason and conscience in these tumultuous times. You are a great man Julius, perhaps the greatest in an era of great men, but I urge you when you return to Rome to mirror the example of Cinncinatus."

Caesar then picked up and glanced over a piece of correspondence from a merchant friend, Trebonius. He reported on how Cato was now ending all of his speeches in the Forum with the phrase "Caesar must be destroyed," echoing his ancestor's warnings in regards to Carthage. Cato had branded Caesar a war criminal, who had created an army which was as much a danger to Rome as Gaul. He was also still doubtless irked by Caesar's humiliation of him in the Forum when he had demanded that Caesar read out a letter that an aid had passed to him. Cato believed that it contained information about a political conspiracy. Instead the note was a love letter from Servilia, Caesar's mistress and Cato's sister. The Forum had erupted with laughter.

Unfortunately the incident had only intensified Cato's animus. If only the old stoic could bear his lamentations with fortitude, Caesar thought to himself and wryly smiled.

But the smile soon fell from his face, as easily as leaves fall from a tree. His joints cracked a little as he rose from his chair. Caesar stood before a polished silver mirror. His complexion was pale. He had lost his tan. Would he soon lose his army, riches, authority? Even possessing the pride of the gods could not gift him the confidence to believe that victory would be easy this time. At best any triumph could prove a Pyrrhic victory. Should he be defeated, or if his army diminished too much, then Cato would receive even greater support in his bid to prosecute him when he returned to Rome. Without his army he would not even be able to rely on Pompey to stand in his corner, Caesar judged. Or because of his army Pompey would see him as a threat and act against him. Their link, Julia, was gone. Caesar had offered his grandniece, Octavia, as a possible bride to Pompey but he had chosen to wed the young widow of Publius Crassus, Cornelia Metella. As Caesar stood before the mirror he noticed a few grey hairs sprouting out from his eyebrows. He would ask his manservant Joseph to remove them in the morning. Not only would he soon be fighting the savages of Gaul, but he also needed to fend off the ravages of time, he mused, the glimmer of a smile returning – and then fading again.

Caesar adjusted the laurel wreath he was wearing and smoothed out the creases upon his tunic. He was an actor, about to go on stage, memorising his lines one final time. What would his final act be? Would he die in battle? Or would he die in bed, an old man, asking if he had played his part well upon the stage of life?

"Evening Joseph. Have the legates and centurions assembled?" Caesar asked his aged Jewish manservant, who was standing at the door.

"Yes."

"I think I'll keep my audience waiting a little longer. It'll give them a chance to enjoy my hospitality. I'm serving them the last of the vintages. Do you think I should shave first?" Caesar asked, stroking his chin.

"Have you not already had enough close shaves recently?" Joseph replied, referring to the recent engagement at Gergovia.

"You have an answer for everything Joseph. Perhaps I should include you in my war council."

"In my experience I have met only one person who has an answer for everything - my wife."

Caesar let out a laugh.

"I'm not sure who I should be scared of more Joseph, your god or your wife. But pray for me tonight my friend. I just hope that your god will be able to hear you above the sound of all the hammering," the general issued, with as much sincerity as satire in his voice.

4.

Caesar dispensed with any notion of retreat or surrender at his meeting with his legates and senior centurions. Their hearts and fortifications would hold he pronounced, with confidence rather than arrogance. They had defeated their enemy before, they would do so again – except that this time their triumph would be greater. The eleven miles of fortifications surrounding Alesia were complete. The army in the town would not be able to break out easily. The second line of defences, which were being constructed to hold off the impending relief force, was also nearing completion. The two enemy armies would but meet in the afterlife, rather than combining on the battlefield, Caesar declared. After motivating his officers and assigning troop deployments Caesar opened the meeting up. Decimus Brutus made some noteworthy suggestions to improve the defences. Not wishing for his fellow officer to hold the floor for too long Antony soon broke in and made a couple of points on the notion of attacking – rather than just defending against – the enemy. He also re-told his joke about the Gauls being able to surrender twice within five minutes. Caesar ended the meeting by instructing his officers to prepare and inspire their men. Have them know their duties. Sharpen their wits and swords. Fail to prepare, prepare to fail, he warned.

As the officers made their way out of the tent Caesar requested that Mark Antony and Oppius remain. What with the centurion having received no specific orders in regards to his deployment for the ensuing battle he wondered if Caesar had a special position in mind for him along the ramparts.

"Would you like me posted at any particular place during the battle general?"

"Yes, fifty miles north of Alesia," Caesar replied and smiled. Oppius knew from experience however that, despite or because of that grin, his commander was being serious.

Either out of curiosity or shock Antony desisted from pouring out the remaining vintage into his cup. Yet again Caesar had concealed his plans from him.

"I have a special assignment for you Lucius. Please, sit down. I am loth to lose you in shoring up our defensive lines – and equally I will miss your experience in leading any attack against the enemy – but needs must. My agents in the north have informed me of a chest of gold, a war chest if you like, intended to fill Vercingetorix's coffers. The coin will prove useful after the battle in bribing some of the tribes and purchasing their support again. Should the forthcoming engagement somehow prove inconclusive – and Vercingetorix escapes – then I cannot allow him to use the gold to re-build his army. I want you to take a dozen men and intercept the chest. My agent will accompany you and lead you to the chest's location. You are one of the only men I can trust with completing this mission Lucius – and equally I know you will not look to make off with the gold yourself."

"Who's the agent?" Oppius asked, fearing that he already knew the answer.

"Livia. I believe that you are already acquainted."

Unseen by Caesar and Antony the centurion rolled his eyes and sighed. Oppius thought how he would rather stay in Alesia and deal with forty thousand savages than face his ex-lover again.

After furnishing the centurion with further details about his Caesar dismissed him. The general proceeded to brief Antony on taking command of Oppius' men in his absence. The two men then shared a cup of wine and swapped gossip and barbs about the aristocracy back in Rome. It was at this point that Antony made his bid to recruit Oppius to his staff.

"When this battle is over – and Oppius returns – I would like to have him serve as my adjutant. I will better be able to serve as your lieutenant, if he serves as mine."

"You have better taste in adjutants than you do in wives, Antony. I cannot assent to your request however. Oppius is of greater value to me than the pearl I gave Servilia," Caesar replied, believing that he was as much serving his centurion's interests as his own by his decision. Should Oppius serve upon Antony's staff he would just as likely be defeated by drinking and whoring, as receive a fatal war wound. Caesar thought to himself too that Antony would ultimately be defeated by a woman. Although he claimed ancestry from Hercules, he was far more akin to Joseph's Jewish hero – Samson.

"Yet surely you can spare one man from your personal staff?"

Partly Caesar was irritated from tiredness, but menace here replaced the friendly glint in his eye as he held up his hand to bid his lieutenant to stop talking.

"Caesar has made his judgement. You have more chance of changing the weather or current of a river than of altering his will once he has spoken, so pray desist. You will not be taking Oppius from my staff. But you can now take your leave."

Antony left, obeying but far from liking Caesar's decision. He marched back through the camp hoping that the virtues, or rather vices, of Brutus' former slave girl would alleviate his black mood.

5.

Strips of cloud scarred the sky the following morning. A winter chill sliced through the air. Fabius stamped his feet to the rhythm of the hammering in the background as he waited, along with Roscius, Teucer and a dozen other legionaries upon the northern road leading out from Alesia. The men were waiting for Oppius and Caesar's agent to arrive and lead them off.

"I'm not sure if I consider myself lucky or not, having been ordered to remain and fight – as opposed to joining you on your mission into enemy territory," Teucer asserted.

"Save any luck you might have for the battle," Roscius replied, scrunching his friend fraternally on the shoulder. "Remember we have a game of dice and jar of acetum to finish off when I get back."

"What do you know about this Livia - Caesar's agent?" Fabius asked, stamping his feet in anxiousness, as well trying to fend off the cold. "Is it true that Oppius and she were once lovers?"

"Aye, it's true. You'll doubtless be inspired to write a poem about the vixen, lad, once you see her. She's half Gaul, half Roman - but all woman," Roscius remarked, as he finished sharpening the edge of his gladius. "By the end of today the pair of them will either be arguing like an old married couple, or fucking like teenagers."

The centurion and agent had listened to Caesar's final briefing intently, but in silence.

"Caesar did not specify who would be in charge on this mission," the woman remarked as soon as they had exited the tent. Livia was in her mid-twenties. She wore a russet coloured peasant dress and cloak made of fox fur. Silken, long black hair flowed down her back and framed an attractive face. Her dark eyes could sometimes beam with coquettishness – but could also narrow in thoughtfulness, or slyness. A small, pert nose and sensual, pink lips heightened her prettiness. Her figure was slender, although her muscular arms and shoulders were no stranger to the practise of archery. A dagger, housed in a scabbard that Oppius had given her, hung down from a belt (which had been given to her by another former lover).

"I'm to command the legionaries. You're welcome to take command of yourself."

"You always did like to be on top," Livia replied, raising an eyebrow and grinning.

Oppius was about to launch into a short stern speech about the need to form a professional relationship, free from any personal enmity that might exist between them, but he grinned too.

A comfortable, or awkward, silence sprouted up between Oppius and Livia again as they proceeded to walk through the camp. The smell of wet grass, garum, ordure and smoke from breakfast campfires filled their nostrils. The sound of laughter, swearing, sawing and hammering filled their ears. Yet the ululations and sound of children crying soon eclipsed all as they walked by the camp of women and their young that resided between the army and the walls of Alesia. In order to save on rations Vercingetorix had ordered that the women and children of the town be banished. With nowhere to go – and in hope that Caesar or Vercingetorix might provide for them – the women had set up camp between the two armies. Yet Caesar had left them to perish. He refused also to allow them through his lines, in fear that they may forage for food in competition with his own army. Even Oppius' face creased in pity as he witnessed the scene before him. The sick, or corpses, were wrapped in blankets and lay on the ground – flies circling around them like vultures. Hollow-cheeked women held children whose limbs were little thicker than a pilum. The centurion could not see Livia's face behind her hair – but he envisioned her expression, anger mixed with sadness. As fierce and cynical as Livia could be Oppius had witnessed her compassionate side too. Although she judged that there were few innocents in this world, those that were so were worth caring for.

"So this is how Rome has brought its light of civilisation to Gaul? Ask these women and children what they would rather have right now: food and water or straight roads and fancy laws for fancy lawyers to profit from," Livia issued, with a scowl which brought an even greater chill to the morning air.

"This was Vercingetorix's doing, not Caesar's."

"It's both their doing."

Oppius kept his thoughts to himself, but secretly agreed.

"So what happened between Lucius and Livia?" Fabius asked, as he took a spare bow string from Teucer.

"She is an attractive woman and an agent of Caesar's. Caesar used her body – and her intelligence – to his advantage. And Caesar and Lucius are not the only ones to have shared her bed," Roscius replied, still unsure as to how good Livia had been for his friend. She had made him happy and unhappy in equal measure - not that many would have noticed much of a change in the tough centurion whilst he was in love, or suffering from a broken heart.

"I was in a neighbouring tent when they had their final blazing row one night," Teucer remarked, shaking his head and wincing as if he were reliving the experience. "She asked Lucius if he would make an honest woman of her – and marry her – if he wanted her to remain faithful. He replied however that it was beyond his powers to make any woman honest, especially her. If you want to know anymore about the affair lad, they're walking this way."

Fabius turned around and was immediately captivated by the powerfully beautiful woman. Oppius rolled his eyes and smiled a little at witnessing the expression upon the young man's face. Had he too been dumbstruck by her in a similar way when he first saw Livia? He couldn't discount it.

"Roscius, are we ready to move out?" the centurion asked, keen to use as much of the daylight as possible.

"Aye."

With just a nod of his head Oppius ordered the men to form two ranks of six and ready themselves and the equipment for the ensuing march.

"It's good to see you again Roscius," Livia remarked, with a playful look in her eye and a smile dancing across her attractive face.

The legionary wanted to say it was good to see her again but somehow he couldn't get the words out of his mouth. Instead Roscius suddenly thought to himself how Caesar could lose an army and his friend his heart over the next few days. The latter was as discomforting a thought as the former, he mused.

6.

Dusk.

Rain spat upon the mud and skeletal trees. Oppius, Roscius, Livia and Fabius crept forward through the woodland. The centurion peered through the trees and took in the scene at the clearing. A dozen or so armed Gauls, either warriors or brigands, sat around a campfire with a joint of meat upon a skewer above it.

"We could go around. It'd take time though. And we would need to set up camp at a sufficient distance from them," Oppius whispered.

"I'd rather take their dinner. And they've also been obliging enough to light a fire for us," Roscius replied, already clasping his sword in anticipation of attacking the enemy.

"Never look a gift horse, or whatever they're roasting, in the mouth. Roscius, take six men and head around to their left flank. I'll head around to their right. Attack when I give you the signal," the centurion ordered.

"What will the signal be?"

"The usual. I'll kill someone. Fabius, I want you to remain here and look after Livia. If somehow one of these bastards is able to escape this way put an arrow through him."

"I can fight too. I do not need a nursemaid," Livia issued, scowling at the centurion and pouting at the same time.

"I know. But I've got plenty of men who can fight. I've only got one agent however who can help me complete the mission. I'd rather not put her life in danger needlessly."

Livia nodded and Roscius headed off, shortly followed by Oppius.

"Lucius speaks well of you Fabius. Of course he'd deny that if ever we put it to him," the woman remarked, tucking her hair back behind her ears to reveal the full lustre and beauty of her face. "You are a young poet, as well as a soldier, I understand. Do you sometimes write your poems in the blood of your enemies to combine your professions – and save money?"

Fabius knew not how to take the enigmatic woman's comments and was too distracted by her looks to perceive the hint of a sly smile on her lips.

"Forgive me, I'm just teasing you," Livia then remarked, the hint of a smile here flowering into an alluring smirk, as she gently clasped his bare forearm. "Tell me, has Lucius ever spoken to you about me?"

"No, but he tends to keep himself to himself," Fabius replied, feeling a little awkward whilst being all too conscious of the woman's touch.

"Too true. As well as Lucius barely ever expressing his feelings to me, he probably did not even acknowledge them to himself."

Yet Livia remembered how the centurion had once declared how he wanted her to be his North Star – forever fixed, shining, so he could always find his way home. As opposed to being a brilliant comet - burning brightly but fleetingly across the sky. They had been in his tent at the time. She hooked her lithe legs around muscular calves. Their fingers were intertwined. He brought her closer, cradling her in his large, scarred arms and they made love. He gave rather than just took as a lover. Her body and heart sang when she was with him. Livia realised that it wasn't just Oppius who had not shared his true feelings. She was guilty of the same mistake.

The wistful looking woman snapped out of her reverie however when she heard the thud of Oppius' knife strike his enemy's chest. The roar of Roscius followed shortly after – and screams succeeded shortly after that – but Livia could not take her eyes off the brutal centurion as he charged towards another foe. A long-haired savage jabbed a spear at the soldier but Oppius deftly avoided its rusty point. Before his enemy could jab his spear again the centurion punched the point of his gladius so far through the savage's stomach that the sword's point protruded out of his back. Blood drenched the centurion's hand and forearm. Fabius noticed how the woman appeared both shocked and enthralled by the violence, unable to avert her eyes from it – or him.

The rest of the enemy were soon bested. Swords finished off those that pilums had failed to deal with. The attack had enjoined surprise with ferocity.

"We came, we saw, we conquered," Fabius heard Roscius contentedly announce, as he retrieved his javelin from his enemy's neck.

Oppius immediately posted sentries around the camp and ordered half a dozen other men to dispose of the dead – and turn any wounded into corpses too.

Dusk slipped off the horizon as darkness slid in, like a knife. The sound of the spitting rain was replaced by the sound of the joint of meat, spitting with fat. The soldiers sat around the campfire, weary yet cheered by the warmth and imminent meal.

"How do you identify a Gaulish soldier? Sunburned armpits," Roscius declared, holding his arms up in a gesture of surrender and booming with laughter. The noise echoed through the trees, out-sounding the eerie nocturnal birdsong.

7.

Alesia.

Darkness visible. The moon flitted in and out behind grey slabs of cloud. Bitingly cold sweat glazed a number of faces, on both sides, as the attack grew imminent. Whetstones scraped along swords. Soldiers stamped their feet to keep warm. Helmets were tapped, for luck. Puffs of breath misted up the air. Mark Antony and Teucer stood upon a viewing platform on the ramparts, facing outwards towards their enemy. A number of defences stood between the ramparts and the besieging forces. Trenches. Large, sharpened stakes pointed outwards. Smaller stakes in holes, camouflaged over, called "lilies" also littered the ground before them.

"Our fortifications may slow our enemy's momentum, but they won't stop them. Roman steel will - both the metal in our scabbards and the mettle in our hearts. Aye, our blades need oiling with blood. Save your arrows, Teucer, for their officers, or any big brute that may cause us trouble. Caesar and Oppius speak highly of you, but I want you to prove yourself to me during this night and the long day ahead," Mark Antony remarked, drawing his razor-sharp cavalry sword.

"Form says I'll be shooting most of them in the back, as when they break they'll doubtless retreat rather than muster themselves and attack again," Teucer replied, attaching his bowstring to his bow. His confidence also sprang out of the events during the afternoon. Shortly after Oppius had headed north the enemy appeared from the south-east. The Gauls, headed by one Vercassivellaunus, Vercingetorix' cousin, looked to test and break part of the Roman line through its cavalry. If Vercingetorix's army could join its counterpart then Caesar would be overwhelmed. Caesar sent out his own mounted force however, containing his veteran German troops, and saw off the attack – but it was a near run thing.

"Don't be so sure. The Gauls have the numbers to defeat us. Our balls are in a vice. But thankfully we know this. This battle is a fight for our lives, not honours. If defeated the legions won't just lose their standards, they'll lose their heads."

Vercassivellaunus' forces moved forward; the sound was akin to the low rumbling of distant thunder. Hands tightened around weapons. Helmets were again tapped for luck. Thousand of Roman eyes squinted in the darkness, trying to gauge their enemy. Their ears were first assaulted as trumpets sounded within both Gallic armies, signalling to each other that they were primed to attack. Cheers went up too between the two armies, as though they had all but routed the smaller Roman force already. Missiles first whistled through the gelid air and then smashed against the ramparts of the outer line of Caesar's defences. At the same time Vercingetorix's army, inside Alesia, launched their attack against the lines and fortlets surrounding them. Under the cover of darkness – and a hail of artillery – Vercassivellaunus' army moved forward, carrying fascines to fill in the trenches and ladders to scale the ramparts. The night air was soon lit up as fire erupted from the Roman scorpions dotted along the fortifications. High-pitched wails spewed forth from their victims, as dozens of Gauls were burned alive. Yet still the enemy advanced - a tide of men propelled by an unseen yet momentous force.

Mark Antony rallied his men and directed forces to where they were most needed. Yet he fought as well as commanded. Teucer was impressed by his energy and bravery. Sometimes he would display unrivalled swordsmanship, but at other times, when needed, his large cavalry sword could be seen slashing and bludgeoning the enemy to death. Teucer shadowed Caesar's lieutenant and more than once loosened an arrow into an opponent about to target him. The Briton also climbed up to the ramparts and fired arrows out into the darkness – blood and screams pockmarking the night.

Yet still the enemy advanced.

Blood – upon swords, clothes and skin – glistened in the moonlight. Howls of agony, clangs of steel against steel, battle cries and the roar of scorpions created a macabre cacophony – but the sounds fell into the background for most of the soldiers. The only thing they noticed was the enemy in front of them, who they had to kill. Or else they would be killed. Some men silently – or audibly – prayed to their gods. Some men, disfigured and dying, called out for their mothers. Or they cursed Caesar and

Vercingetorix alike – the authors of the horror story that they had been written into. Death and chaos feasted on Alesia that night, as if a rich banquet had been laid out before them.

Caesar somehow always managed to be where he was needed, riding on his white horse and marshalling his reserves. Holes were plugged and troops were given a second wind by their commander's words of encouragement. His sword was as bloodied as any infantryman's weapon. Caesar orchestrated his army as if he were conducting a piece of music. Flagging legionaries fell back on their drills and training. They fought on out of a duty and pride, not wanting to let down the men fighting beside them. And they fought on because if they didn't they'd perish.

During a lull in the fighting Mark Antony and Teucer took in some water.

"How many of the enemy have fallen?" Teucer breathlessly asked, hoping that the legate knew something that he didn't.

"Not enough," Mark Antony answered, his muscular body trembling with energy and exhaustion.

"A good answer. But surely we're through the worst of it? How many waves of men can keep coming?"

"How many times can a blacksmith strike a hammer on his anvil?"

"A blacksmith needs sleep and victuals though."

Yet still the enemy hammered upon the defences. But the defences and the thin red line of legionaries held. Caesar continued to use his reserves wisely. Mark Antony, Trebonius and Decimus

Brutus led their troops with wisdom and courage. The tide of men began to draw back, on both sides of the Roman defences.

But Vercingetorix and Vercassivellaunus would attack again during the day.

8.

Both Roscius' laughter and the evening birdsong had ceased. Even some of the stars in the sable sky appeared to lose their sparkle, as if too tired to shine in the dead of night. Yet Livia and Oppius were still awake. Livia had deliberately slept near the centurion. Not only did she feel safer, warmer, near him but she hoped – like now – he would be awake and she would get the chance to speak in private to the man who had never been far away from her thoughts.

"I'm sorry, for everything," she whispered, her expression filled with kindness and contrition. Oppius had rarely seen her look more beautiful.

"I'm sorry too," Oppius replied, smiling a smile that was seldom to be witnessed upon the soldier's face. Perhaps Livia alone had been privy to it.

"I need you to know that it was never business, but a pleasure, when I was with you. At times I may even have found happiness. I got to make love to a friend, rather than a patron or source. Take it from me, you're worth ten Caesars," the woman issued, feeling both emboldened and vulnerable by sharing her feelings in such a way.

"Cato may well agree with you on that score, but few others would," the centurion wryly asserted.

"I loved being with you Lucius. But too often I felt like I was your mistress and the army was your wife. And she has you under her thumb at times. You once told me that you fought for the glory of Rome, but really you fight for the glory of Caesar. They are not one and the same thing. Things will end badly for Caesar. He is forever risking everything on a roll of the dice. The Sword of Damocles hangs over him – but one day it will fall and impale him."

"I'm not sure how much of a wife the army is to me - my first wife was far more demanding if that's the case - but certainly it's my home."

"What if I told you that you could make another home for yourself? What if we could run away, live prosperously and peacefully far from the reach of Caesar and Rome? I'd make an honest woman of myself, for you. You could lay down your sword. What if I told you that we could write a new chapter into our lives?" Livia whispered, passionately and imploringly, her eyes as bright as the still flickering campfire.

"I would say that you were talking in your sleep - dreaming."

Livia, feeling frustrated or excited, was about to reply but then she caught her breath and stopped. Instead she just grinned at her former lover and declared,

"If I'm talking in my sleep then you know what you have to do?"
"What?"

"Stop my mouth with a kiss."

9.

Their luck was in, Oppius thought to himself. Sunlight poured over the scene like honey, albeit the ground was still damp and bracken broke noiselessly beneath their feet. A plume of smoke spiralled up out of the chimney of the stone hut that stood before them. Livia's intelligence seemed to be correct. Ideally the centurion would have liked to see some evidence of the gold being housed at the property, but he trusted the agent.

"Would you like your agent to join in the fight now, or stay behind again?" Livia asked, whilst tying her hair back.

"As you once told me, women should make love, not war. I want you to hold back, here with me. We'll work this similar to the attack on the camp last night. Roscius, take half the men and line them up in a semi-circle on the left. Stay well within the woods and move slowly up to the treeline. Have the men just carry swords, shields and pilums. Quintus, I want you to take the rest of the men and ready yourself in a similar fashion upon the right. Fabius and I are going to remain here and have the two sentries outside of the hut sound the alarm, so to speak. Once the alarm is sounded I'm hoping that the men inside will rush out into the open ground – the kill zone. I'll give the usual signal."

Quintus, a stone-faced veteran, and Roscius nodded and assembled their men. Now Fabius I want you to wound, rather than kill, the sentry on the left. Shoot the bastard in the groin. His screams should catch the attention of his comrades. We're then going to step out into the open, entice the bastards to avenge their friends.

As with the previous evening, it was a massacre. Oppius and Fabius struck true with their arrows. The screams of the sentries curdled the air. The Gauls rushed out, carrying their weapons. A couple quickly saw the Roman archers and rushed towards them. Their high-pitched battle-cries and fearsome appearance disconcerted Fabius and he delayed in nocking his second arrow. Oppius however calmly let off his second bolt, firing it into the face of the barbarian racing toward him with his sword raised above his head, ready to kill. Just as the centurion was about to draw his knife and launch it at the Gaul targeting Fabius he heard a whistling sound by his ear and watched as Livia's dagger struck the barbarian's chest.

"A woman can make love and war, if you find the right one," she exclaimed and grinned, as both men turned towards the agent and nodded in thanks.

The rest of the legionaries appeared from out of the treeline and launched their pilums. Many, but far from all, struck the enemy force, which numbered around twenty. Some of the Gauls appeared to be veterans and some of the spears which were launched in reply found Roman breasts. Oppius and Roscius were soon at the heart of the fighting though and tipped the balance of the encounter. A few of the Gauls attempted to flee, but although they may have been able to out-run their enemy they could not out-run their javelins.

A few Gauls retreated back into the hut. Wary of losing more men Oppius ordered Fabius to fetch the fire arrows that Teucer had given him before they left Alesia. The enemy were soon smoked out. They surrendered, but Oppius had no need of prisoners.

The tang of blood and stench of death soon infused itself into the air. An increasing number of birds were perched on the surrounding trees, anticipant of a feast. After attending to the wounded and letting the fire die out Oppius, Livia and Roscius entered the hut. He had doubtless died from wounds sustained during the fighting, but a charred corpse covered a strong box in the kitchen of the dwelling. Even Roscius grimaced as he drew his sword and cut away at the blackened, sticky flesh, in order to free up the box from the body.

Roscius and Oppius then pulled the box outside, delivering themselves from the unholy smells of the hut. Oppius broke the lock with a few well-struck blows with an axe and opened the chest. The sunlight had a rival, as hundreds of polished gold coins glistered before them. Their eyes were stapled wide with wonder. The box contained more wealth than the centurion had ever seen, than perhaps anyone had ever seen, he thought.

"We could buy up any property in Rome with this, and still have change for a vineyard and coastal villa," Oppius remarked, smiling in wonder and also in satisfaction, that he had completed his mission.

"Or Caesar could use the money to finally pay our arrears and bonus," Roscius replied.

"I didn't say it was that much."

"He may even have enough gold here to pay the gods and buy back his hairline."

"Whilst you mention Caesar I should now divulge another part of our mission that I was asked to keep secret until we discovered the gold," Livia announced, as she too marvelled at the contents of the chest. It may seem strange but we should talk out of earshot of your men. Roscius, you should join us too. Also, it wouldn't do any harm to involve Fabius."

Oppius looked confused. He was far from surprised that Caesar and Livia could keep something from him, albeit he was at a loss as to why they needed to talk in secret behind the building.

"Please, trust me," Livia issued, as she led the trio off.

10.

Once they were securely out of sight around the back of the cottage Livia gazed into the forest intently – and then began to speak.

"I wanted to say two things. Firstly, thank you. And secondly, sorry," the wily agent exclaimed, her face a mixture of contrition and satisfaction. The three men creased their faces in bemusement in reply, before their expressions were pictures of shock and pain. Half a dozen armed men appeared from out of the trees behind the soldiers (Livia had positioned herself so that her audience would have its back to the forest). Before any of them had a chance to draw their swords or offer up the alarm Oppius, Roscius and Fabius were wrestled to the ground and bound and gagged. Fabius was able to elbow one of his assailants in the face as he was pulled to the ground, but his attacker knifed him in the thigh in reply, once the young legionary was safely bound and gagged.

With Oppius secure Livia nodded her head in the direction of one of her warriors – and he swiped his axe down to signal the attack. The legionaries, who had executed two ambushes in the past twenty four hours, were now ambushed themselves. A force of two dozen barbarians, formed from all manner of tribes that had fought Caesar in the past, stormed out of the tree line and launched their spears into the unprepared Romans. Screams frightened the birds from the trees. Oppius heard the clash of arms and hoped that at close quarters his legionaries could muster some form of defence – and attack – but his unit was outnumbered. He coldly stared at Livia as he heard his men die behind the stone hut.

"You shouldn't look at me like that Lucius. I've saved you and your close friends from being killed have I not? I also gave you the chance to come away with me – and the gold – last night, but you wouldn't listen. I realise now that you'll always choose your wife over your mistress," the bewitching agent said as she bent down, removed the centurion's gag and tenderly stroked his cheek.

"Why?" Oppius asked.

"Why steal a chest full of gold? I would have thought you cynical enough to know that the answer lies in the question. Or has your noble soul corrupted your sense of cynicism? For years I have been suspected of serving Rome by the Gauls and of serving Gaul by the Romans. Yet really I have been serving myself. And why shouldn't I? Everybody else serves themselves. Except you perhaps."

Cries still sounded in the background, as the barbarians finished off the wounded. As stony-faced as the centurion tried to remain, he winced inside a little each time a cry of pain shattered the air.

"If your next question is why did I need you to capture the gold, when I could have used my men to do so, I'll tell you. I need the tribes of Gaul, whose gold this is, to believe that Rome has their stolen war chest. I want them coming after Caesar, not me," Livia expressed, smiling.

"Your soldiers have not died in vain. They've provided us with an alibi, a scapegoat," one of the barbarians pronounced and laughed. By the way in which he was dressed and how others deferred to him Oppius judged him as being Livia's lieutenant. He was well built and well armed. A greasy beard covered most of his broad face, aside from his baleful grey eyes. Even when jesting there was a cruelty in his expression. "So you are the best that Rome has to offer? I'm disappointed. It didn't take long for my men to teach your soldiers a lesson. It's a shame that I won't be able to teach you a lesson too."

"School's not out yet," Oppius replied.

Livia issued a number of orders. She allowed her men to plunder the Roman corpses for loot. The chest was loaded upon a cart. Oppius and Roscius were both bound to tree trunks.

"Caesar won't be happy about this. He'll come after you," Oppius remarked, as Livia walked by him.

"By the end of today or tomorrow Caesar will probably be dead, perhaps by Vercingetorix's hand himself, which will make a lot of people happy."

"So what's your plan now? Leave us to die here, strapped to a tree?"

"My plan is to live prosperously and peacefully in a faraway land. I will take Fabius with me and after a time I'll send him back, to release you. He may well have time to compose a poem about his adventure. It was a pleasure knowing you Lucius, but this is business. For what it's worth I think that you've made me become

108

a better person – but just not good enough," the darkly alluring agent issued, with a fleeting but genuine look of regret or sadness in her eyes.

"Good bye, Lucius."

Livia soon gave the order and led her warriors off. A limping Fabius attempted to put on a brave face but he was understandably fearing for his life as he looked back one more time at his comrades. Tears welled up in the young soldier's eyes. Anger welled up in the centurion's heart. Again he tried to move and loosen his bounds, but it was futile.

The sound of their enemies moving north faded. The sounds of the forest returned. Such was the black look upon the centurion's face that Roscius allowed his friend some time to deal with his thoughts. The wind through the trees made a shushing noise too. Yet finally Roscius broke the ice and spoke.

"I think I'm sitting in some piss, where one of the bastards used this tree as a toilet. Also the cold is making my nose itch. I think I'd rather be back in Alesia, with half of Gaul trying to kill me."

Oppius only half heard his friend however and knew not how much he was joking. All he knew was that they were out of luck. He just hoped that Caesar and the Tenth were faring better.

11.

Alesia.

Joseph looked out and shielded his eyes from the glare of the afternoon sun. If only he could have shielded his eyes from the violent scenes before him too. Such was the peril of the situation that he even fleetingly wished that he was back home, in the company of his wife. Vercassivellaunus' forces were beginning to clamber over the ramparts. Would the dam soon burst? He watched as a young legionary fought off three men at once, using his sword, shield and helmet to attack the enemy. Joseph stood in admiration and fear for the young man. He nicknamed him David. Yet no sooner had the old manservant cultivated a spark of hope that David would prove victorious than an arrow struck him in the shoulder. The legionary fell from the rampart to the ground, opening his eyes to find a flame-haired Goliath standing over him, his axe-head having seemingly been dipped in blood. The brawny savage let out a war-cry as he raised the weapon above his head, ready to bury the blade into the stricken legionary. Yet the war cry was suddenly eclipsed by the sound of a horse's hooves. Mark Antony launched himself from his grey gelding and brought the Goliath to the ground. Antony rose quicker than his opponent and plunged his cavalry sword into the barbarian's stomach, before chopping off his head in a single blow.

"Teucer, take a group of men and plug the gap," Antony ordered. He then attended to the young legionary. "I saw you. You fought well. How many of the enemy do you think you've killed today?"

"Not enough."

"Good answer. I thought you were worth saving. I also thought that this long-haired bastard here was worth killing. What's your name?"

"Enobarbus. Domitius Enobarbus."

Teucer fired off five arrows within a minute; each arrow found the chest of an enemy combatant and cleared the stairway up to the rampart. Teucer drew his sword and ordered half a dozen men to help him drive the barbarians back. A hare-lipped Gallic infantryman was armed with a long spear however and was fending the legionary off as his feral-looking comrades scaled ropes and ladders and made it onto the platform. Just as Teucer thought that there was no way past the point of the Gaul's bloodied spear tip the hare-lipped opponent was knocked to the ground by a legionary's helmet striking the side of his head. Tiro Casca followed up his unorthodox attack by wading in with his sword and shield and killing the remaining attackers who breached the walls.

"Now fuck off and find some arrows Teucer. You're about as useful with a sword as a eunuch is with a whore," the veteran legionary growled, as he picked up his enemy's large spear and commenced to jab down with it at the next wave of assailants scaling the walls.

The individual clangs of steel against steel produced one long metallic ring, pealing out like a giant bell. War is a conflagration – and Alesia was on fire. Roars of pain, triumph and intimidation stained the air. Blood stained the ground. Caesar thought how, from the sky, the battle might look like one insect colony invading another. His attention was wrested from his brief conceit however as one of the fortlets crashed to the ground. The enemy had used grappling ropes to pull it down. Caesar rode towards the danger, his distinctive red cloak billowing in the wind, to rally his forces and direct his ever dwindling reserves towards the danger. His thin red line was growing thinner. Caesar was like a surgeon, trying to suture the wounds of an ailing patient, as he looked to fill the gaps in his defences. Yet the veteran commander knew that no army could ever win a battle by just defending.

Mark Antony crouched behind the defences, blood pouring down his cheek. Missiles – stones and arrows – flew overhead or thudded into the wall. One such missile, a stone from a peltist, had ricocheted off the top of the wall and struck him upon the side of the head.

"Bastard," the officer cursed, as loudly as any legionary – albeit he could barely hear himself over the ringing in his ear. "Right, let's see how good a shot you really are Teucer. If you can put an arrow through the dog who hit me then I'll duly reward you. If we live through this carnage."

"What's he look like?" Teucer said simply in reply.

"Black hair. Your build. Red trousers. He's probably also got a love bite on his arse from his sister."

The archer first popped his head over the rampart to spy his target. He then carefully selected one of his few remaining arrows. In a fluid movement he proceeded to stand, pull back the bow and fire off the bolt, ignoring the chaos and danger within his peripheral vision. The bowstring sang and the arrow struck the right note as it punched into the peltist's chest.

Antony did not know whether to nod in approval at witnessing the shot, or shake his head in disbelief at the archer's skill.

"We both need to live through this carnage now, just so I can tell the story of what you've just done. What are they putting in the water over there in Britain?"

"Wine."

It was not just the line of the Roman army which was weakening however. Vercingetorix and Vercassivellaunus had lost more men than Caesar. Vercassivellaunus had yet to break in. Vercingetorix had yet to break out. Caesar saw his chance to counterattack as he committed reserves (both cavalry and cohorts) to aid one of his legates, Labienus, fighting out of a hilltop fortlet in the defences. The smell of sweat and death hung like a fog in the air. The air was thick with pilums too as they rained down upon the Gallic forces. The legionaries then waded in with their swords, cutting a swath through their enemies as if they were scything the harvest. Caesar sensed his opportunity. Although conscious that it could prove his only, or last, throw of the dice he ordered his cavalry to break out from his outer fortifications and flank his enemy. It worked. Those that did not retreat were slaughtered as Caesar's cavalry rumbled like thunder and struck like lightning, cutting down the Gallic forces outside of the town. The cohorts broke out too and dispatched or dispersed the enemy. Caesar willed his cavalry on, to trample his enemies – like insects. The fields surrounding Alesia would soon be streaked with blood and gore and littered with corpses. Teucer soon found himself having to shoot upwards into the air, rather than downwards, for his arrows to reach their targets.

Realising that the relief army had been routed, Vercingetorix's forces inside the town also faltered and retreated.

Caesar had finally won Alesia – and Gaul.

12.

Fabius returned. Blood stained his right leg. Livia had ordered one of her men to attend to the wound upon his thigh but when the legionary was finally ordered to return to his comrades he was given the parting gift of a forceful kick on his leg, which opened the gash up again. The young soldier, his usually olive complexion rendered ashen, cut Oppius and Roscius free and then collapsed on the ground.

The all too familiar noxious stench of death filled the centurion's nostrils. Oppius briefly paused to take in the scene, strewn with Roman corpses, and closed his eyes – as if offering up a silent prayer for the dead. There were no gold coins to place over their eyes to offer up to the ferryman however. His eyes then snapped open and Oppius proceeded to drink any water and eat any food he could get hold of, sharing it with his friends. After taking in some food Fabius drifted off to sleep and Oppius allowed the youth to rest. Whilst he did so the centurion asked Roscius to gather up as many re-usable arrows as he could – and also bundle together a dozen pilums. Oppius did the same. He also went around and cut the heads off numerous others pilums and barbarian spears, before finally constructing a make-shift crutch for Fabius.

"Wake up lad, you'll have enough time to sleep when you're dead," Roscius uttered as he gently kicked the young legionary's foot. "We're heading out."

"Where to?" Fabius asked, wincing a little in pain as he stood up.

"North. We've still got a mission to complete," Oppius grimly said, handing the crutch to the youth.

"But –"

Roscius here looked at Fabius and shook his head, conveying that it would be useless to protest or try to reason with their centurion. He had seen his friend like this before. Oppius could only be satisfied now by avenging the deaths of his men. Usually Oppius only wore such a storm upon his brow in private, when he dwelled on his father's death. A legionary in the Ninth legion had baited his sword with poison during a tournament and murdered him.

Roscius, like Fabius, was all too aware of how suicidal their mission now was, but to abandon his friend would prove a more uncomfortable fate. Roscius knew that only the blood of his enemies could aright Oppius – and he was happy to help him shed it. They were not just comrades who the barbarians had slaughtered, but friends. Roscius silently cursed his enemies too for killing Quintus, before he had the chance to pay him back the money he owed him.

"We'll carry everything. Just get us back to the point where they released you, so we can pick up their trail while there's still some daylight left. This mission isn't just about getting that gold back now, it's about getting back our pride," Oppius announced, tossing a gladius to the young legionary.

Fabius caught it, nodded and led his comrades off. Between Alesia and facing Oppius' ire for disobeying his orders, perhaps facing the thirty barbarians – with a force of three men – was the best course of action, he ironically thought to himself.

13.

Even in the darkness the lake shone with a silvery-blue hue that was a mirror to the clear night sky - studded with stars and the brooch of a bulbous moon above. The barn sat close to the shore of the lake. A couple of half-drunk sentries stood around a small campfire outside the structure. Oppius could still hear plenty of voices from inside, carousing or cursing in various languages. Thanks to the ruts in the ground that the cart made, heavily laden with gold, the prey had been easy to track. The centurion kept his distance as he made a reconnaissance of the scene. He would head back into the forest and join his friends. They would rest, but then return and set out their strategy in the dead of night. And in the morning they would kill.

Whilst Roscius stood sentry Oppius and Fabius finished off the wild mushrooms they had cooked upon the campfire. The pair remained silent for some time, before the pensive looking centurion spoke.

"I promised your father that I would keep you safe. I fear that in ordering you to complete this mission I've broken that promise."

"My father would understand."

"More so I hope that you understand Fabius. And if you do understand, please explain things to me," Oppius quietly said and half-smiled, the hum and crackle of the fire nearly drowning out his words. Fabius noticed that the melancholy centurion was talking as much to himself as anyone else. "Why am I doing this? Out of revenge, duty, pride? None or all of those things? Perhaps I just want to see her face once more – see her smile. Although I doubt that she'll have a smile on her face when she sees me." Oppius' smile briefly broadened at the thought, but then vanished.

"She spared your life. She must care for you," Fabius replied, trying to console his friend. But the centurion here waved his hand in front of his face. Fabius was unsure if his centurion was gesturing to dismiss his comment, or brushing away an insect.

"It was unwise of her to spare my life."

"I read a poet recently, who set down that to be wise and to love exceeds man's might. It may well exceed a woman's might too."

"I could use some wine rather than poetry right now. Caesar will owe us some Falernian after this walk in the woods."

"How do you think we will fare back at Alesia?

"If we can hold our nerve then we can hold the ground. The relief force for the Gauls will have supplies for one day or so. They must either taste victory quickly, or not at all. We will give them a bloody nose and hunger will kick in. Once the relief force loses its appetite for a fight it'll break up and retreat. Vercingetorix and his army inside of Alesia will surrender soon after, not having the food and stomach to fight on either. Vercingetorix is no Hannibal and the Gauls are no Spartans."

"Hopefully victory will bring peace."

"Ha, there's more chance of having Roscius recite poetry than victory bringing peace. Battles beget battles," Oppius answered whilst closing his eyes and resting his head upon the ground in the hope of finding a shard of peace, before he gave battle again.

14.

The blood appeared black in the moonlight as it oozed from the necks of the sentries. Oppius and Roscius dragged their bodies into the trees. Fabius started to plant a number of "lilies" between the barn and tree line, camouflaging the javelin heads as he went. A majority of the enemy wore but flimsy sandals, or went shoeless. Oppius and Roscius set their position around ten feet apart from one another at the tree line, which stood at around fifty feet from the barn. They dug their scutums into the ground, should they need to duck behind them (or they could also take cover behind the large neighbouring birch trees should the enemy launch a wave of arrows or spears). They also planted a dozen pilums in the ground, within easy reach next to them. Fabius meanwhile selected a position to the side, where he could conceal himself and flank the enemy as they came out of the barn. He also planted a few "lilies" in the open ground before his position, in case any of the enemy decided to rush him.

Oppius crept up to the building and doused oil upon the barn door, before returning to his men and giving them one final briefing.

"Fabius, make every arrow count. Put the bastards down. As long as they stay down you can move onto your next target. If one of our traps fells an enemy let him lie there in agony too. Wounded will be as good as dead. Victory must come quickly, or not at all. Should they organise themselves and there's too many of them to defeat then you know where you should retreat to. But let's try not to give them our backs as targets or give them material for jokes about Romans running from Gauls."

All three men smiled fleetingly and tried to give one another encouraging looks, but a grim seriousness soon took over.

Dawn gradually bled upwards into the night and the sun's rays beautifully sparkled upon the even more silvery-blue lake. Occasionally a fish popped its head out of the water and swished its tail.

Oppius and Roscius stood in plain sight, unflinching, as a scar-faced youth came out of the barn to relieve himself, while the morning light cut through the gaps in the planks of the side of the barn. He squinted at first at the scene, either because of the brightness or in disbelief. He quickly called to his comrades however, sounding the alarm in three different languages, drowning out the trill of the birdsong. Some men rushed out immediately, some men more slowly, rubbing the sleep out of their eyes as they did so. A brace of the enemy wasted little time in throwing their javelins at their Roman foes, but they were launched more in hope than expectation. Teeth were bared, curses were fired off – for want of a hail of arrows to succeed their words. Livia's lieutenant finally made an appearance. Oppius caught his eye and wryly smiled.

"I'm here for that lesson you wanted to teach me," the centurion declaimed, although by the time he had finished his sentence the hulking barbarian had gone back into the barn to retrieve his sword. Livia was nowhere to be seen, Oppius noticed.

Oppius nodded to Fabius. The first arrow felled the man nearest to the entrance to the barn; his corpse barred anyone opening the large wooden door easily. The next was a fire arrow, which set the oil doused door ablaze. Livia's lieutenant was not only prevented from joining the fight but he was also unable to communicate his orders above the roar of the flames and the howls of pain outside. The sound of the fire was soon accompanied by the whoosh of arrows and pilums as Oppius, Roscius and Fabius launched attacks from the front and side. Half a dozen men soon roused themselves and ran towards the two Romans in front of them, drawing their swords and issuing battle cries. The "lilies" flowered beneath three of the men's feet however. Screams cut through the air, as metal sliced through skin and bone. When the remaining enemy reached Oppius and Roscius their battle cries proved more accomplished than their swordsmanship. The Romans efficiently skewered the barbarians and then swiftly continued to launch their remaining pilums at the men inside the killing ground, outside the burning barn. A group of Gauls retreated into the forest, having been paid by the agent – and a few barbarians from differing tribes followed them. Fabius continued not to waste his arrows and took his shots as if Teucer were watching or whispering into his ear; the youth controlled his breathing and aim. A number of the enemy believed that more than one archer must have been firing at them from within the woods.

Another wave of spears was launched in their direction but Oppius and Roscius took cover in the trees from those that flew close to them. The barbarians then launched an attack carrying swords and axes; their offensive however was slowed through their caution at stepping upon one of the camouflaged holes in the ground, housing a spike. As the enemy delayed their attack the Romans felled a couple in the group through burying pilums or knives into their chests. Oppius then drew his gladius and cut through their defences, armour and rib cages in short time. Bodies, some half alive, some half dead, were littered around him – groaning in pain or cursing him. The centurion barely noticed them however, as he took to the task of employing his remaining javelins usefully. His blood-lust was up, compensating for his body being sapped of half of its strength. Killing remained as much of a science as a desire in the mind of the soldier. Roscius too grunted in satisfaction as another pilum struck the sternum of an opponent. More of the enemy retreated. Once out of missiles the two soldiers, wielding their scutums and swords, advanced. Arrows continued to zip through the air. The wounded moaned upon the ground, or played dead (a dress rehearsal for the fate that would soon await them). The air still crackled with the sound of the entrance to the barn burning. All was confusion – for the enemy.

Roscius redoubled his offensive upon receiving a wound to the shoulder, his blood-strewn face making him appear even more fearsome. An arrow pierced the neck of a barbarian, which gave pause to the enemy and another half a dozen barbarians scrambled into the woods. Just when they believed they had no one left to fight however, Livia's bearded enforcer – accompanied by a brace of men – appeared before them, having escaped from the burning barn. A pilum and arrow soon hit their mark to dispense with the men which flanked their commander.

A roar issued forth from a mouth missing half its teeth, as Livia's lieutenant raced towards Oppius, armed with his large cavalry sword and shield. His face was black and red from the fire and smoke, his great beard singed. The centurion deflected the first blow with his gladius. A heavy clang rang out and Oppius felt the blow jolt throughout his arm and shoulder. The barbarian was skilled but yet often used his sword as a club, as he tried to bludgeon his way through the Roman's defences. He's only a pounder after all, Oppius thought to himself in regards to his over confident enemy. The centurion looked to be in trouble a couple of times, but he ordered his legionaries not to help him when they offered to finish off his ferocious adversary. Oppius formed a plan.

He first retreated a little and then skirted around the barbarian, turning his man.

"Are you going to fight or keep dancing Roman?" the barbarian goaded - and then attempted to spit at his enemy.

"Both."

Oppius quickly feinted to the left but then moved to the right to get inside his attacker's defences; once close enough Oppius tripped and shoved his opponent to the ground. Fabius flinched at the sound of the steel crunching upon the back of the barbarian's skull. The tip of the spike from the lily protruded from out of his bloodied mouth and beard.

"End of lesson," Oppius remarked, although his enemy could no longer hear him.

Roscius, Fabius and a timely shower helped put the fire out. Livia was still nowhere to be seen, although Oppius could surmise from the gap in the planks at the back of the barn how she had escaped. She had escaped with some of the gold, as well as her life, but Oppius was little concerned about the value of Caesar's war chest. More so he was content, from having satisfied his honour and the honour of his slain unit.

Oppius gazed out at the serene, still lake, desiring that his heart could find the same sense of repose and quietude. A couple of song birds swirled around in the vast space between the water and sky, in courtship. Sunlight glittered across the skin of the water, its beauty as hypnotic as *her*. He breathed out, partly in a sigh. Perhaps not even the centurion knew if it was a lover's sigh, or a sigh of regret.

"Are we going after her?" Roscius asked, wounded and exhausted but still willing to follow his friend to the gates of Hades.

"I'm ready," Fabius said with the confidence that victory brings, whilst extracting one of his arrows from an enemy corpse.

"I could say that she's not worth it, but she's carrying a wealth of gold. Yet we're going back. Fortune favours the brave, not the foolhardy," Oppius expressed, unsure whether tiredness, or his feeling for Livia, was influencing his decision. The centurion thought how she would be able to live prosperously and peacefully in a faraway land, but not forever.

The centurion was also keen to return to Alesia, Caesar and the Tenth Legion – just to make sure they were all still there.

15.

Alesia.

"I've known some costly whores in my time, but Livia is now in a class of her own," Caesar remarked, his pinched expression conveying how he was not as amused as his comment might have suggested. He was unsure whether to be angrier about the theft of his gold, or for being taken in by the guileful agent. Woman - that was the gods' second mistake, he was about to express, quoting one of his favourite philosophers. Such was his ire that for a moment Caesar was persuaded by the thought that Oppius might have allowed his former lover to escape with some of the gold, or he had hoarded some for himself, but then his thoughts and expression softened towards the loyal soldier. Caesar's centurions must be above suspicion, he posited.

Oppius stood before his commander, having finished his debriefing in regards to the mission. The centurion recounted how he had buried the chest of gold in a secure place in the forest. The danger of having the chest taken from them – and the fact that it was too heavy for three men to manage – meant that he couldn't bring the gold back immediately. He sought permission to arrange for Fabius to lead a cohort to the location and transport the chest back to the camp. Caesar granted permission for the officer to take care of things.

"I find myself in your debt again Lucius. But I am now in a position to repay this debt to you. I shall grant you and your men a leave of absence, as well as some spending money to enjoy on your leave. My only request is that you visit Rome in your time away from your duties. I have some letters I would like you to personally deliver – and receive a response to. But all this can wait until tomorrow. Rest, and then enjoy yourself tonight with all the wine we recently liberated from our enemy."

Caesar dismissed his centurion, yet just as Oppius was leaving his commander asked, in a tone of both considerateness and curiosity,

"Did you love her? Are you still in love with her?"

The centurion here paused and thought of those things he did love – his mother, friends and even the army - before pensively answering,

"No."

It was mostly lust, as opposed to love, Oppius concluded.

Mark Antony's muscles bulged on carrying the large jar of wine, before setting it down next to Teucer, who was sitting around a campfire accompanied by Roscius and Fabius.

"Your bonus, as promised. If you can still shoot straight after drinking all of this then you too may well be descended from the gods," Antony said, his swollen cheek bone and bloodied lip from the battle still unable to mask his handsome and genial features. "That shoulder looks painful Roscius."

"You should see the other guys," the legionary replied, grinning with pride as he remembered their recent feat of arms as he also got up and stirred the broth in the pot above the fire, receiving a face full of aromatic steam as he did so. "Would you like to stay for some food?"

"Even if you could cook as well as you can fight Roscius, I must take my leave. I just came along to give Teucer his reward for keeping me alive this past day or so. Britain's loss has been Rome's gain. It was a pleasure fighting with you," Antony affectionately said to the archer and clasped his forearm in a Roman handshake.

"The pleasure was mine as well, although let's not arrange to repeat the experience too soon," Teucer replied, genuinely impressed by the legate – as both a man and soldier.

"But look who it is! It's Caesar's golden boy, so to speak," Mark Antony exclaimed at seeing Oppius join them. The centurion knew not if Antony was mocking him a little, or pleased for him. In truth Oppius was too tired to care. Nevertheless he was glad that Antony had survived the battle.

Antony departed, to interview Enobarbus for the position of his adjutant, whilst Oppius wearily sat down. He closed his eyes briefly and emptied his mind, whilst hoping to relieve his body of its numerous aches too. But then he gave his men the good news.

"We have been granted some leave and expenses to travel to Rome. I've got to deliver some correspondence for Caesar, but otherwise we'll be off duty," the centurion announced, affording himself a smile in knowing how much his men would be cheered by the news. They had fought hard. Soon they would play hard. The spirits and faces of his men lifted immediately, particularly in regards to Roscius.

"Although off duty, there will still be some campaigns to be fought. Fabius, we need to get you laid in the finest and filthiest brothel. The two things are one and the same when it comes to houses of ill repute. Teucer, you will no doubt try to campaign to drink more than me. But be prepared to be defeated in this cause, my friend. And what will our golden boy campaign for whilst in Rome? Nothing other than to avoid bumping in to his ex-wife - whose campaign will be to rob him of his spending money – and joy – should she see him."

The four friends gave out a laugh and proceeded to work their way through a pot of broth and jar of wine, remembering and toasting their dead comrades deep into the night.

16.

Joseph instructed a servant to further fuel the braziers, lighting and heating the chamber. Caesar appeared oblivious to any change in light or temperature though, as he continued writing various letters. Joseph gazed at the proconsul with fondness and also, even after all these years, wonder at his master's tireless energy and ambition. Yet as well as admiration Joseph's feelings were mixed with pity, for Caesar could all too often be a slave to his ambition and pride. As close to defeat as the army had been at Alesia, Joseph knew it would not satiate Caesar's appetite for war and power. Whilst the night before he had prayed for Caesar to find a way to win the war, tonight he would pray for him to find peace.

"Firstly, how are you progressing with your studies Octavius? Did you receive the books I sent? Your sister may well steal and read them first, but make sure you read them afterwards. I sent you a copy of Cicero's latest work. It is not his best, but it is still superior to any other's best. I received a letter from Cicero recently and he wrote something that I'm compelled to pass on. He expressed that man's intellect is the sum of his reading - so the more we read the greater the sum of our intellect will be, he argued. In short, keep reading. Immerse yourself in philosophy and literature each day, as if you were a soldier drilling yourself in swordsmanship. You were born for greatness Octavius, but it'll

take more than my prophetic judgement for greatness to come to fruition... Work hard. Don't disappoint me...

...There are those who will question my motives and actions in regards to my campaigns in Gaul but History will be kind to me – for I intend to write the History myself... The Gauls fought well, but not well enough...Libienus, Mark Antony, Decimus Brutus, Trebonius all proved to be inspirational commanders, yet it was perhaps the case that they were moved to greatness by the inspiration of each lion-hearted legionary too... But we must thank the gods as well as the legions. It was the closest of close run things. To adapt the quote from Pyrrhus, another such victory over the Gauls and we are undone... I will punish some tribes, bribe others. As for Vercingetorix he prostrated himself before me, but even Caesar's famed clemency has its limits. He has been responsible for spilling too much Roman blood for him not to pay a price, in blood, himself. He ventured out from Alesia to surrender in his finest armour, riding upon his best horse. But a beggar is still a beggar, even if dressed like a king... To the victor, the spoils. I may well have taken enough prisoners to grant a slave to every deserving legionary... I have won a great victory Octavius but there will still be those ingrates and backward-looking senators who will call for me to disband my army, now that it has secured our northern borders. Anyone who wishes to disband my army though will have to do so by force, rather than self-interested legislation... Caesar must be Caesar..."

Sword of Rome: Gladiator

1.

"She kept me up all night, even when I was dreaming of her in my sleep," Roscius expressed, still smirking fondly, remembering the previous evening's drinking and whoring. The hung-over soldier then reached for a nearby jug of water and gulped down its contents in an effort to rehydrate himself.

"Was she clean?" his centurion asked. Lucius Oppius did not mind his men enjoying themselves, but he did not want them catching a pox either. He had let his unit sleep in, but he finally roused them. He wanted to reach the city by the close of day. They had both time and money to spend in Rome over the coming days – a reward from Caesar for having completed a special mission for their general during the battle of Alesia. Oppius brushed his hand in front of his face, but it did little to diminish the thick odour of sweat and wine which hung in the air of the room at the inn.

"No, fortunately she was filthy," the hulking infantryman replied, giggling like a schoolboy at his own joke. "She was uncommonly attractive, for a whore. Thankfully she was common in all sorts of other ways though. But still my piece couldn't compare to the girl we picked out for Fabius, eh lad?"

The young, studious legionary, who owned aspirations of becoming a poet, blushed and grinned sheepishly in the corner. His blushes could still not disguise his red-rimmed eyes however.

"Her breasts were an eyeful, handful and no doubt mouthful," Teucer, a skilled archer from Britain who Caesar had recruited to the Tenth Legion, exclaimed whilst simultaneously yawning.

Fabius rolled his eyes, as he considered how he was planning to introduce the unit to his mother over a supper at his family home just outside of Rome.

"The lad has probably already run out of ink, writing poems to her," Roscius remarked.

"He certainly must have run out of something for her. He didn't get back until only a few hours ago," Teucer added, winking at the youth.

"She's doubtless taken his heart," Roscius said, following up his jug of water with a swig of sour wine.

"More likely she's taken the contents of his purse. There's always fresh meat to fuel the oldest profession," Teucer posited.

"Aye, and the one you picked last night was so old she could have been one of the founders of the trade."

"I would try and defend her honour and virtue but I fear she lost those during the reign of Sulla," the Briton joked.

Despite having warned his men not to have too raucous a night the officer would refrain from saying anything to Fabius, partly because he was also guilty of staying out late. Oppius had spent the evening with one of the servant girls at the inn, Florentia. He had

136

not long left her side. Oppius had promised the pretty, blonde girl that he would see her again on his way back. Florentia had promised that she would stay faithful to him until that time. Both would break their promises, though neither would be broken-hearted as a result. Nevertheless the lissom, fun wench had proved a welcome distraction. For once he had not spent half the night awake, thinking about Livia - a former agent of Caesar's and Oppius' ex-lover. She had betrayed him in Gaul, yet had spared his life. Memories and images of the seductive woman often still jabbed through the ribcage of his thoughts.

"Was she worth it?" the centurion remarked, turning to the youth.

The once sweet-faced Fabius nodded in reply, whilst this time wolfishly grinning.

Oppius had frequently asked himself the same question in regards to Livia. The answer was not always the same. He knew not if he would kiss her – or kill her - should he ever see her again.

2.

Oppius gave a few coins to a farmer heading towards the city so that the four soldiers travelled in the back of a wagon on the final leg of their journey. Rome never ceased to take a man's breath away, or give him a crick in the neck, as he craned his head upwards to take in the famed seven hills – from the Subura to the Palatine, with its gleaming white villas. Clouds scudded across the sky above but they could still not shut out the will of the gods to have the sun bathe the Olympus-like city in light. Streaks of smoke poured upwards from Rome's various bakeries and forges. The murmur of thousands of voices could be heard from outside the walls; the voices were separate, yet also bound together in an inexplicable chorus – or sometimes dirge - of sound. Traffic streamed in and out of the city gates, kicking up dust. The city swallowed up an endless procession of mules and wagons laden with olives, grapes, barley, salted pork and other assorted produce. A white bull slowly – and seemingly sadly – entered the city, perhaps foreseeing its role in an imminent pagan sacrifice. Immigrants of all colours and creeds, dressed in rags and carrying all their worldly goods in small bundles, gaped in fear and wonder at their new home. Rome and the surrounding view, as the soldiers made their way along the Via Salaria, was also home to various gardens, fields, theatres, monuments and snaking aqueducts. The roads were lined with tombs, from the austere to the elaborate. Fabius mused to himself how all roads led to Rome, but really all roads lead to one's grave. He made a note of the concept, in order to include it in a future poem.

Oppius thought how Rome was a monster; it fed itself on a diet of martial glory, dramatic spectacles, political demagogues and religious fervour. Rome had also seemingly thirsted for blood over the centuries too. The walls had run red with Tarquin the Proud, the Gracchi, the supporters of Sulla and Marius - and Catiline and his conspirators. The walls were currently painted with graffiti about Caesar and Pompey – but would the paint be ultimately washed away in the blood of a civil war between the great men?

Before Rome imploded again though, Oppius would enjoy the city. He who is tired of Rome is tired of life, he had heard Fabius once say, quoting another poet. The centurion looked forward to visiting a bath house and feeling the water, strigil and massage oils upon his skin, soothing body and mind. He would doubtless also accompany his unit when they ventured down to the bars and brothels in the Subura one evening; the Subura was the place where everyone liked to visit but no one liked to live. He would decline an invite to any gladiatorial bout however. Although Oppius could understand the popularity of the spectacle and the crowd baying for blood that did not mean that he appreciated the "sport". The centurion had witnessed enough death and cruelty through his job. He could do without their spectres when free from his duties.

As the wagon passed through the Collina gate Teucer gently whistled through his teeth in awe at the scale and other-worldliness of the city, albeit he was less enamoured with the pungent smell of horse dung assaulting his nostrils.

"Not even you could drink this town dry Roscius," the Briton exclaimed, thinking how London had a long way to go to match the wonder and enormity of Rome.

"No, but I'm going to have fun trying," the legionary replied, licking his lips in anticipation of the days ahead. "I'll begin by working my way through Fabius' family cellar during dinner this evening. Most of the vintages are even older that the whore you slept with last night."

"But will they taste as sweet?" the Briton replied with a lewd grin and wink.

"Yes. Because the wine will be free."

"You'll pay for the wine if you drink too much though. We've still got some business to attend to tomorrow morning, delivering some correspondence for Caesar. Roscius, you and I will be venturing over to the Aventine Hill to deliver a letter to a merchant, Sextus Mallius. Fabius, I want you to deliver a letter to Caesar's great nephew, Octavius. Teucer, you can accompany him."

"Do you not want to visit the young Caesar yourself? He could prove to be a powerful patron in years to come," Fabius asserted.

"Having one Caesar as a patron is proving dangerous enough. If the young Caesar starts ordering me around too, it could prove the death of me," the centurion humourlessly joked.

3.

Titus Fabius still had the same distinctive scarred, shaven head from when he had been a soldier, but the former officer's once flint-like features had softened with age and good living. His waistline had grown as had his income since retiring from his twenty-five years of service in the army. Titus was now a wealthy merchant, having invested in a number of mining projects in Greece. He lived in one of the largest properties on the Quirinal Hill, having bought the villa because the bedroom overlooked the Campus Martius. "It's nice to be reminded about where you've come from," Titus remarked to Oppius, who had once served as a raw recruit under the veteran centurion.

"The pornography's mine. All the serious books are his," Titus exclaimed, smiling and nodding towards his son. Fabius rolled his eyes and looked embarrassed - akin to any youth in the presence of a half-drunk father. Oppius and his unit were being given a tour of Titus' house. They were in the library, where the merchant's slaves commenced to serve his guests with wine and various dishes of finger foods (olives, mixed nuts, dates, figs, plums, mussels and snails).

"I must thank you again Lucius for taking care of Marcus. He left here a boy, but he has returned a man. He was as wet as a sardine when he first joined the legion, but there's now more of a hardness to him," Titus said, looking fondly at his eldest son and admiring his new soldierly physique.

Roscius was here about to add that there was certainly a hardness to Marcus the night before in the brothel, but thankfully his mouth was more concerned with making the most of the food than making a joke.

"He's taken as much care of me as I have of him, I dare say," Oppius replied, modestly.

"It does seems you need looking after sometimes my old friend. I read about your act of bravery, or rather lunacy, on the shores of Britain, when you helped take the beach. The despatches about the engagement had men cheering and raising their glasses to the standard bearer of the Tenth. Women probably swooned too. When I asked you to take care of Marcus I thought it was implied that you should take care of yourself too."

"It wasn't reported in the despatches, but Marcus saved my life during the invasion – I'm glad to say. I'm not sure how glad he was about it though, after all the drilling and dangerous situations I've put him through since. But Marcus has turned into a fine young man and soldier, Titus."

"I believe you. I do not provide him with a generous enough allowance to bribe you into saying complimentary things. But I warrant that I do not just have you to thank for keeping an eye out for the lad. I suspect that you too have also had a hand in his protection and education," Titus remarked, turning towards Roscius and Teucer.

"Aye, I guess I taught the lad how to hold a bow and shoot straight," the archer wryly conceded.

"And I taught him how to hold his drink and not shoot his mouth off," Roscius added, grinning with visible pleasure and pride at the witticism he had just come up with.

"You have my thanks," Titus warmly exclaimed, clasping his hands upon the two men's shoulders. "My door will always be open to you. But right now let me open up my kitchen and wine cellar to you both."

Just as Teucer had once believed that the attacks upon the Roman defences at Alesia would never end, so too he wondered if the procession of slaves bringing out different dishes of food would carry on throughout the night. Various foodstuffs on silver plates covered all three tables in the opulent dining room: leeks in mushroom sauce, spiced pork, salted tuna upon a bed of lettuce, stuffed eels, lamprey, wild fowl, radishes in garum, partridge in garum, asparagus in garum, sardines in garum, wood pigeon, various cheeses and more. Even though their host was discussing the fate and future of Rome, the archer could not help but be transfixed by the aromatic feast before him.

"It's a matter of simple arithmetic. There can only be one First Man of Rome. This city will not be big enough for the both of them. Caesar and Pompey will clash, as sure as the seas crash against the shores. Pompey will not permit any equal, Caesar will not admit any superior. Any hope of a peace between them died with Julia I warrant – Caesar's daughter and Pompey's wife. For

Rome, it was a match made in heaven. Pompey has yet to officially break with Caesar, but I know that Cato has been whispering poison into his ears, as well as openly denigrating Caesar in the Forum."

"Who do you believe will be the last man standing?" Marcus asked his father, losing his appetite at the thought of a conflict which could tear the world in two. He blanched, imagining that the bloody battles and scorched plains of Gaul could spread to the Italian peninsular and pit Roman against Roman.

"Caesar has spent the last ten years sharpening the swords of his legions, whilst Pompey has exited the theatre of war. His military prowess may now be akin to an old, unused blade – which has spent too long housed in its scabbard. Yet Pompey currently holds the ground, Rome itself. As you know military thinking dictates that an attacker normally needs three times the force of the defender to take a fortified town. Yet Caesar may only raise a third of the forces that Pompey could have at his disposal. So again it could just come down to a matter of arithmetic. But Caesar has defied the odds before. Cicero once made a speech about how Pompey possessed the key virtues of a great general, namely courage, military knowledge, authority and good luck. Caesar not only possesses a surplus of the first three of those virtues but I warrant that he could even turn Pompey's good luck into better luck. However, the storm brewing between Caesar and Pompey is on the distant horizon. I would have you look to the clouds that could be hanging over yourselves right now."

"What do you mean?" Oppius asked, topping up his men's wine with water.

"Caesar is not the only person to employ agents to keep him informed and watch his enemies. Cato and Pompey doubtless are aware of your presence in Rome – and your task to deliver some of Caesar's correspondence. Watch your backs lads. The backstreets of Rome may prove more dangerous than the battlefields of Gaul. At least you faced your enemy there and knew what was coming. My advice to you is to keep your heads down and lay low."

A short pause here ensued while the four comrades looked at each other, unsure of how much they should trust in their host's warnings and advice. Even Roscius paused in necking his wine. Yet after draining his cup he spoke:

"I intend to spend many an hour lying low – below the female population of the Subura. It'll be fine. We're off duty. I'm no more an agent of Caesar's than I am a fishmonger."

Although off duty Oppius still ordered his unit to sharpen their blades that evening, before they went to bed.

4.

Morning.

A watery light seeped into the narrow streets as Teucer and Marcus Fabius made their way across the city to deliver Caesar's correspondence to his great-nephew. The Briton could not help but be amused and captivated by the sights, sounds and – less so – smells of Rome. He swung his head left and right to take in the colourful and novel scenes of Rome waking up, yet at the same time he needed to keep an eye on the ground as the archer dodged left and right to avoid stepping into the excrement beneath his feet.

"This city is full of history – but it is also full of shit," Fabius remarked, quoting a line from one of his own poems.

The streets soon grew wider – and cleaner – however, as they made their way towards the Palatine district and their destination.

The slave who opened the door to the legionaries seemed to have had his nose broken more times than Teucer had broken his bowstring. Grunts supplanted speech as the attendant – a former gladiator who now served as one of many bodyguards to the young Caesar – led the soldiers through the large house out into the garden, where they found Octavius sitting beneath a cypress tree, reading.

The boy immediately removed his sun hat and got up to greet the messengers as soon as he saw them. He wore a white tunic with a subtle purple border. His hair was fair, his complexion pale – to the point of appearing sickly. Yet his blue eyes shone with friendliness and intelligence. His build was slight and Fabius thought to himself how Caesar's great-nephew had spent more time in the library than on the Campus Martius.

Fabius, who had spent a similar amount of time exercising his mind – rather than body – as a young teenager, looked over to see what Octavius had been reading, after handing over the letters and exchanging pleasantries and news about his great-uncle and the campaign in Gaul. The would-be poet raised his eyebrow in pleasant surprise to discover that the youth was reading Catullus.

"Now he is treading that dark road to the place from which they say no one has ever returned."

Despite the weak light Roscius still squinted as he gazed up at the sky, accompanying Oppius to hand Caesar's letters over to Sextus Mallius at his house on the Aventine Hill of Rome. In answer to the accusation of being hung-over the legionary replied that he was just "tired". The property was extensive – and expensive. Crassus had once owned the house. Suffice to say the build quality of the residence was superior to those houses that the former triumvir had constructed for his numerous tenants. Mallius had been described – and labelled in graffiti – as being a "new Crassus". The first man to call him such had been Cicero (the satirical statesman having given him the nickname in order to denigrate the affluent and influential merchant). But Mallius took pride in the title and thought it a compliment. Mallius even took to adopting some of Crassus' business practices, as well as his maxims, as a result. "Loyalty and friends can be bought, rather than earned." Although the merchant and banker often trumpeted that he was a self-made man in terms of his income (he owned property and mining interests, as well as a string of gladiator schools) most of his wealth stemmed from a fortuitous inheritance.

Oppius and Roscius were led into a half-lit triclinium. When someone once asked Mallius why he kept his house so gloomy he replied that "darkness is cheaper than light". Yet still the light was good enough for the merchant to look at – and look down upon – the soldiers cum messengers. His eyes were two slits – full of idle, or active, disdain for the world. His face also housed a downturned mouth and aquiline nose. His skin was leathery, his build was lean. Titus had given his opinion of Mallius at dinner the previous night, yet the centurion would have come to the same conclusion about the merchant on his own accord soon enough. Mallius viewed Rome as not something that he should serve, but something that he could exploit. He lay upon his couch as if it were a throne.

"Well don't just stand there you fools! Which one of you slabs of meat possesses these letters from Caesar?" There was a slight sibilance and shrillness to the merchant's voice. Roscius would comment after the meeting that Mallius owned both a "woman's voice and girl's figure".

Oppius walked over to Mallius and handed over the correspondence. The merchant neither thanked nor looked at the soldier as he did so – but merely thrust out his arm and grabbed the packet.

"Now wait here whilst I go through them, in case I need to give a reply immediately," the sour-faced financier remarked. Mallius proceeded to read Caesar's letters upon the large sofa, often adjusting his toga whilst he read, as the garment failed to cling comfortably to his slight figure. He neither offered his guests refreshments nor permitted them to sit down.

The centurion was already aware of the nub of Caesar's message, as his commander had confided in him. Mallius was in possession of certain pieces of intelligence in regards to which senators were for or against him retaining his legions, should he return to Rome. The aged merchant's eyes both widened and narrowed whilst he read the letters. He hummed and grunted a couple of times but by the end he seemed content – to the point of licking his lips in satisfaction or expectation.

"You are Oppius?" Mallius remarked; this time fixing his eyes upon the centurion intently, as a critic may appraise a new piece of sculpture.

"Yes."

"Now you are - mine," the wily looking merchant replied after a pause, his downturned mouth transforming itself into a serpentine grin.

5.

"My mind's sunk so low, Claudia, because of you, wrecked itself on your account so bad already, that I couldn't like you if you were the best of women, - or stop loving you, no matter what you do," Fabius exclaimed, quoting his favourite lines from Catullus. He briefly paused as he thought of Oppius and Livia in relation to the extract, before adding that,

"Unrequited love is perhaps the only true love."

"Then give me plenty of a love that's false," Teucer replied, in between mouthfuls of his honey-glazed pork.

The young Octavius smiled, enjoying both the idealism of Fabius and the cynicism of his comrade. Octavius had asked the soldiers to stay for an early lunch and questioned them more in regards to Caesar and the Gallic campaign.

"You have an accent. May I ask where you're originally from?"

"Britain. You can take the boy out of Britain, but you can't completely take Britain out of the boy," the archer answered.

"And how would you describe your countrymen?"

"They are mad when they're drunk – and mad when they're sober," Teucer concluded, after a brief moment's thought.

"I do not mean to give offence to your homeland but I have heard that Britain is still largely a barbarous land, especially in the north. It is in need of laws – and bread and circuses. Once we start providing these then we might be able to civilise the people, wean them off their drink."

"Stop the British from drinking? Now who's mad?" Teucer remarked, amused at the proposition.

"I am but mad north-north-west," Octavius wryly replied, quoting a line from a play which was familiar to Fabius also. "Let me thank you again for having come so far, from the north-west, to deliver these letters though. I hope I will see you both once more before you return. I may have letters for you to give to Caesar if so."

"You may wish to give them to Lucius Oppius, our centurion. He has Caesar's ear and can deliver any messages personally," Fabius said, increasingly impressed by the boy's intelligence, politeness and wit. He was mature beyond his years – possessing genuine virtues as opposed to just being precocious.

"My great-uncle has mentioned him in his correspondence. He called him one of the bravest soldiers in his army."

Teucer thought to himself how Oppius was as bloody-minded as he was bloody brave. He was intrigued as to how the studious youth and tough centurion would get on however, should they ever meet.

Oppius' face began to screw itself up as much as his fist as he read over the letters. The first was addressed to Mallius and mentioned how Caesar was willing to lend him the use of his centurion, as well pay him handsomely, for the information he wanted. The second letter, contained in the packet, was addressed to Oppius himself. Caesar first apologised for the position he was putting his centurion in, but the intelligence the merchant possessed was extremely valuable to him. Caesar also stated how he would financially compensate Oppius and his unit should Mallius make use of his offer during the soldier's stay in Rome. Oppius cursed his commander beneath his breath as he read his orders – and Mallius spoke whilst he took in the letter again.

"I am a merchant and one of the commodities I trade in is knowledge. As you are discovering I have a piece of knowledge to sell – and I have a buyer. Caesar has offered me a sum of gold, as well as your services and labour, as payment for this knowledge. I'm willing to accept the terms. As you may already be aware I own a number of gladiator schools. I also arrange gladiatorial contests for the populace in various arenas in and around the city. The mob's manners may be bad, but its money is good. I have arranged an event for the day after tomorrow in a sizeable arena just outside Ostia, but I am one combatant short due to injury. I could of course call upon a piece of meat from one of my own schools, but it strikes me that you might add a certain glamour to the bill. You are the famous standard bearer who led the charge during the invasion of Britain. You have just come back victorious from the siege of Alesia. Yes, you will provide something extra I believe. You are an accomplished soldier. Let us hope that you prove an equally competent gladiator, for your sake more than mine," Mallius issued, and then let out a nasty little laugh.

As much as he felt he owed Mallius nothing (or less than nothing, such was his growing dislike for the odious merchant) Oppius still owed a duty to Caesar. Caesar had promoted him and taken the centurion into his trust. He had rewarded him well for his service – and felt his commander would display a similar loyalty to him should somehow their roles be reversed.

"You can of course refuse, but nobody will win if that proves the case. Caesar will not receive his intelligence and I will not get paid. You may also find yourself earning your commander's displeasure. Not an enviable fate I suspect. If you have any doubts, I can assure you that your opponent will not be of the highest standard."

The effete merchant took a visible pleasure in wielding a certain amount of power over the centurion. He thought to himself how yet again brains were conquering brawn. Rome was Rome because of the patrician and merchant classes. The mob merely existed to raise their superiors up even higher. Even the success of the Roman army was due to the few leading the many – lions leading donkeys – Mallius concluded.

"So, centurion, do we have an accord?"

"Put together the names on a list for Caesar – and you can put my name down on the bill for the contest," Oppius answered, looking as though the next person that he would kill would be the merchant, as opposed to any rival in an arena.

6.

Oil glistened all over the gladiator's muscular body. He snorted and grinned, revealing a set of yellow teeth pillaged from the mouths of his various victims in the arena. Although "Aulus the Mauler" was not of the highest standard of combatants, as Mallius had promised, he was still of a "high" standard, Titus Fabius had assured Oppius. The centurion stood next to his fearsome opponent in the tunnel. As an extra piece of theatre, or authenticity, Mallius suggested that the soldier wear his uniform when fighting the veteran gladiator. Oppius carried his gladius and scutum. Mallius had also ordered one of his attendants to clean-up the centurion's breastplate and greaves.

Aulus tensed up next to his opponent, flexing his muscles in order to intimidate the slightly smaller soldier. The gladiator's body was a lattice-work of scars. His long, lank hair could still not hide his large cauliflower ears. Aulus turned towards Oppius and gifted him a hostile, unblinking look whilst flaring his nostrils. Titus warned his friend how the gladiator would attempt to intimidate him beforehand, "There's many an opponent that he's defeated even before they have stepped out onto the sand... Aulus is quicker than his bulk suggests. He also knows as many dirty moves as a legionary. Even more perhaps. Yet his weaknesses will be his over-confidence and his need to play to the crowd. A few more like Aulus however and Spartacus might now be residing in a villa on top of the Palatine. He's a brutal bastard that even his mother would have trouble loving."

Oppius merely rolled his eyes in reply to the gladiator's attempt to overawe him.

"You all set?" Roscius asked, warmly clasping his friend on the shoulder.

"Aye. Are we all set? Did you get a good price?" the centurion replied, making reference to the bets that Oppius had asked his legionary to place on his behalf.

"I got a great price. You're far from the favourite."

"I'm unsure as to whether that's good news or not."

"The prize may not just be your winnings. I've heard that the wife of a senator will invite the victor back to her villa. Apparently she likes gladiators, or soldiers," Roscius said, raising his eyebrow suggestively.

"Some trophies are not worth keeping. I've seen her. She's even too old for Teucer. If she likes soldiers tell her I'm a gladiator. If she likes gladiators tell her I'm a soldier."

Roscius wished his friend good luck and then disappeared to join his comrades at their seats in the arena.

"I'm gonna make you wish you never left Gaul and your legion," Aulus remarked in a rasping voice, sneering at his opponent.

"I wish that already."

"I'm gonna teach you the meaning of the word pain."

156

"You sound like my ex-wife. If your tactic is to bore me to death then you're succeeding."

Aulus snarled, but before he could utter anything else the gladiators were instructed to follow the umpire and arena slaves out onto the sand.

The roar from the crowd assaulted his ears to the point that Oppius even flinched a little. A thousand cheers and jeers were spat forth. Some called out Aulus' name, either in denigration or celebration. The centurion briefly took in some of the enraptured spectators. Many were wide-eyed, lusting for violence. Wine-stained teeth were also bared, in smiles or hisses. Women shrieked. Oppius became slightly disorientated as hundreds of people he neither knew – nor desired to know - called out his name. He squinted in the light of the sun and placed his hand in front of his face. Many were dressed in their brightest and best clothes; perhaps the men folk had told their wives that they were visiting the temple. The audience undulated as it rose and sat down together.

Aulus acknowledged the crowd, which only fuelled the frenzy. The retiarius (or "net man") jabbed his spear up in the air and also swung his net, fishing for their attention and adulation. A cold sun hung in a pale blue sky. His muscles rippled, the oil upon his skin gleamed as if he was made of polished bronze. Oppius observed his opponent, scrutinising his body for any past injuries he could exploit. The centurion had spent the previous day training with Titus and Roscius, working through the offensive and defensive capabilities of the retiarius. One had to get past the point of the spear, whilst also avoiding the danger of being trapped or tripped by the net. Titus drilled him hard; by dusk Oppius began to win as many practise bouts as he lost.

"Hear that centurion? That applause is for me. You may be a big noise in the theatre of war, but this is my stage – and I'm the lead actor on it. I intend to put on a show."

Again the gladiator raised his arms up triumphantly, as though the bout was over and he was already victorious. Oppius watched the arena slaves scatter extra sand on the ground, to soak up the puddles of blood – as Aulus continued to soak up the atmosphere. "The Battle of the Beasts," a contest between a drugged up rhinoceros and elephant, had preceded the gladiatorial combat. From the amount of blood and gore Oppius could discern beneath the sand it appeared that both had perished in the fight.

A trumpet sounded and the arena's umpire made a brief announcement. Oppius drew his sword. The centurion had taken down bigger, stronger and quicker – but not like this.

The umpire ordered the combat to commence.

Aulus the Mauler took his customary wide stance. He then spread his arms, turned his head up to the sky and gave out a mighty roar. It was the last line the colourful gladiator would ever deliver upon his stage. Noticing his bare torso as a wide open target and his eyes averted towards the sky Oppius grasped his chance. The sharpened gladius cut through the air – and cut into his chest and lungs, choking out the net man's battle cry.

A stunned silence was swiftly succeeded by an explosion of cheers and boos, even greater to that of before the bout. Some spectators felt cheated out of a proper fight, yet others marvelled at the soldier's audacity and skill. In the stands Roscius offered up a silent prayer of thanks to Mars and Fortuna. Teucer meanwhile clapped his hands, before dashing off to collect the unit's winnings.

The boos soon started to outnumber the cheers as Oppius ignored the audience's clamour for him to acknowledge them, or his triumph. Didn't someone tell him that he was here for their entertainment? Coriolanus was less contemptuous of the people, a senator who was in the crowd commentated to his mistress. The soldier continued to ignore the abuse and praise from the crowd as he walked over to his slain opponent. The colour was already draining from his face. His tongue poked out from his crooked set of teeth.

"Show's over," Oppius remarked, as he removed his sword from the still twitching corpse.

7.

News of the centurion's victory – and the novel and dramatic manner of Aulus the Mauler's defeat – travelled back to Rome before even Oppius and his unit were back inside the city walls. The tavern in the Subura, where Roscius and Teucer spent most of their evening, was abuzz with reports (some accurate, some fictitious) about the day's events in the arena at Ostia. Some considered the soldier's victory unsporting and that the spectators should have demanded their money back. Others felt a sense of pride – and security – that the centurion had defeated a gladiator; it augured well if ever a new Spartacus rose up to take on the legions.

When Roscius and Teucer returned to Titus Fabius' villa, in time to soak up the wine with another feast their host had arranged for them, they recounted a list of nicknames that Oppius was now being called: "Soldier of Fortune", "Caesar's Champion", "Oppius the Aulus Mauler". Marcus Fabius added to the list, by reporting upon a fresh piece of graffiti he had seen.

"The cartoon labelled you as the "Sword of Rome". I'm not sure it'll catch on. The image had you with a sword between your legs. Unfortunately for you they drew a gladius, rather than spartha."

"You have made a name for yourself it seems," Roscius exclaimed, feasting his eyes at the new batch of dishes that were being placed before him (red mullet, goose liver, pumpkin, beans in garum, wild boar chops in garum, lobster claws in garum). The legionary also feasted his eyes upon the dish of the serving girl who was attending to him. Either she was afflicted with a facial tic, or the buxom slave was winking at him whilst she served the soldier.

"Making a name for yourself can be as much of a curse as a blessing in this city," Titus posited, Cassandra-like in his tone and expression.

"You worry too much father," Marcus replied, just about winning his fight to separate the meat from the bone upon his chop.

"It's wisdom, as well as worry, which has turned what little hair I have left grey lad. Caesar's enemies might look to attack Caesar's Champion, in the absence of Caesar himself. You may also have become a victim of your own success in the eyes of Sextus Mallius. He'll reason that your new found fame will be able to put bums on seats."

"We had a deal. One fight, in exchange for the list."

"Never trust a banker Lucius. He will change his mind as easily as he'll change his rates of interest. Given the current state of affairs, the safest place for you may well be in the arena," Titus stated, wishing that he could have been solely joking.

8.

"I've known whores, or politicians even, who are more honest," Oppius exclaimed as he came out of Sextus Mallius' villa, accompanied by Marcus Fabius. Their meeting with the merchant had been brief. Mallius had given the centurion half the list, but argued that as he had added to the intelligence over the past day he wanted to alter the contract so that Oppius would fight one more time for him in the arena. Such was the promoter's confidence in Oppius - that he would sell out the arena - the merchant was even willing to give the lowly soldier a cut of the profits – a gesture that was unheard of normally, Mallius added magnanimously.

"I can help furnish you with both riches and fame," he uttered, jangling as he did so from all the jewellery (amulets, bangles and rings) he was wearing.

"I don't want fame or riches. I just want to go home," Oppius replied with frustration, remembering how he had still to visit his mother. Home however was perhaps now the legion, he considered. Either way, home was not the politic and decadent city of Rome he realised.

"Your home isn't going anywhere, however you are! Half the city wants to see you in the arena – and the other half wants to see you dead! It's perfect. Caesar, more than anyone, would want you to fight again too. You are his champion!"

The merchant's eyes gleamed like two gold coins, envisioning the spectacle and gate receipts of the famous standard bearer fighting again.

"You have a talent for killing it seems. It would be a crime to let your gift go to waste," Mallius softly said, looking to flatter the soldier, as he also lasciviously eyed two young slave boys standing in the corner, ready to bathe and massage their master.

"My talents extend to killing outside the arena too – and I don't just specialise in killing gladiators," Oppius replied, menacingly. The centurion was tempted to slit the man-snake's throat there and then. Yet unlike the state sponsored murder of gladiatorial combat he would be put on trial for killing the financier in his home. As "Caesar's Champion" the Senate would also hunt him down and prosecute with extreme prejudice. Not even Cicero would be able to save him, should he serve as his advocate.

Mallius left him to think over the new proposal and to give his answer in the morning, but both men knew that Oppius would strap his sword on again and enter the arena. The centurion hoped the next bout would be as equally brief and undemanding as the first. Mallius assured the soldier that his opponent "would not be the best that Rome had to offer".

Rain spat down from a sky as grey as a wolf pelt. Oppius thanked Fabius for accompanying him but the centurion now dismissed the young legionary.

"Consider the rest of the day your own Fabius. You might like to compose an ode and elegy for me, in light of the forthcoming fight.

That way you will be covered regardless of the outcome," Oppius grimly joked, but smiled not.

Once his legionary was out of sight the centurion sighed and his shoulders dropped. His first thought was that he needed a drink. Mallius was even running his ex-wife a close second for the person who had heaped most misery upon him inside the city walls. Oppius also felt a creeping resentment towards Caesar. A drink, or several drinks, would help take his mind off things. He also thought how he was a short walk away from one of his ex-lovers, Fabia. She had been the wife of a quaestor then. He was now probably a praetor – and as such would seldom be spending time at home. She always dressed to impress; her outfits would take an age to put on, yet a moment to take off. He could still hear the rustle of her silk stola as they made love in her curtained litter. If time had not ravished her, he would. Yet more than any patrician's wife Oppius missed and desired Livia. But it was a desire infected with grief. She had to be dead to him now. Should he go and visit Fabia, to see if she was home? Or, as he had money in his pocket, he could just as well visit a whore to help take his mind off things. There was little difference between them. Indeed Fabia would want him to buy her a piece of jewellery as tribute (she called such pieces of jewellery from her lovers "trophies"), which would end up costing him more than an hour or two with any prostitute.

"You Lucius Oppius?" The voice was stern, rough and abrupt.

"Are you asking me a question, or telling me I'm him?" Oppius answered, sizing up the man who had accosted him.

"My name is Rufus Glaber. I am an attendant to Marcus Porcius Cato. You will accompany me to see him. This is an order rather than question."

Oppius noticed how he was surrounded by four other men, all wearing identical white tunics with a black border. All had the build of former soldiers or gladiators, yet such were their severe and drear expressions that Oppius fancied they could have been former lictors also. He surveyed Glaber in particular. He stood – attempting to be imposing – with his arms folded across his barrelled chest. His body was taut and athletic, his jaw firm and neck bull-like. His green eyes were cold, yet focused. Oppius recognised a fellow officer when he saw one. The centurion weighed up his chances of fighting, or fleeing.

"You're quick and you're good Oppius, but you're not that quick and that good," Glaber remarked, reading the centurion's thoughts. With a nod of his head the four men surrounding Oppius moved in a little closer. "You're a rat caught in a trap. It'll be pointless to run or struggle. We don't mean you any harm, yet."

"I hear Cato keeps a good wine cellar. I'll come willingly."

Glaber's men subtly walked either side of Oppius as they made their way over to Cato's residence.

"I served in the Ninth, should you be wondering. Thankfully I was given a way out of the army though. The pay is better this side of the fence. I still possess a vine stick to keep discipline. I am also free from latrine duties," the ever alert mercenary remarked, wishing to either put himself above the centurion or instil envy in him.

"It's my experience that everyone has to deal with some sort of shit every day, no matter what they do."

"You're right. Today I have to deal with you," Glaber replied, with thinly veiled contempt.

"If ever you have to deal with me in earnest, you might wish you were back on latrine duty." Steel glinted in his eye. Oppius had encountered many an officer like Glaber before. Those that had tried to break a vine stick over his back had ended up with a broken nose. Respect needed to be earned through more than just possessing a bull-neck and superior attitude. Perhaps Mallius could arrange things for Cato's "attendant" to enter the arena too.

"Caesar's Champion also possesses Caesar's arrogance it seems."

"What might prove unfortunate for you is that Caesar's Champion is lacking in Caesar's clemency." The steel grew even harder, and sharper, in the centurion's gaze as he wryly smiled at the scowling mercenary.

9.

His grey eyes were red-rimmed from drinking, as Oppius recalled Titus' comment the night before:

"If Cato does speak the truth then it is wine-truth, such are the amounts he imbibes. He is temperate in everything, aside from his intemperance."

Although it was mid-afternoon the shutters to the austere triclinium were still half closed. Cato squinted in the half light however, as though suffering from a headache. The famous senator had a ruddy complexion, unkempt hair and wore an unwashed toga. Glaber warned Oppius that his master might seem tired, as he had spent the evening debating philosophy and politics with a number of other patricians and philosophers. Most that had attended would have said they spent the evening drinking. The senator put down his book, rose up from his cedar wood chair and took in his guest. "He looked like he was chewing a wasp," Oppius would tell Titus later that evening, in regards to describing the aristocrat's expression when addressing the soldier. "If it's any consolation Cato looks down on everyone; he considers himself the best of the best of men, the champion of the optimate cause and embodiment of the Republic," Titus added.

Many a time had the centurion witnessed Caesar roll his eyes, curse the stoic's existence or wryly smile upon hearing Cato being mentioned. He was renowned for his incorruptibility, his honesty and also his vehement opposition to Caesar and the triumvirate. Caesar and Cato had first famously clashed over the sentencing of the Catiline conspirators. Caesar had eloquently argued for clemency, yet Cato's forceful argument for condemning the guilty won out. The two men – the two unofficial figureheads of the opposing optimate and populares parties – clashed again over the reform of land rights. To help settle Pompey's legions Caesar passed legislation as consul to re-distribute the land of Cato's fellow patricians. Although the zealous senator often won the respect of colleagues for his integrity and sense of justice – all too often he was on the losing side in regards to Caesar and the triumvirate getting their way. He fought and lost his cause to root out bribery and end its power in deciding elections. He tried yet failed to prevent Caesar obtaining his governorship in Gaul. If Caesar would say it was day, Cato would call it night. Yet whereas Caesar now had his legions, all Cato possessed were words to champion his cause – and though he could be eloquent, he could also be obtuse and conceited. As Oppius had once heard Caesar joke, Cato would never use one word when ten could suffice.

"So you are the famous standard bearer? Yes, I have read the accounts of your heroic acts. My cook uses less garnish than the author of your deeds. Or should I call you the Sword of Rome? - A sword that Caesar would use to stab the heart of the constitution. You are of course just a mere soldier, not a philosopher or orator, but answer me this question standard bearer: are you a servant of Caesar or the Republic?"

His voice and words were measured, but underneath Oppius sensed that the stoical senator was as much a slave to his passions – and vanity – as most men. Perhaps more than most men. He was a dam that could break at any time. When younger, Oppius had heard about Cato nobly sharing the same conditions as the soldiers he commanded during his military service. Cato also battled to reform the cronyism and kleptocracy of Rome's bureaucracy. Yet the gnarled man standing before him now seemed but a shadow of the Cato of those stories. It seemed Caesar was not the only one who garnished the truth as much as Titus flavoured his dishes with garum. Before Oppius could reply Cato raised his hand.

"You do not have to answer. I know where your loyalties reside. I also have no desire to hear your lies. If I wished to fill my day with lies I'd read Caesar's colourful despatches from Gaul." Cato uttered Caesar's name as if brought a bad taste to his mouth, or was a curse.

Oppius here thought to himself how he would rather be filling his day differently, in the company of Fabia or a barmaid. Oppius thought about saying something, to either defend Caesar or just to let someone else speak, but the soldier had encountered politicians before. The sooner Cato finished what he had to say, the sooner he could be dismissed and get on with his life. Before he started to speak again however, he nodded to one of his slaves and his cup was topped up with wine.

"You think him a hero? A new Gracchus? Even should he wish to raise the people - or rather the mob – up, Caesar would still desire to stand atop of them and tread the mere mortals into the ground. Aye, even after all I am saying he will still remain a hero in your blinkered view of the world. But in the eyes of myself and the constitution Caesar is an outlaw and a war criminal. The governor of Gaul will not become a king of Rome. He must be brought to justice. I remember having to stomach the company of the dictator Sulla when just a boy. I would sit as close to him as we are close to each other now – and I vowed to myself that should I have been given a sword, I would have killed the tyrant then and there. More than the Gracchii your master desires to be Sulla. He is even more ambitious – and cynical – than Pompey. Caesar will be the death of the Republic, unless I can be the death of Caesar first. Yet I do not necessarily want to be the death of you, standard bearer. I do not doubt that you are brave but I would like to appeal to a love of reason and a love of the Republic – which hopefully still resides wuthin you. Or perhaps I will appeal to your survival instincts. You have been summoned here in order for me to ask you to pull out of your next gladiatorial bout. Caesar's Champion must sheath his sword. You can feign injury, or say you have been called back to Gaul, but you must instruct your sesterces-loving promoter that you cannot fight again. I will not allow Caesar to gain any more triumphs in Rome, even by proxy."

Cato's voice was now rough from wine and resentment. A film of sweat glazed his brow and the senator bared his teeth in a snarl when he mentioned Caesar.

"There is a good chance that I might be defeated. Surely then the triumph will be yours."

"There is more than a good chance that you will be defeated, should you face the opponent that Glaber believes you'll share the arena with."

Oppius raised his eyebrow and his face betrayed a fleck of surprise, that his opponent had already been chosen – and that Cato was in possession of the name before he was.

"You look a little shocked standard bearer. I know more than you might think. For instance I know about your fund-raising mission in Alesia and also how you tracked down and killed an agent from Rome in Britain, who was recruiting men to fight against Caesar in Gaul."

"I wasn't aware that was common knowledge," Oppius answered, steel replacing surprise in his expression.

"There is nothing common about the sum of my knowledge, standard bearer. I know that you are a hard man to kill."

The soldier was tempted to reply that his ex-wife had once judged him to be "a hard man to love", but he allowed Cato to finish.

"Therefore I would rather not leave anything to chance, as much as Glaber here posits that you do not stand a chance against your prospective combatant. Should you go ahead with the match however, then you will stand little chance of survival afterwards – no matter what the outcome. I can assure you of that. I will prove that you are a hard, as opposed to an impossible, man to kill."

10.

Evening.

A bulbous moon, assisted by a quartet of braziers, helped illuminate Titus Fabius' garden. Oppius sat alone on a bench, downed another wine and then re-filled his cup. After his meeting with Cato the centurion had found the nearest tavern. He was soon approached by the establishment's resident strumpet but he was not in the mood to raise a smile, or anything else, in relation to her advances. He just wanted a drink, or several. After an hour or two of attempting to drown his sorrows he headed back to the villa. Oppius slept off his bout of drinking and, when awake, found the nearest slave and asked him to bring a jug of wine to the triclinium. The centurion proceeded to give an account of his meetings with Mallius and Cato to his friends. Titus immediately instructed a couple of his attendants to visit some relevant contacts and discover the name of Oppius' mystery opponent.

As ever Titus was a generous host and all manner of dishes were laid before his guests. Roscius paid his compliments to the chef, although he bestowed even more compliments upon the slave who served him the food, Helena.

"She is a woman with great attributes," Roscius remarked to his host.

"Aye, I've noticed you've been admiring her attributes – both of them – all evening."

The joke did much to relieve the tension in the air, created by Oppius' news and dilemma.

At the same time as a course of fruit was brought out towards the end of the meal, one of Titus' attendants returned and whispered the name of Oppius' prospective opponent in his ear. The colour drained from Titus' face and he briefly closed his eyes, as if praying that the news could have been otherwise.

His opponent would be the Sicilian, Decimus Baculus, Titus revealed.

"His nickname is "The Doctor", due to the clinical nature of his victories and his custom of retaining body parts as trophies from his defeated opponents. He sometimes wears a necklace, with fingers hanging from it. Mallius has been a snake again. Baculus isn't the best gladiator in Rome – that title belongs to Brutus Matius – but it could easily be argued that he's the second best the profession has to offer. The Doctor has killed more people than the pox – and the deaths have been just as agonising in many cases. He won his freedom some years ago. The optimates still employ him to come out of retirement every now and then though, when a gladiator gains favour with the populares and needs to be put in his place. He is fast, strong and vicious. He is also proficient with sword, spear, shield and dagger. His armour and arms are first rate. I have seen him kill – and kill easily – as a retiarius, secutor or murmillo. There would be no shame for prudence to defeat valour,

Lucius, and for you to pull out of the match. Glaber is right in that you cannot be considered the favourite for the contest. Baculus will not look to merely wound you and have the crowd decide whether you should live or die. Or you may triumph, but still leave the arena crippled or disfigured. And from what Cato is saying, even if you win you will lose. Rufus Glaber is not a man to be toyed with. If Cato and the optimates unleash him, he will not hesitate in killing you should you survive the bout. I urge you to re-consider if you are still thinking about fighting, my friend. Caesar would understand. He can also doubtless think of alternative ways of extorting the list of names out of Mallius. The man is a snake, or insect, and Caesar can crush him as such."

The centurion merely nodded in reply, to convey that he understood and appreciated his friend's advice, but then just silently rose from the table, grabbed a cup and jug of wine and made his way out into the garden. Titus was about to say something, either in protest or support, but Roscius gently clasped his host's arm and shook his head. The legionary knew better than anyone when his centurion just wanted to be left alone.

"A rat caught in a trap," was how Glaber had described him, Oppius thought to himself. But rather the soldier judged others to be the rats, taking bites out of him. Feeding upon him. All of them – Mallius, Cato and even Caesar. If he fought then it would surely mean either death in the arena by Baculus' hand, or death just outside the arena by a dagger in the back from Glaber or one of his mercenaries. And so the easy option would be to pull out of any contest. Caesar would lose his intelligence, or at best be delayed in obtaining it. At least he would not lose a centurion. Mallius would lose money, but Oppius wasn't about to lose any sleep over that. Titus had argued that there would be no shame in refusing to fight. Better to lose one's honour than one's life. Yet the soldier could not wholly embrace such arguments. He recalled something that the young Fabius had said whilst the unit travelled to Rome from Gaul. The youth had quoted from his favourite poet after Teucer had asked what he was reading:

"Mine honour is my life; both grow in one;

Take honour from me, and my life is done."

It started to rain. The wind howled in the background, whether wildly or mournfully. Oppius heard a hiss and sizzle as spots of water fell over the hot coals of the braziers. He picked up his cup and jug and headed back inside to join his friends. Oppius forced a smile and clasped a fraternal hand on Roscius' shoulder. The unit greeted him with an apprehensive silence and forced themselves to smile reassuringly in return, albeit their expressions soon returned to being downcast.

"Don't look so glum. You're not at my funeral quite yet."

"What have you decided to do?" Titus asked, looking more apprehensive than most.

"We're going to head back to Gaul," Oppius replied. His host sighed in relief and nodded in support of the centurion's decision. "But not immediately. After all, I wouldn't want to miss my appointment with the Doctor."

11.

Gaul.

Caesar sat in the inner sanctum of his tent and adjusted the laurel wreath on his head. He wryly smiled, being reminded of a piece of graffiti in Rome that someone had recently reported to him. "Caesar does not want to wear a crown because he desires to be king, but rather because he wishes to conceal his bald head." Although slightly amused by the comment the satirist would be smiling on the other side of his face if ever Caesar found out who it was.

Joseph, Caesar's aged Jewish attendant, shuffled in at twice the usual pace of his doddering gait (his mind, or wit, however was as quick as any man's in the camp).

"This is from a messenger. Once he recovered his breath, he mentioned that it was urgent."

The general opened the message from Titus Fabius and read it intently, his expression conveying both intrigue and disappointment.

"How did your Solomon express it Joseph? "There is nothing new under the sun." It seems that Oppius has been loyal and Sextus Mallius disloyal, choosing to serve Mammon rather than Rome. The former shall be rewarded, whilst the latter shall be punished. Here, read this," Caesar stonily said and handed the letter to his man-servant.

"At least you could not ask for a better soldier, fighting as Caesar's Champion," the wizened attendant remarked after taking in the message. Joseph liked and admired the centurion, who had risen from the ranks. Unlike many of his master's officers and legates, who came from moneyed or aristocratic backgrounds, Oppius married a sense of duty to his position of power. Too many of Caesar's officer's were serving in the army in order to further their political careers – and in regards to their political careers they would ultimately look to take from the system rather than give something back. He could never envision Oppius toadying up to Caesar in order to vie for the position of collecting taxes in a province, or bidding to become a praetor.

"I agree. But even Lucius' best might not be good enough this time."

Caesar read the name Decimus Baculus again and shook his head, either in despair or disbelief. Caesar had recently purchased his own gladiator school (in the long term it would prove cost effective for him to possess his own gladiators, rather than pay someone else when financing a season of games during elections or a triumph). He had looked to hire the veteran fighter to train his new men, but was advised that Baculus was already in the employ of the optimates. Caesar's brow creased in worry and Joseph wondered whether his master's thoughts were dwelling on potentially losing his centurion, or on having his prestige tarnished should "Caesar's Champion" be defeated.

12.

It was agreed that Baculus would fight in the role of a hoplite. Oppius, again, would fight as a centurion.

"At least you might garner a few more cheers of support, fighting as a soldier," Marcus Fabius remarked to his commanding officer, trying to offer him a morsel of consolation. The friends were once again gathered in the garden. They were also joined by Roscius' cousin, Sergius, a former gladiator. The afternoon sun did its best to come out from behind clumps of pink-grey clouds. The smell of the freshly-baked bread before them warmed the air however.

"I wouldn't be so sure. The people are all for soldiers in a time of war, or immediately after a great victory, but otherwise they do their best to forget about us. They'll complain about the cost of an off duty soldier, pass by a crippled veteran whilst walking to the temple, or condemn his drinking or whoring," Oppius replied, with disappointment rather than rancour infusing his tone.

"Aye, I'll make you right. The people much prefer their soldiers conquering foreign lands, than a full local barracks bringing down the value of their properties," Sergius said. Sergius looked more like Roscius' brother than cousin, such was the resemblance between them. They shared the same large build, square shoulders and even squarer jaw. But even more so they seemed to possess similar temperaments. Sergius' nickname had been Hilarus ("The

Cheerful") outside the arena, but Hercules inside of it. When he had first joined the party of soldiers earlier in the afternoon Teucer had asked Sergius about his history.

"I signed up as a gladiator after being found guilty of killing a man. I had a disagreement with a tax collector. He struck first, but I struck harder. I tried to knock some sense into him. Unfortunately I knocked the life out of him... Gladiator school was tough, but others found it tougher. I was already in good condition and could handle myself. Some were former slaves, some former prisoners and some were volunteers, looking to make their name or fortune... My first fight was nearly my last. I was seriously wounded by a Numidian who was as strong as Roscius' love of wine. But thankfully I defeated the savage. He sheathed a dagger in my leg. But at the same time I sheathed one in his neck... There are plenty of worse fates to that of being a gladiator. The food is good and regular. Some of my fellow gladiators knew how to have a good time and laugh, as well as knowing how to fight. There were plenty of loners and sullen brutes as well though... The crowd liked me. I pretended to like them back. Make no mistake - the mob can be as vicious and as merciless as any combatant. Victory brought certain bonuses, so to speak, however. The wife of a governor requested to "see my scars" one evening after a contest. She inspected my scars again the following night and I became her lover. In some ways I had to perform and exert myself more in her bedroom than I did in the arena. She also often hired me out to her friends, for them to inspect my scars too. But I don't want to complain. I was getting paid for something that I would have paid for. Eventually she even paid for my freedom and I bought a small farm just outside of Corfinium. I still, however, keep abreast of who is making a name for themselves in the arena."

"Never mind about the property prices coming down. How do we bring down this bastard Baculus? Does he have any weaknesses?" Titus exclaimed, re-focusing the group.

"I hear he has a weakness for blondes, but that's unlikely to be decisive in the arena," Teucer joked, albeit the group all but ignored the satirical Briton's comment.

"Baculus has few weaknesses. Indeed if I were given favourable odds I might even bet on him to defeat Brutus Matius – Charon – Pompey's prize gladiator. Baculus possesses stamina and speed, strength and skill in abundance. Yet you may have a chance if you frustrate him. Anger may provoke a mistake, although you'll still need to get inside the point of his spear to best him. Aye, if we can somehow heat his blood so he sees a red mist, we might blind him. But you'll need to be armed with Caesar's luck, as well as his steel," Sergius remarked, whilst arming himself with a cup of wine and slice of bread (before his cousin could finish off both).

"We'll still need to beat the point of that spear. How can we turn his main weapon into a source of weakness? I don't doubt that Lucius can use his shield to defend against the jab of the hoplite spear, but how can he then counter-attack successfully?" Titus buried his head in his hands due to being deep in thought, or despair.

"I have an idea," Teucer announced, with a gleam in his eye that didn't just come from the wine. His friends, this time, gave the archer their attention.

13.

"Will the Doctor find a cure to defeat Caesar's Champion?"

"Unlike lightning, can the Sword of Rome strike twice in the same place?"

So read some of the advertising and graffiti discussing the bout.

Rain slapped down throughout the early afternoon but it still could not dampen the spirits of the crowd inside the arena on the outskirts of Rome, which housed the much anticipated contest. The cheers – and laughter – had only recently subsided from the event which preceded Oppius' match. The promoter had organised a spectacle in which condemned prisoners were armed with swords and given special helmets, restricting their sight. Arena slaves then pushed them towards each other; the prisoners would slash wildly and look to defeat their opponents. The last man standing would gain his freedom. Bloodied corpses, some with their faces half cut off or their bowels hanging out of their stomachs, were wheeled past Oppius as he stood in the tunnel. He shook his head in disgust, lamenting the cruelty and waste. He could have made something of these men should they have been made to enlist in the army. But Rome had deemed them fit but for the charnel house. Blood and garum seemed to be the Empire's two most prevalent trades nowadays.

"Are you ready?" Titus asked, hoping that this would not be the last time he ever spoke to his old friend.

"As ready as I'll ever be. What are my odds?"

"Bigger even than the balls you've needed to go through with this."

"Should I not upset the odds today my friend I want you to make sure that my mother is provided for. Collect any payments from Mallius and Caesar that you need to."

"You have my word. But you make sure you defeat this bastard, otherwise I'll have my son read out one of his poems at your funeral. Good luck." Titus shook his friend's hand and departed, passing by Oppius' opponent as he did so. Both Titus and Oppius squinted slightly in the dimly lit tunnel – such was the polished gleam of the veteran gladiator's armour and weaponry. His breastplate and greaves were inwrought with silver and gold. Roscius could eat his dinner off the small hoplite shield, Oppius fancied – although Roscius could and did eat his dinner off any surface. The gleam from his helmet and shield could also temporarily blind an opponent in the afternoon sun, Sergius had warned the centurion. An attendant had even polished the gladiator's sandals. Should it be a fashion contest, then Oppius had lost already. He was an amateur to his opponent's professional. Decimus Baculus had dark features and a trimmed, black beard. He was slightly taller than Oppius – and his reach slightly greater, the soldier judged. His figure was an alloy of both strength and athleticism. Baculus was as well conditioned as any soldier he had encountered. There was an air of coldness and precision to the undefeated fighter. Sergius had said that "The Doctor" had a block of ice for a heart. Oppius had drily replied that his ex-wife had at least provided him with a sparring partner to deal with such an opponent.

The stone-faced gladiator nodded cursorily at his combatant and stood next to him. As he did so, Baculus tightened his grip around his long hoplite spear, his forearm bulging with muscle. He also twisted the spear so that the leaf-shaped blade caught the attention of his would-be victim. Oppius had seen many a spear-head before, albeit none so polished or recently sharpened.

Both men stood patiently next to each other as they heard the murmur of an announcer and a few bursts of cheers from the arena through the tunnel.

"I have read about some of your exploits in Gaul. You are a genuine war hero. It'll be a shame to kill you," Baculus said flatly. "You probably hoped that you would die upon some distant battlefield, clutching an enemy standard."

"Actually I hoped that I would die of old age in my bed, clutching a servant girl."

The veteran gladiator let out a grunt cum laugh.

"I have a cousin who serves in the Tenth in Gaul. He said you were a good officer, unlike most of the martinets or aristocrat's sons playing at soldiers that the army is filled with. You shouldn't be here centurion. I shouldn't be here either. I should be back home, with my wife and family. Yet still we remain puppets. Caesar pulls your strings. Cato has pulled mine."

"We could always cut our strings and agree not to fight."

For a moment Baculus paused and thought about the novel proposition. He wryly smiled but soon wanly shook his head.

"The stage is set and the audience are expecting a performance."

14.

A crescendo of sound greeted them like a blast of hot air from an oven as they walked into the arena. Baculus remarked to his opponent to try not to be distracted too much if the crowd called out the gladiator's name. Oppius could not quite tell whether he was intending to intimidate him, or if he was offering words of support. The roar of the arena eclipsed that of the rain. Again Oppius felt, at best, indifference towards the mass of blood-thirsty spectators – at worst he held them in contempt. He ignored most of the comments emanating from them, although he was amused by the odd one or two.

"Kill him... Shove his own sword down his throat... It's Greece versus Rome. The legionary will always defeat the hoplite... Send him back to Caesar in a box. Better still, in two boxes..."

Oppius gazed around the crowd to try and pick out where his friends were seated but things all blurred in to one rolling sea of faces and colour. However, due to their white togas – and designated area – the centurion could pick out where the senators were seated. Most were sat still, popping olives into their mouths – attempting to appear impervious and imperious compared to the animated crowd. Oppius wondered which ones were on Mallius' list and would be for or against Caesar in his bid to become consul again. Cato, his brow knitted together, gave the centurion a look of daggers; he looked as though he was chewing upon two wasps, Oppius fancied. He had failed to reply to Cato's numerous messages over the past day or two, which warned of the consequences of Oppius entering the arena again as Caesar's Champion.

Oppius also recognised the famous round face and distinct quiff of Pompey (it was rare for the First Man of Rome to leave his estate outside of the city and attend a gladiatorial contest, especially when his champion fighter "Charon" was not taking part). Time, or the tragic death of Julia, had aged him considerably since the last time the centurion had seen him. Caesar had once called his friend "a double-edged sword of charm and cruelty". Pompey the Great's original nickname, during his time under Sulla's command, had been "the teenage butcher". Both names had been earned. Age had not only changed his appearance though. The once dictatorial triumvirate had grown more conservative in his politics and sought the approval and love of the Senate, as well as the people, in recent years.

Finally, looking along the row of seats, Oppius spotted the odious figure of Mallius. One of his young slaves was fixing the pleats in his toga, whilst another filled his cup with wine. The merchant noticed the centurion, smirked and raised his cup to him. Oppius was tempted to reply by raising his own hand in a somewhat different gesture.

Cheers and rain swirled around in the arena. Thunder rumbled in the background; so did the low chant of "Bac-u-lus, Bac-u-lus".

Clouds scraped across a marble-grey sky. At least the sun would not be strong enough to reflect off his opponent's armour or shield and blind him, Oppius thought to himself. The centurion wiped his hand on his tunic, not knowing if his palm was moist from sweat or rainwater. He drew his sword, breathed deeply and nodded to the umpire to convey he was ready. His heart beat fast, as if he was perched upon the transport ship again - about to invade Britain.

Baculus skipped swiftly and smoothly towards him, his spear jabbing out like a lizard's tongue. Oppius easily brought his shield across and sidestepped to deflect the blow. Immediately the soldier was impressed and wary of the gladiator's speed. Keep moving, keep surviving, Oppius told himself as Baculus stabbed the spear forward again, after the odd playful feint to do so. The centurion sensed that the gladiator was merely sizing him up, checking for any weaknesses in technique or fear in his opponent. The Sicilian had also satisfied his curiosity in regards to discovering that the centurion had reinforced his shield; it would take an almighty effort for him to punch through the scutum.

Baculus leaned back but then quickly skipped forward, stabbing low and then high. Parts of the crowd gasped with each offensive. Although heavier than the regulation legionary's shield it still appeared light on the soldier's arm and Oppius blocked both thrusts. The veteran gladiator nodded, either in appreciation or because the attack had confirmed something about the soldier in his mind. The centurion was growing a little anxious – solely defending – but he remained patient. Keep moving, keep surviving.

Sweat and rain chilled their faces. Baculus circled around his opponent, prey; sometimes he prowled, sometimes he almost danced. The voice of Tiro Casca, a veteran legionary, crept into Oppius' head. He would perhaps have castigated the gladiator with his mantra of "Stop dancing and start fighting" when teaching swordsmanship. Yet the soldier quickly shook off such idle thoughts, shaking his head as if there were cobwebs between his ears.

The gladiator probed and then sprung forward again. This time however Baculus' momentum took him much too far forward. Years of drilling meant that Oppius stabbed rather than slashed. His sword clanged upon the bright hoplite shield, but for the first time the centurion found himself momentarily inside Baculus' spear point. Oppius punched his own shield forward and knocked his opponent backwards. The gladiator soon regained his balance but a cheer of encouragement rang out around the arena for the underdog. The cheer was succeeded by the chants of "Cae-sar" and "Opp-i-us". Roscius, Teucer, Fabius – and dozens of other current and former soldiers who Titus had bought tickets for – led the chants of support.

Baculus seemed initially distracted, or disconcerted, by the dramatic change of support in the crowd but his aspect soon grew as steely and cold as the blade on his spear. He rushed forward again and unleashed a flurry of attacks. The jabs were more powerful, but less controlled. Oppius moved back and then sideways, so as not to get cornered against the sides of the arena.

Keep moving, keep surviving he voiced beneath rasping breaths. To gain a brief respite – and put his opponent on the back foot - the centurion pretended that he was about to throw his gladius (as he had famously done so to defeat Aulus) but Baculus flinched not and merely raised his shield a little higher in precaution.

Again the hoplite gladiator launched another wave of attacks, sometimes feinting, sometimes creating new angles in which he stabbed his spear forward. Still the crowd chanted for himself and Caesar – which fuelled rather than perhaps diminished Oppius' chances of defeat, he fancied.

For once the centurion's defensive technique was flawed and with a flick of his wrist Baculus altered the trajectory of his spearhead and it sliced through Oppius' unguarded thigh. The soldier stumbled backwards but remained on his feet. More changeable than the weather, the crowd gasped – and then ominously began to chant "Bac-u-lus" again. Perhaps the chanting this time had been led by Oppius' ex-wife.

Blood dripped over and darkened the sand. The centurion witnessed a hint of a smile – a triumphant smile – upon the gladiator's face. In nine bouts out of ten Baculus would have bested Oppius. But it was just this one bout which mattered. The Sicilian sensed victory. But so did his opponent. Oppius would use his injury to his advantage, pretending to be more wounded than he actually was. He hobbled backwards and raised his shield up higher, as if cowering before the superior fighter. His actions bred an even greater confidence in the gladiator. The Doctor could afford to be less clinical. The crowd smelled blood – and defeat – too. Cato could afford to look more stoical and indifferent in regards to the outcome, believing now the result would be in his favour.

It was time to roll the dice and gamble on Teucer's plan. Baculus moved forward. Oppius retreated, sluggishly. The gladiator could almost afford to toy with the soldier, like a cat would with a mouse. The spear was jabbed forward again. Oppius however moved quickly, deliberately, so that the tip hit – and slid through – a designated part of his shield. Teucer's idea, in order to disarm Oppius' opponent of his spear, was to cut and disguise a slot in his scutum. The spear head would be suddenly, unexpectedly, trapped and Baculus would be left temporarily vulnerable.

Once his spear was caught in the vice of the shield Oppius moved his arm out to further unbalance his opponent. Baculus, although caught unawares, still instinctively brought his small shield close to his stomach and chest but the shield was too little and it was too late. The centurion stabbed his sword down fast and hard into the gladiator's thigh, twisting the blade when he reached bone as he did so. Baculus howled in agony; the unholy sound could have woken the gods. The gladiator stumbled backwards fell on the sand. The blackness of unconsciousness nearly swallowed him up but the veteran warrior still instinctively drew his sword as he lay upon the ground. As soon as the blade had left its scabbard though it was flying through the air, as Oppius kicked it from his hand. Baculus, in the last throw of the dice, weakly threw his shield at the centurion but the soldier easily deflected the missile with his scutum.

The crowd erupted in a thousand cheers, or just a mighty one. If the sound had woken the gods then Oppius hoped the gods would punish them for the disturbance. Roscius and his unit didn't even need to prompt the chanting of their officer's name. In time to the calling out of "Opp-i-us" the bulk of the crowd jabbed down their thumbs, instructing the centurion to finish off the wounded gladiator. The rain and sound of the crowd swirled around him more violently as Oppius stood over and looked down at his stricken opponent. The once triumphant smile had been washed away. The blood too had drained from his face. Baculus closed his eyes, either in resignation or a final prayer. He opened them again on hearing the chants of "Opp-i-us" turn into a chorus of boos and hisses. He gazed up to see that his opponent had sheathed his sword and was raising his arm – and thumb – up to the crowd. The centurion had of course been tempted to raise his hand in a somewhat different gesture to the mob in the arena.

"I would kill you, if I was standing there," Baculus said, emotionlessly.

"I know. Cato – and my ex-wife – would have rewarded you handsomely for it as well."

"Caesar has a worthy champion."

"Caesar has Caesar. He doesn't need me. Nor should you need Rome. You fought well, but go home to your family and retire. Kill time rather than people."

The hint of a smile came over the gladiator's face once again.

Mallius smiled so widely it looked as though his grin was wrapping itself around the whole of his head. Already the merchant was thinking about how he could entice or blackmail Oppius to enter the arena again. Perhaps he could even fight – and defeat - Pompey's champion, Charon.

15.

At least Mallius had arranged for a coach to take him back to Rome after the contest, even though the coachman was slightly confused at first, as he believed that his passenger would be going by the name of Baculus. Titus and his unit would make their way back on their own.

The muscles in his injured leg both throbbed and tightened at the same time as he rested in the coach. Mallius provided his own surgeon, who had once been in the employ of Crassus, to attend to his wound after the bout.

"I must look after my prize asset," the merchant explained, before leaving to check upon ticket receipts.

As the surgeon stitched up his wound Oppius received an unexpected visitor. Pompey stood before him in a gleaming white toga and ran his hand through his hair, attending as much to his famous quiff as to the centurion. Pompey smiled gently, although his hard eyes struck a hard note compared to the softness of the rest of his face. He initially just surveyed the soldier, without uttering a word. He stared intently, as though he were almost taking in the soldier's past, present and future as well as his physical appearance. At the same time as feeling that he was the centre of Pompey's attention, Oppius also felt that he was but of

196

vague secondary importance to the senator; a lesser mortal (if indeed Pompey considered himself wholly mortal).

"You fought well centurion. You are a credit to the army. Although it seems that Caesar's Champion possesses Caesar's good fortune, it also seems that Julius has infected you with his weakness for clemency. Should you have somehow been in a position to spare my gladiator, Charon, he would have despised you all the more and murdered you in your sleep afterwards. As much as you have won a battle, you have not won the war," Pompey exclaimed, sneering a little as he mentioned the words "Julius" and "clemency". Before Oppius could reply – although he was at a loss as to how to – Pompey took his leave.

Sunlight finally melted through the clouds and rain as Oppius entered the city, though dusk was about to melt the day. Mallius had arranged for a litter but Oppius never felt comfortable travelling in them. They were for over-indulged women, or overweight patricians. He walked gingerly, but made his way through the streets towards Titus' house. Oppius was mindful of his injury – and also watching for Rufus Glaber and his men. He spotted one not before long, just as Oppius was about to enter a small fruit market. He was wearing the same distinctive white toga, bordered in black, from before. The soldier soon saw two more. As he looked in their direction they averted their glances. One pretended to buy some grapes whilst another bent down to re-fasten his sandals. Yet Oppius still couldn't see Glaber. He would want to be here to finish the job, the soldier suspected. This was one of the few opportunities when the centurion would be isolated and vulnerable.

Night slowly moved in, as did Glaber's men. Oppius moved as quickly as he could, his crutch clacking upon stone, away from his pursuers. Sharp twinges of pain ran up and down his wounded leg. There was an argument for staying in the crowded marketplace, but it would be all too easy to receive a blade in the small of his back in such an environment, he judged. Blood trickled down his thigh from his wound opening up as he walked briskly down a side street. The side street turned into an alley. The alley turned into a small courtyard. Yet the courtyard was a dead end. Its entrance was also its exit. The courtyard was made up of three high stone walls. Overhanging the walls on one side were balconies from an apartment block. Even if uninjured, the walls were too high for him to scale. Oppius turned around – and finally saw Glaber.

"I would say that you're a lucky bastard, given your victory earlier, but given your situation now, I'm not so sure," the mercenary said - relishing having captured his quarry so easily. With a movement of his head he instructed the two random citizens in the courtyard to depart. They did so without protest. He was flanked by two pairs of his men either side of him, and two of his men stood guard behind. Oppius instinctively moved backwards, ending up not far from the graffiti-filled back wall of the courtyard. Glaber's unit looked capable, if unexceptional. There were six of them. In his condition he would just about be able to defeat two of them, at best.

"I bet against you and lost money on the bout. I'm not happy Lucius. Cato is also unhappy." Glaber drew his dagger. The clouds bound themselves together again, shrouding the city in the dullest of lights.

"He should learn to bear his lamentations with fortitude," Oppius drily replied, reciting the philosophy of the stoic.

"You shouldn't be so hard on Cato. He suggested that I only go so far as to prevent you from ever fighting again. But I argued that I needed to be more thorough. Partly because if I don't end things for you now, you might end things for me later. Ideally I would have liked to make you suffer – blunt the Sword of Rome – but we are where we are. You are where you are. A rat caught in a trap."

"You're right. But I'm not the rat – and you've not set the trap."

Teucer and Marcus Fabius appeared from out of one of the apartments and stood on a balcony above the courtyard, their bows drawn. Titus and Roscius appeared at the entrance to the courtyard, blocking off any possible retreat by Glaber and his men.

"Ideally I would have liked to have made you suffer, but we are where we are. You are where you are." Oppius drew his dagger.

Enraged and desperate Glaber sprang forward and made to attack the centurion but Teucer's arrow caught him in the chest and knocked him off his feet. Marcus Fabius felled the enemy in his sights too. Roscius and Titus made short work of the two men closest to them. Roscius swung his elbow into the face of his enemy, breaking his nose. Blood then blurred his opponent's vision – and he saw not the legionary punch the gladius into his chest. Titus' opponent blocked two of his sword strokes, but he did not block the third. The former centurion moved in close and buried his sword up to its hilt in the mercenary's stomach. The remaining enemy received arrows in their backs as they looked to retreat and attack Roscius and Titus standing at the mouth of the courtyard.

"Have mercy," Glaber pleaded, as he looked up at the centurion.

"I'm afraid I used up all my clemency in the arena," Oppius replied – and then buried the bottom of his crutch into the mercenary's eye-socket. Titus and Roscius slit the throats of the wounded. Their white togas, with black trim, were now awash with blood.

"Thank you," Oppius remarked to the approaching Titus.

"No need. I should be thanking you my friend. It's about time my sword was covered in blood again, as opposed to just rust."

Teucer and Marcus Fabius jumped down from the balcony and retrieved their arrows, as if plucking them out of the dead from a battlefield in Gaul. The men looked around at the courtyard littered with corpses and just nodded to one another.

"Can we go eat now?" Roscius finally asked, ending the eerie silence.

16.

Oppius woke and squinted in the light of the early afternoon sun the following day. In the distance he could hear the sound of a cohort being drilled outside the city walls. He suspected they were raw recruits, being broken in. Even if they were doing everything perfectly the legionary in charge would still find fault and drill them again. He may even drill them once more, just to amuse himself. The raw recruits' reward would finally come when they could drill a future batch of raw recruits and amuse themselves accordingly.

Oppius and his own unit had feasted well the night before. They turned in early however, tired from the day's events. Roscius worked his way through various courses before leading the servant girl Helena off so he could have his "dessert". Titus also retired and went to bed early, explaining that he had to run an errand in the morning.

Titus returned to the house as Oppius sat down to eat a lunch of bread, pork, olives and figs.

"We have been grateful for your hospitality Titus but I think it's time we moved on. Instead of another one of your banquets I must have a home-cooked meal, in my mother's kitchen," the centurion explained to his friend.

"I understand."

"Before I leave Rome however, I must first call on Mallius and retrieve the other half of the list for Caesar."

"I already have the full list in my possession. He would have broken his promise again and forced you into the arena. For all of his wealth, the only money he needs now is for the Ferryman. I bloodied my sword one more time. Suspicion will fall upon his two young slaves, who I paid off and instructed to leave Rome immediately. Few will mourn the death of a banker, especially one who was owed so much money by so many people."

"Will Cato not be suspicious? And how much should I worry about him coming after me, for defying him and killing Glaber and his men?"

"Cato has far too much pride to consider that a mere centurion could merit being his enemy. He is far more obsessed with battling and defeating Caesar, to the point where he will even join forces with his former enemy Pompey to do so. No, out of sight means you will also be out of mind. As well as the list, I must also give you some letters from Octavius to pass on to Caesar. Marcus visited the boy again this morning."

"What does he think of him?"

"Marcus was impressed by his intellect and good manners. He thinks that Octavius will be a student rather than a soldier though – a poet rather than a politician."

"You may have once said the same about Marcus. Perhaps Octavius will surprise a few people too."

"We'll see. Time will tell – far more accurately than any augur. I trust that you will return to Rome soon my friend. You are always welcome at this house. I hope that this visit has not put you off returning, although I wouldn't blame you if you kicked the dust from your shoes in regards to the city. You've been thrown into the arena twice to be slaughtered – and you've seemingly made more enemies than a tax collector whilst here."

"It could have been worse."

"How so?"

"I could have bumped in to my ex-wife."

Both men grinned and decided to drink one last jug of wine before Oppius departed.

Sword of Rome: Rubicon

1.

Ravenna.

Sunlight sliced through the shutters and illuminated the cottage, turning the motes of dust in the air into glitter. Lucius Oppius lay next to Atilia in bed, furs covering half their bodies.

"And where's this one from?" Atilia asked, her finger lightly touching the star-shaped scar on the centurion's shoulder. The olive-skinned woman slotted her body into his, her slender leg hooking itself around his calf. A log fire purred with heat in the corner.

"Our second invasion of Britain. We encountered a band of barbarians on the south coast. I was struck by an arrow during an ambush," Oppius replied, breathing in her perfume.

"Did it hurt?"

"Not half as much as when I caught up with the archer and my sword struck his collar bone."

The woman winced slightly, but then smiled broadly. She gazed lovingly into the soldier's eyes, before tenderly kissing the spot where he had been injured all those years ago. His muscular arm curled around the woman and brought her closer. Atilia was a widow. She had been married to a quaestor who had served as a senior administrator in Caesar's army. He had passed away the previous summer from a fever. Oppius had known Quintus and believed him to be decent, for a bureaucrat. The centurion and the widow had finally become lovers, after being friends, a month or so ago. They were physically attracted to one another, but their relationship was founded upon something more. They eased each other's sorrows. Atilia still grieved for her husband and worried about her future – bringing up her young son on her own. Although she had expressed her sadness and anxieties to Oppius, the centurion's sorrows remained unvoiced. Yet should he have given voice to his gloomy thoughts the soldier might have spoken about a former lover, Livia; the ghost of his father, who he was still trying to earn the respect of; of what he had seen – and done – upon the battlefield; or of the impending civil war.

"And this?" Atilia softly said, whilst tracing her fingertip along the thin line of a scar which ran down Oppius' forearm.

"This was from a brawl in a tavern just outside of Ancona. He had a knife. Fortunately I had a Roscius." Oppius smiled, recalling the image of Roscius tossing the knife-wielding drunk out of the window as if he were a rag doll. The hulking legionary had saved his life during many a battle, as well as brawl, over the years. Atilia leaned over and kissed his arm – and then seductively ran the tip of her tongue along the scar. The soldier drank in the sensation and the image of his lover looking up at him. Atilia's face glowed with kindness and affection. Her lustrous auburn hair fell down to her shoulders. She was older than him, but time had lined her face with wisdom rather than decay. Atilia's hazel eyes were warm. Livia's darker aspect had all too often blazed with a passion, which had burned both of them.

"And this one?" She rubbed her leg against his thigh beneath the furs. A playfulness mixed with devotion infused her expression and tone.

"An arena outside of Rome. I was a famous gladiator, for all of two weeks, would you believe it?" Atilia continued to stroke her leg against his and for a moment or two Oppius might have even been grateful to his opponent for inflicting the injury and leaving him with the legacy of the scar. Atilia ducked her head under the furs and kissed him upon the thigh. Her hand commenced to caress him too.

"And this one?" she finally asked, reappearing from below. She smiled and pointed her finger at a round, pink scar the size of a small coin upon his broad chest.

"Rome again - from a fight with my ex-wife. She tried to break my heart – with a chisel."

Atilia raised her eyebrow but then soothingly kissed Oppius on the chest, before passionately kissing him upon the mouth – all the time wondering whether he was being serious or not.

2.

Rome.

Tiro noted the untouched food - and the careworn expression across his master's face bespoke of another sleepless night. Cicero held his head in one hand and a stylus in the other.

"Are you not going to eat something?" the secretary asked, placing a blanket around his master's shoulders, concerned that he might catch a chill from the draft coming through the bottom of the door to the library.

"I've just had to stomach reading a feast of fawning petitions, from the likes of Metullus Scipio and Lucius Lentulus, asking that I condemn Caesar more openly. And that I should lead us into a civil war. I have lost my appetite."

All manner of correspondence was strewn across the statesman's desk. Cicero's knife had even grown blunt, from having to constantly sharpen his stylus. Patricians, merchants, clients, sources of intelligence, and senators with a lack of intelligence, were all seeking his advice – or trying to direct him towards a certain course of action. Their words and demands were akin to the constant buzzing of insects, he thought.

"You need to keep your strength up," Tiro remarked, worried about the strain that this latest political crisis would cause to 'the Father of his Country' as the people had once fondly called his master (having saved Rome from Catiline's rebellion and a possible civil war some years ago). The secretary yearned again for the time spent in the family's villa in the country. Back then Cicero had filled his days writing elegant philosophy rather than endless letters to political allies. Similarly Tiro did not have to endlessly copy out such letters - and decrypt correspondence lest they fall into the wrong hands.

"I doubt history will record that Cicero saved the Republic because he took in some lentils," the usually equitable statesman gruffly replied. Tiro was taken back somewhat by his master's tone and lowered his head in chastisement. Cicero witnessed the hurt on his faithful secretary's face – and felt far more chastised by his expression than any words he could have uttered.

"My apologies Tiro. I should have eaten those words, rather than have spewed them out. I know you mean well. Leave the plate. I will eat a little after finishing off this letter to Atticus."

"*Dear Atticus,*

I feel like I'm tied to two horses, champing at the bit to gallop off in opposite directions. Or rather I'm tied to two asses – Pompey and Caesar. Each faction wants me to openly side with them. I can only tell you that I am on the side of peace. But far more than for myself, I am worried that Pompey and Caesar will tear Rome apart. Their great prize will be a bankrupt estate, or a charnel house, once war has had its way. We must have peace. I am becoming so desperate I am considering dressing Tiro up in a stola and having him appear before Pompey at night, and, pretending to be Julia, urging him to maintain good relations with Caesar (as Julia did when she was alive).

At least Pompey is finally waking up to the prospect that this crisis could indeed lead to war, which may instil in him a greater desire to negotiate and compromise. He may remember the more barbaric aspects of Sulla's dictatorship. Liberty is rendered even more precious by the recollection of servitude. I believe that our once 'Teenage Butcher' does not have the appetite for a bloody civil war. For a time his pride convinced him that Caesar would fall into line. He could not think of Caesar as an equal. When Pompey was asked, "Suppose Caesar keeps his armies?" he haughtily replied, "Suppose my son took a stick to me?" The First Man of Rome's pride may ultimately cause more suffering than the pride of Achilles.

Unfortunately we can also add the ingredient of the pride of Cato – and his fellow patricians – into the recipe for disaster. Cato is looking to block every suggestion of a compromise, whether it comes from Caesar or Pompey. His animus towards Caesar is such that he would rather see Rome burn than see Julius as consul again. He would rather even give up wine than give up his determination to see Caesar put on trial for war crimes. Caesar's latest offer is for him to relinquish his governorship of Gaul and to give up all but two of his legions, in exchange for being able to run for consul without having to enter Rome. Yet Cato and his pack of bloodthirsty aristocrats have rejected this compromise out of hand.

If Caesar wants to run for consul he must do so as a private citizen, they argue. Yet Julius knows that without his imperium he will be vulnerable to prosecution – a prospect that Cato is licking his lips in delight over. The Senate is right to posit that his legions are not his to command or give up, but Rome's. But whenever have right or wrong been integral to politics?

But I should not talk solely of politics my friend, lest I bore you – and myself. Have you purchased any interesting pieces since our last correspondence? Perhaps you could purchase enough sculptures so as to replace the Senate with statues. Some would perhaps then blessedly talk less – and also be less hard-headed or hard-hearted. And how is young Caecilia? Please thank her for the recipes she sent me last month. She should put her dishes together and write a cookbook. Such is the inevitable decline of culture that I dare say sales of such cookbooks will eclipse sales of philosophy books one day. Why be given food for thought when you can just be given food?"

Cicero was in little mood to be trivial, however, in his letter. The black thought occurred to him again that perhaps History was not a story of peace and progress, punctuated by chapters of war. But rather History is a story of warfare, punctuated by brief episodes of peace and progress. The elder statesman's eyelids weighed as heavy as his grim mood. He took one mouthful of his lentil soup, but that was all. Drear clouds clung together, like a giant tumour, and blocked out the morning sun, leaving the chamber cold and dark. Yet still Cicero would end his letter to his friend with the words, *"Where there's life, there's hope."*

3.

A chill wind whistled beneath the door. Oppius sat up in bed with a distracted look on his rugged face. He thought upon how his friends, Roscius and Teucer, were faring in Rome. They were accompanying Mark Antony, who had been sent there to act as a tribune and advocate for Caesar's cause. The centurion had appeared even less anxious during the siege of Alesia, or the invasion of Britain. A few grey hairs had even sprouted upon his temples over the past month or so. The thunder cloud of civil war hung over everyone, from Ravenna to Rome, Iberia to Egypt. Oppius believed that the soldiers of the Tenth would follow their general into Italy, but did Caesar want to lead them into a war – of Roman against Roman? Sulla had been Caesar's enemy all those years ago, after the dictator had triumphed over his uncle Marius, but it was Sulla rather than Marius that Caesar could now emulate. The atmosphere had been tense, even eerie, in Caesar's tent of late. Their commander shifted between being angry, confused, morose and bellicose, with a pained expression sometimes hauting his looks. Caesar would pace about, giving voice to his private thoughts and contempt for his enemies.

"My dignity will not countenance their calumny... There was no such clamour to prosecute Pompey and Crassus for their misdemeanours during the triumvirate... They are jackals, envious of the lion's majesty... I will not submit to their painted authority... A man should be tried by his peers... They are parasites upon the state, sucking upon the glory and riches that Caesar brings to Rome... If I do take up the sword against my homeland it will not be out of ambition, or to defend myself, but rather to free the people from the Senate's yoke... These so-called optimates, best men, are merely the best at serving their own interests. They all too often defy or pour scorn upon the people and their representatives, the tribunes. Taking office is just a means to take from the treasury. When young they are all educated together, these tics in togas, and then serve as an assistant or special adviser to a senator – before their fathers die and they can afford to buy a place in the Senate themselves. He who knows only of politics knows nothing of politics however. The political world is not the real world. How much time has Cato spent living in the Subura, like myself?"

Would Caesar plunge the peninsular in to a state of war merely to satisfy his pride? Unfortunately Oppius already knew the answer to the question.

Atilia's voice and the smell from a steaming pork chop, cooked in a mushroom sauce, brought the soldier out from his gloomy reverie.

"You seemed a world away just then. What were you thinking about?" the woman asked, curiosity missed with concern, as she passed the plate of food to the soldier.

"I was thinking about last night. And not just what we did, but rather what you said," Oppius replied, lying. They had spoken about returning to Rome together. Atilia needed to see her son again. She had urged the centurion to give up his commission – and he was tempted to do so. She argued that she did not want to be a war widow twice before she was forty - and that he would be able to find employment in Rome (Oppius had mentioned before how his friend Titus had offered him a partnership in a business). After Alesia and his last mission to Rome, Oppius reasoned that he had now done more for Caesar than Caesar had done for him. And even if he was somehow competing with his father's ghost, had he not already eclipsed his achievements in the military too? But could he marry again? His first marriage had been a mistake, but he had been young then. And Atilia was nothing like his first wife; Atilia was perfect.

Oppius hummed in pleasure as he tasted the food, although the hum of pleasure may also have had something to do with Atilia playfully sliding her hand beneath the furs and caressing him.

"If you come back to Rome you can have plenty more home-cooked meals. You'll also be able to have me on a plate every night."

Lucius Oppius was even more tempted to return to Rome as a civilian rather than a soldier.

4.

The cold air of the Subura was stained with the pungent odours of wine and sweat. Laughter, slurred words and the clinks of numerous cups sounded out in the dimly lit drinking establishment.

Roscius whipped his brawny arm across; the point of his elbow connected with the side of the drunk's head and knocked him unconscious. Vomit slapped upon the sawdust-strewn floor as Teucer kicked the man he was fighting in the groin, making him retch. He duly collapsed, knocking a table and several drinks to the ground as he did so. Bone crunched against cartilage as Mark Antony broke the nose of his antagonist.

Caesar's lieutenant had caused the fight in the tavern, 'The Cock and Bull'.

"She belongs to me," a rasping voice had abruptly expressed. The craggy-faced drunk pointed to the whore sitting upon Mark Antony's lap as he spoke. Two equally craggy-faced drunks stood beside him.

"For the right price she belongs to anyone it seems," Mark Antony replied. The girl, merry with wine, smiled – flattered from having two men fighting over her (if they were willing to raise their fists for her, perhaps they'd be willing to raise what they would pay her for the night too).

"Take that back!" The drunk had been with the girl for the past three evenings, having declared his love for her on the second. He also promised that he would talk to her master and buy her freedom, so he could then marry her. He warned the girl how he would have to first pay off his bar bills however.

"The only thing I'll be taking back is your girlfriend, to my rooms. Now fuck off before I bruise your face, as well as your pride."

Teucer rolled his eyes at this point and hoped that Antony's diplomacy skills would improve when dealing with the Senate. Unsurprisingly the drunk broke out into a rage attacked his rival. The three men quickly departed after the fight. The whore shot curses at the soldiers as she was left sitting on the floor, as opposed to Antony's lap.

"At least we now have a cock and bull story to tell Oppius when we get back," the archer joked to his legionary friend as they came out onto the street. It was now Roscius' turn to roll his eyes.

"Now my friends, the night is still young – and so are the actresses I'll introduce you to," Caesar's lieutenant announced whilst fraternally clapping his arms around the shoulders of the legionaries as they made their way out of the Subura. "I dare say you'll want an encore from them after their performance, if they don't tire you out too much."

Although Roscius and Teucer were naturally keen to experience the next act in the evening's entertainment they were also slightly concerned by Antony's behaviour. He was due to meet representatives of the Senate in the morning to put forward Caesar's case for retaining his imperium. The soldiers were half tempted to encourage Antony to cut short their evening. Titus Fabius, their host, had promised to lay on a banquet for them. They could not help but be curious however about the feast of flesh their friend was promising to lay out before them.

5.

Caesar tapped his foot impatiently, but otherwise sat still and appeared calm as his aged servant Joseph finished shaving him.

"You may not always enjoy your job my old friend but I warrant that there are many who would pay a king's ransom to be in your place right now, holding a blade to Caesar's bare throat. The most powerful statesmen in Rome would love to trade places."

"I'm not sure if I'd be able to do the job of a politician though. I find it too difficult to say one thing and do another," the Jewish manservant drily expressed as he rubbed oil into Caesar's skin.

"Indeed. Integrity is far too heavy a burden to carry when attempting to climb up the political ladder. I must trust in Cicero though," Caesar remarked, reaching to the desk and holding up a letter. "He has tabled another offer, although how much power he has to cement any negotiations is debatable. But I have acceded to his requests. I do not seek war although I also will not run from it should it seek me out."

Caesar's hand reached down and he began to repeatedly pull his sword from his scabbard by a couple of inches and then return it.

"Cicero also encourages me to return to Rome as a private citizen, but accept Pompey's offer of his personal protection. I have no need or desire to have Pompey as my protector. Nor would

I wish to offer him the opportunity to be my betrayer. I can scarce understand the Senate's enmity towards me. Can you?"

"Unfortunately enmity often exists outside the realms of reason and understanding."

"I have furnished our state with riches, glory, security and spectacles. Yet they dress up their envy in the weeds of justice and aim to condemn rather than congratulate me. It is a crime against nature and the gods to act so ungratefully. The honour of a second consulship should be mine - else we dishonour the name of honour. I should be now planning a campaign against the Parthians, not my homeland. It was said that Pyrrhus possessed a countenance which conveyed terror rather than majesty. It is my intention however to convey majesty rather than terror, should it come to war. Should they not give me what I have earned by right, I shall take it by force. When I enter Rome it will be as a liberator rather than conqueror though."

Joseph's wrinkled face creased even more, in melancholy and trepidation, as he stared at his master and wondered how much Caesar believed in his words. Or did he know that he was dressing up his naked ambition in the finery of honour and virtue?

A gust of cold air blew through the tent and Caesar wrapped his large, red woollen cloak around him. His stern expression softened as he caught the scent of perfume upon the cloak, from the senator's wife he had bedded the night before. In between bouts of lovemaking she had professed how loyal her husband was to Caesar's cause – to the point where he thought the lady protested too much. He just hoped that the senator would prove more loyal towards Caesar than his wife had been towards her husband.

6.

The air was crisp. Marcus Fabius sat beneath a bare oak tree on the hard ground yet looked out across the winter landscape as if it were in bloom.

"Where both deliberate, the love is slight:
Who ever lov'd, that lov'd not at first sight?"

Fabius considered the lines again, struck by their wisdom and poetry. He was also tinged with sadness and envy, that he could not compose something similarly poignant to echo the sentiment. Yet overall the young legionary was happy – for he was in love.

Caesar had recently organised a party for his senior officers and people of influence in the town. Oppius had arranged for Fabius to attend too. Fabius saw her through a crowd of people. He could not help but wear an expression filled with admiration and desire. She looked away, but then looked back. Blonde ringlets hung down to frame a sweet face, encrusted with sparkling blue eyes. Mustering up his courage, in a similar yet different way as he would if he were about to go into battle, Fabius made his way over to the young woman. The wine also helped dissolve his nerves and inhibitions. Her name was Claudia. She was well-read and possessed a lively – and mischievous – sense of humour. Unfortunately she was also married. Yet mutual affection and attraction eclipsed their sense of propriety and Fabius asked if he could see her again. There were a hundred reasons why she should have said no, but she said yes. Her heart fluttered as much as her eyelashes as she did so.

Fabius and Claudia met the following afternoon. And then the next day. They made love. Claudia confessed how unhappy her marriage was.

"I am but an ornament to him that is locked away until I can be brought out and shown off at a party... I could be as desirable as Helen of Troy or Dido. My husband however would prefer the company of Paris or Aeneas. Ours is a marriage of convenience, to help further his political career."

Oppius, who knew of Rufus Scorpus, the unpleasant yet well-connected official who Claudia was married to, advised his legionary to keep one eye on his heart and the other on his back. Yet he could not help but smile fondly at his friend after offering his advice. The boy had become a man. Not only was he in love, but he was cuckolding another man – and a client of Cato's to boot. The centurion fondly smiled again as he approached Fabius. The youth had a distracted, lovesick look plastered across his face. The stylus in his hand meant that he was doubtless in the process of composing another poem to Claudia.

The sound of Oppius' caligae on the hard ground brought Fabius out of his reverie.

"Any word from Roscius or Teucer?" the legionary asked. Fabius had volunteered to accompany his friends and Mark Antony to Rome, but Oppius had turned his request down, explaining that if

223

he left as well then he would have no one to shout at and give orders to. The centurion was also conscious of keeping the promise to his friend Titus, Fabius' father, that he would keep a watchful eye over the lad.

"No. Any words may well be slurred that we hear from them though. They're probably spending half of their time in the tavern, despite or because of Mark Antony."

"Or they're drinking my father's cellar dry."

"Now I have heard from your father however."

Oppius kept to himself how Titus had made him a business proposition – and how he was thinking about accepting the offer and leaving the army. He did report though how his father was in good health, in contrast to the fractious body politic in Rome. The economy was beginning to falter, in light of a possible civil war. The optimates and populares were finding more things to fight about, than agree upon. Only the paint sellers seemed to be thriving, such was the amount of graffiti sprouting up all around Rome. Titus' favourite mural commented how for once the people wanted politicians to be politicians – and just sit around and talk whilst not actually doing anything.

"But we've no time to stand around and idly gossip like fishwives. It's time."

Oppius had met Fabius to accompany him to a fencing session between a representative of the Tenth legion and one from the Thirteenth. The soldiers often arranged such sparring sessions, where the bets and sometimes blood flowed, to pass the time. The centurion briefly paused, as the legionary gathered his things, and bleakly recalled how his father had died during one such fencing bout. He was determined that he would not lose his young friend in a similar way – who had become something of a surrogate son to the veteran soldier. Under his tutelage he had grown in skill with both the sword and bow. In return the studious Fabius had furthered his officer's education. Marcus still occasionally helped re-draft Oppius' correspondence; so too he checked the endless accounts that the centurion had to go through.

"Have you remembered to sharpen your blade, as well as your stylus? I'll let you borrow my shield too. It's reinforced. I wouldn't want you suffering any injury. Claudia would prefer to see all of you intact this evening I warrant," Oppius remarked with a wink. The centurion found out about the affair through his young legionary asking him for the use of his cottage. He had said yes.

"Even I was young and in love once. Or thought I was in love," Oppius had said with a wry smile.

"Were you in love with your first wife?"

The officer part coughed and part laughed in reply.

"By the gods, no. Maybe I was in love with her for an hour or two upon our wedding night. After that things went downhill quicker than a herd of Carthaginian elephants. She soon drained me of any emotions or savings I had and purchased enough shoes to fit out, again, a herd of Carthaginian elephants. It was one of the happiest days of my life – when I got divorced. But don't let my cynicism taint your affair, Fabius. Love exists; it's just as rare as a courageous Gaul or sober Briton."

7.

Grey clouds, like flagstones, slotted together overhead. The carriage rattled onwards, towards Pompey's estate. Tiro insisted that he be allowed to wrap another blanket around his master. It was cold – and growing colder.

"The atmosphere may be even chillier at Pompey's house, when I join our host and Cato for our meeting." Cicero buried his chin in his chest and remained impassive as his secretary placed another blanket around his shoulders. The statesman had been wrapped up in a gloom for most of the journey. Tiro thought that he looked like a man who had just received news that a close friend had passed away. Usually Cicero would take in the scenery when travelling. The intelligence and beauty of nature was perhaps proof of a divine creator, he would conjecture. Or the statesman would run through the latest gossip he had heard and waspishly make comments about certain corrupt politicians – and their even more corrupted wives.

"Surely they will listen to reason."

Sometimes his secretary's good-natured optimism tipped over into naivety, Cicero thought to himself. Yet he would not have traded his ever amiable, ever loyal assistant for the world.

"Hah. When has a politician ever listened to reason? And even if we deem Cato a philosopher more than politician, when has a philosopher ever listened to reason?"

Cicero's smile did not last long and his brooding expression returned as he thought how Caesar too had abandoned his reason, allowing the toxic – and intoxicated – Mark Antony to act as his ambassador and present a letter to the Senate. Caesar had first, in an obtuse self-glorifying manner, listed his achievements in the document. He then demanded that, should he have to relinquish his command, then so too should Pompey. Either make Caesar consul, or Caesar would make war, the letter implied. Was Caesar hoping that the Senate would pander to his demands if he threatened war? People who play with fire often get burned, Cicero sadly mused to himself.

Yet where there is life there his hope, Cicero posited again – forcing himself to believe in his own maxim. He carried with him a letter from Caesar, written in a far more mollifying tone, offering a far more reasonable compromise. In order to keep busy Cicero also brought a number of other letters with him on the journey. He read over his last correspondence from Marcus Brutus and grimly thought how the noble statesman would experience his own species of civil war should a compromise not be met. Caesar was all but a surrogate father to Brutus, having helped bring him up during his time as Sevilia's lover. He remembered many years ago how Brutus had entertained the guests at a dinner party by showing off a trick that Caesar had taught him – that of being able to run up and leap upon a horse from behind – and looking to his teacher for approval. Caesar had also paid for Brutus to study philosophy in Greece. The other father figure in Marcus' life however had been Cato. Everyone would have to choose a side, but Brutus would be conflicted more than most. The studious statesman also enclosed a poem that he had recently read and enjoyed. Cicero wryly smiled, in light of its pertinence and wisdom.

The Waggon of Life

Though creaking sometimes with the load,
Life's running waggon scarcely rocks.
Grey Time conducts us down the road;
This driver never leaves the box.

We climb upon the boards at dawn
Full of wild devilment and crowing;
Spurning the languid life with scorn,
We cry, 'Go on, get fucking going!'

But by midday we've lost that boldness,
Feeling the waggon shake and judder.
Dread are the heights and dizzy gorges.
We cry, 'Slow down, you silly bugger!'

On goes the waggon round the bend.

By evening well we know the rhythm.

Nodding, we ride to our journey's end,

Time's waggon ever-onward driven.'

8.

Half read – and unread – correspondence littered the chamber. Half eaten – and uneaten – dishes of food lay on top of the bedside table. Pompey's attendants departed, having finished dressing their master in his toga. Pompey barely recognised the figure staring back at him in the polished silver mirror. He blamed his pallor and tiredness on an illness he was still recovering from. He scrunched his face up in irritation as he gazed over to see the fire dying out. The cold numbed his bones. Although it may sometimes be charmed by a woman, time waits for no man - he realised. His once strong and handsome face had become drawn and flabby. Grief, for Julia, had aged him as much as the passing of time. He was fond of Cornelia – and attracted to her – but he still missed Julia and often still felt like a widower, rather than a husband. Sometimes he would ask Cornelia to wear Julia's perfume. Would she had survived, then so might have their child. Would she had survived, then so would have his alliance with Caesar. Their conference at Luca had but delayed, rather than averted, their collision course however. Pompey sometimes felt disappointed in regards to Caesar, as if he were a father betrayed by his favourite son. Or he felt indignant towards his ungrateful subordinate, for defying his former patron. But sometimes, increasingly, Pompey experienced a shard of fear when he thought of Caesar.

Yet his courage and pride would get the better of any trepidation he felt in dealing with Caesar. Someone had to stop him. The Senate were a bunch of squabbling children, or a pack of scavenging dogs concerned with taking a bite out of the fatted calf of Rome; Cato and Marcellus could not be trusted with combating Caesar – either with besting the force of his personality or the force of his veteran legions. The First Man of Rome was the *only* man in Rome who could save the Republic.

"They're here," Flavius Laco remarked, appearing at the door, little disguising the contempt he held for the deputation of senators who had gathered in Pompey's triclinium. Flavius Laco was more commonly known as Charon – his name in the arena. A former legionary and celebrated gladiator, Laco had been recruited from the Ninth legion to Pompey's personal staff many years ago. Rumour had it that Laco tracked down and killed Spartacus as he was escaping across the Alps. When due to fight in the arena, Charon was advertised as being *"Forged from the fires of Brutality and Guile."* Although he had served as the proconsul's bodyguard – and as his champion in the arena – Pompey had also employed the loyal soldier as an enforcer and assassin.

Pompey nodded – and sympathised with the soldier's contempt for the gaggle of politicians waiting for him. What had Cato's war of words with Caesar achieved over the years? He took in Laco and thought to himself how little he had appeared to age since he had first caught his eye. Perhaps Time was scared of approaching the fearsome looking warrior. His hair was free from grey, his body as well conditioned as a man half his age. A few scars lined his torso but Laco had inflicted far more injuries on others than he had received himself. Perhaps one of the scars was formed from having any sense of mercy or remorse cut out of him years ago, the great statesman mused. The gladiator had earned his nickname from having ferried so many opponents to their deaths. It was likely that spectators also muddled up the nickname with Charun, the demon that an arena slave would dress up as before finishing off any suspected wounded combatant with a large hammer at the end of each bout.

"Come my friend. Let us meet our guests. Cato has no doubt already started drinking my wine. Some of the vintages may even be as old as the resentment he bears towards me."

9.

Marble statues of Alexander the Great and Scipio Africanus flanked the entrance to the triclinium. A large, elaborate mosaic, inlaid with gold, depicting the defeat of Spartacus ran around two sides of the room. In the same way that the mosaic commissioned by Crassus had not included Pompey in the narrative of the slave leader's defeat, Pompey had here erased his old rival from history. The rest of the triclinium was tastefully furnished, containing art and furniture picked out by Julia. Paintings, recommended by Atticus, hung upon the walls. Some of the furniture was made from the timbers of pirate ships, captured by Pompey. Cornelia had recently wanted to re-decorate but her husband had forbidden it.

Pompey greeted Cicero warmly but cast a sterner gaze over the rest of his guests. Those that were sitting rose to their feet as Pompey the Great entered. They nodded at their host respectfully; some almost bowed. The ardent stoic Cato had even deigned to wear a laundered toga – and footwear. Along with Cato it was the consul Gaius Claudius Marcellus and Quintus Metellus Scipio who moved towards Pompey, as if it had been decided that they would be the principle speakers for the group. Representatives from a number of other patrician families were also present. All had, at one time or another, attempted to stymie Pompey's rise to power and block his land reforms to re-settle his army veterans.

The influential optimate senator Metellus, who was also father-in-law to Pompey, moved forward to address their host first. Metellus had offered his daughter to the First Man of Rome for both political as well as financial reasons. Metellus had for years been a staunch opponent of Pompey and Caesar, referring to them both as "low born". Cicero had referred to the self-important aristocrat as being "more kin than kind" in his relations with Pompey but his hatred – and fear – of Caesar eclipsed that to what he felt towards his son-in-law. Cicero rightly surmised that Metellus was not the only figure in the room to have reasoned out that the enemy of his enemy should now be his friend. With his beak of a nose pointed upwards – and his pigeon chest proudly pointed outwards – Metellus spoke:

"Thank you for seeing us at such short notice. But as you well know time is of the essence. Caesar stands upon the borders of Gaul and Italy, no doubt amassing his forces. As with Hannibal years ago, an enemy is at the gates.

"Aye, that is what we must now classify Caesar as – an enemy of the state. Who does he think he is, to dictate terms to us? And he dares to threaten Rome with soldiers belonging to Rome! No, we must stop him. We have the law on our side." Marcellus was unable to contain his ire any longer. The consul had long been an enemy of Caesar. "His slick-backed hair is as oily as his manner," Cicero had commented to Tiro on their journey to the meeting.

"What is the point of quoting laws when your opponent carries weapons?" Pompey wryly replied.

"Rome possesses its own weapon though, capable of defeating Caesar," Marcellus exclaimed whilst producing an ornate sword and walking towards the great commander. He bowed and offered the sword with a sense of solemnity and ceremony, conscious that he was making history.

Cicero smiled to himself, albeit with a heavy heart, at the irony of the scene. Cato and Marcellus had spent half their lives berating Pompey for acting like a dictator – yet now they were encouraging him to assume the role. Pompey must have known that they were flattering him into armed conflict with Caesar, but Cicero knew that Pompey might still take the bait.

"Let us fight for peace, before we surrender to war, gentlemen," the elder statesman announced, just as Pompey was about to clasp the proffered sword. "I have in my possession a letter from Caesar, offering to relinquish his province. He only asks that he retain one of his legions and be able to bid to become consul in absentia. Even if each soldier were a Hector or Achilles, he cannot pose a serious threat to the state armed with just a single legion."

Pompey raised an eyebrow in slight surprise at Cicero's news. He could be content at such a compromise. Pompey, once nicknamed 'The Teenage Butcher', had seen enough Roman blood spilt over the years to not want to see anymore, lest it was necessary. Julia would have argued for the merits of peace over war too, he believed. With just one legion at his disposal, compared to the forces that Pompey had under his control, Caesar would still be the junior partner in their alliance, even if he secured a consulship again. And there was no reason why he should not ally himself to Caesar again, as opposed to Cato and Metellus – who would have few scruples in turning upon him once Julius was defeated.

"Can you be sure of the sincerity of Caesar's offer?" Pompey asked Cicero, consciously or unconsciously drawing back from the sword that Marcellus was still holding out in front of him.

"I believe that he is acting in good faith."

"Hah! Punic good faith, I warrant," Lucius Cornelius Lentulus, Marcellus' co-consul, interjected - making reference to the treachery of Rome's former enemy, Carthage.

"Caesar is in no position to negotiate and make demands. He must face trial for his crimes. He cannot set himself above the law," Cato argued, shaking his head vigorously, to the point of nearly spilling his wine.

"The safety of the people should be the highest law. If you persist in your animus and personal grievances against Julius then you will end up breaking that law," Cicero stated.

"Be quiet old man. You have no stomach to even hold down spicy foods, so we do not expect you to have the stomach for a fight," Lentulus spat out in reply, looking to diminish Cicero's influence over their host.

"Should you insult my friend again in my house, Lentulus, then you may have another kind of fight on your hands." The colour drained from the statesman's face at Pompey's rebuke. Just as the chastised consul was about to apologise, to both his host and fellow guest, Cicero approached Pompey directly and spoke to him as if the rest of the party were invisible.

"Let us not listen to those who think we ought to be angry with our enemies, and who believe this to be great and manly. Nothing is so praiseworthy, nothing so clearly shows a great and noble soul, as clemency and a readiness to forgive," Cicero calmly expressed, his sage aspect boring into Pompey's soul.

"Cicero may be right. If Caesar is content with such a settlement then we should be too."

"But for how long will Caesar be content? His career has shown us that once he secures what he wants, he then looks to secure even more," Metellus countered, screwing his face up in detestation upon positing his enemy's name and ambition.

"It is not a question of Caesar being content either. The Senate has no desire to negotiate with Caesar as to how many legions he unlawfully retains. The law dictates that he must become a private citizen again to run for office. His demands are unacceptable. Caesar must be destroyed," Cato steadfastly decreed.

Pompey sighed, from sadness or tiredness. Time had not only caught up with him. Fate had too, for he knew that it would always come to this. Caesar must be Caesar. But Pompey was the First Man of Rome - and as Caesar himself had once said, it was better to be the first man in a village than the second man in Rome

"I do this not from pride, but rather out of a duty to protect the Republic," Pompey proudly exclaimed – and held out his hand to receive the ceremonial sword from Marcellus.

Cicero sighed, from sadness and tiredness.

10.

A fire blazed away and heated the cottage. Atilia rested her head against his chest, still wearing her crumpled stola from the night before. Oppius closed his eyes and the usually stern looking centurion appeared content and at peace for once. He breathed out, in a sigh of pleasure.

"Have you spoken to Caesar yet?"

"Not yet."

Atilia held back from saying any more – the awkward silence shattered his moment of contentment. The soldier felt her body tense up a little beneath the furs. Oppius had told himself that he would leave the army but he had still to tell Caesar. He dreaded his commander's anger or enmity, but more so Oppius worried that he would disappoint his friend in his hour of need. Caesar engendered and rewarded loyalty. Perhaps he would still serve with Caesar until he reached Rome. He might have little need of the centurion if he became consul again.

Oppius was more worried about how he would tell Roscius however. Perhaps, if Caesar had any goodwill left for his officer, he would permit the legionary to leave the legion too. Perhaps Titus could purchase his freedom and have him work for him also. And what of Teucer? Would he want to remain in the Tenth after they left? Although his native land held many painful memories for the archer, home was still home. The island even had its charms perhaps, although they were difficult to see through the constant haze of rain. Maybe Oppius wasn't the only one who wanted to settle down. A love of life in the army can wear as thin as quickly as the soles upon one's boots during a march. Or would he ultimately end up like his father, married to the army? His father had given everything for the legion, including his life. He had died during a fencing match with a soldier from the Ninth legion. Rumour had it that the legionary from the Ninth had baited his blade with poison.

"And how is young Marcus? I saw him out in the town with Claudia yesterday. You may want to warn him to be more discreet. Although Rufus Scorpus cares little for his wife, he cares a great deal about his reputation."

The hint of a smile returned to Oppius' face as he thought about the love struck youth. He had even caught him reciting snatches of love poetry as he cleaned out the latrines the other day.

"I will warn him, although I'm not sure how much my words will register over the sound of his beating heart."

11.

"Dear Atticus,

If politics seems increasingly like a stage play to you then we are entering into the second act of our tragedy. Caesar has been declared an enemy of the state. And Pompey is its greatest friend. After all those years attempting to prevent Pompey from becoming a dictator the Senate has now asked him to act out the role. It appears it takes a dictator to stop a dictator.

When asked how he would defend Rome, Pompey answered, with no little bluster, that "I have only to stamp my foot upon the ground, and there will rise armies of infantry and armies of cavalry." Let us hope that ultimately the sound of Pompey's feet stamping on the ground does not spring from the scenario of him running away. I worry that it has been some time since he last drew his sword. He has been worshipping Julia and Cornelia, rather than Mars, these past years. He is like a veteran gladiator, having to come out of retirement one last time. Hopefully the arena will not seem strange to him. Caesar however is the young challenger, who has just won a string of victories.

I remember giving a speech some years ago, which I have just had Tiro dig out (I wouldn't want to misquote myself). The speech concerned the threat of the pirate, who afflicted our state back then. "There can be no trusting him, no attempt to bind with mutually agreed treaties." The same thought may apply to Caesar. Despite my will to negotiate and reach a compromise the storm clouds would have only moved slower towards us, rather than dissipated. Pompey may bend the rules which keep the Republic's shape, but Caesar will have no qualms about breaking them. Should Caesar prove victorious then civil war will be succeeded by a revolution. Yet should Pompey win then I suspect that he will be more focused on screwing Cornelia and his mistresses again, rather than the Republic. We will have to compose new songs for him, but few new laws.

The one piece of good news I do have is that I have heard that Mark Antony's life is now in danger, now that his commander has been judged an enemy. I'm not sure about the Republic, but certainly a few marriages will now be saved from our arch-cuckold having to leave Rome. The city's vintners and brothel owners may be wearing black in a show of grief however.

You will not be surprised to hear that I have never seen Cato so happy. Finally he has found someone else to agree with him that "Caesar must be destroyed." Such has been the smile on his usually sour face that anyone would think peace, rather than war, has broken out. Only the gods know how much drink he has had to celebrate the good news. Metellus is also smiling, perhaps at the thought of raising taxes in the name of raising arms. Marcellus is walking around with his chest puffed out, as though he has already won the war. I'm not sure the people share the Senate's confidence or sympathies though. Marcellus may be overestimating the

Senate's popularity – and also crucially underestimating Caesar's. I love the cause but hate the men. The Senate has also suspended the powers of the tribunes, to help pass its ultimate decree and give Pompey and the Senate all "necessary" sovereignty. Democracy has been slain, in the name of democracy. It is not the best piece of legislation to come out of the Forum (unfortunately it has also not been the worst I have been witness to).

Pompey has already been given command of two legions, those that were formed for the prospective Parthian campaign. As well as possessing considerable forces in the East, Pompey can also call upon seven legions in Spain, which may be able to attack Caesar's rear before he gets to Rome. On the other side Caesar is in possession of eleven legions, although he will not be able to muster them immediately. These legions are travelling down the road to ruin – and such are the state of Roman roads that we may get there quicker than anyone expects.

Cicero."

12.

The morning's apricot sunlight washed over the scene. The smell of the dewy lawn filled his nostrils. Pompey sat on a bench in his garden and gazed into his fish pond. A brace of koi carp swirled around just beneath the surface in a dance of colour. Pompey wistfully recalled how he would often come here with Julia in the morning, after their breakfast together. They would sometimes spend hours just sitting and talking. She would sit, her legs tucked beneath her – and just lean into him, their warm bodies as one. Pompey thought how he genuinely cared for his present wife. Cornelia was refined and beautiful and could arouse him; she was accomplished, educated. He would often listen with pleasure as she played the lyre, or she would engage him through discussing the various books on philosophy and geometry she voraciously read. Cornelia also turned a blind eye to his indiscretions with mistresses and slave girls, whilst at the same time remaining faithful to him. He was attracted to his wife, but he didn't love her. Not like he loved Julia. Although Julia had been much younger than Pompey, she was wiser than him. He sometimes affectionately nicknamed her "Julia the Great". She made him want to be a good – better – man. Tears welled in the widower's eyes as he remembered again her sudden death – and the death of their baby son a few days later.

A cold wind numbed his face. Pompey fancifully wished how it could numb his feelings too.

The statesman was snapped out of his maudlin daydream by the purposeful footsteps of Flavius Laco on the marble path. The former soldier's forehead was creased in duteous gravity, causing his bushy eyebrows to enjoin. The polished pommel of his sword gleamed in the sunlight. So too Laco wore a couple of daggers and a non-military issue breastplate over his tunic. A round shield hung on his muscular arm. Flavius Laco was ready for war, albeit his orders would be to just kill one man. It was Pompey's desire to end the war before it could commence. Laco would lead a small force and intercept Caesar on the border, before he could bring together all of his legions. *Cut off the head and the body will die.*

"Are the men ready?" Pompey asked, having cast off his grief-stricken expression.

"They are."

"Are they good men? Can they be trusted?"

"I trained them myself – and the gold has purchased their loyalty."

"Then let it be done."

Laco nodded. Pompey turned his head and stared again into the pond as the agent marched back along the path towards the house. His temples were liver-spotted, his eyes red with sleeplessness. The skin hung down from a face dripping with sorrow. He would mourn his friend, a fellow soldier and former son-in-law. But he would welcome the death of his rival and Rome's enemy. Pompey just hoped that Julia could understand and forgive him. He was doing this for Rome, out of his duty to the Senate. So too he was looking to stop Caesar in such a dishonourable way so that countless soldiers and civilians would not suffer needlessly. The blood would be on his hands alone. Indeed the only person who Pompey convinced himself that he wasn't doing this for was Pompey.

13.

Finally – like Oppius, Roscius and Teucer – Fabius had had his nose broken. Blood ran down his chin. Rufus Scorpus stood over him, smiling as the young legionary winced in pain. The haughty bureaucrat nodded to his burly attendant, Pullo, again. This time Pullo's punch was directed at Fabius' body – and the soldier felt a couple of his ribs crack. An hour or so ago he had been in the company of Claudia, walking from the market towards Oppius' cottage. A carriage had pulled up beside them however, carrying Scorpus and half a dozen of his attendants. Both Fabius and Claudia were abducted and taken back to the bureaucrat's house. The seething husband first struck his wife, calling her a whore - and then she was locked in her room. Fabius had his hands bound behind his back and was then strapped to a chair. Pullo stood before him in the triclinium, flexing his fingers – his hand either smarting from the last punch or readying itself for the next. Scorpus paced, prowled, behind the brutal attendant. Half of Fabius' body felt numb from the cold and the other half throbbed in pain. He trembled, either from the winter wind or from the growing torment he felt.

"Did you think that you could try to embarrass me and not face any repercussions? You've had your bit of fun, but now I'm putting an end to things. I may even put an end to you," Scorpus stated, his face screwed up in contempt for the lowly soldier.

"This isn't about me having a bit of fun. I love her." Perhaps there was still some shadow of hope for the idealistic soldier; if he could make his case then he could persuade Scorpus to divorce Claudia and they could live happily ever after.

"Don't make me laugh. You've fucked her and felt good – and have mistaken that feeling for love, that's all. Maybe I shouldn't altogether blame you. You merely observed some low hanging fruit and plucked it. I always thought that the selfish bitch would take a lover. I just imagined that she wouldn't lower herself to start rutting with a baby-faced soldier. Should she have given herself to a Caesar or Pompey then I would have turned a blind eye. I would even be willing to pimp her out to the right man, if it served a purpose. But you're no better than the shit on the bottom of my shoe, boy."

Fabius' expression was either contorted in pain, or disgust. He struggled, in vain, to free himself from his binds.

"And now I am in a dilemma. You need to be punished for your transgression. I'm unsure whether to allow you to walk again, screw again or even breathe again. I am nothing if not fair however. Be assured that I will be punishing my slut of a wife too. I'll break her, like a horse, so as to never need to punish her again. I'll leave your fate to Pullo though." Scorpus nodded to his attendant again, looking also at the dagger upon his belt.

Pullo first held the glinting blade beneath his victim's eyes, before quickly, sadistically, slicing his cheek. Again Fabius struggled to free himself but the ropes only bit into his arms and wrists the more. He tried – but failed – to contain his terror as a smirking Pullo raised the knife up to the soldier's face again. Fabius shook his head, in either an attempt to persuade his torturer to desist or to prevent himself from sobbing, which he felt like doing.

The grin across the face of Rufus Scorpus widened as Pullo slowly pressed the point of the dagger into the young man's thigh – and then twisted the blade. Fabius' scream curdled the air. He first begged the attendant to stop - and then called him a bastard. After finally withdrawing the knife from his thigh the former butcher smeared the bloody blade across the legionary's face, laughing as he did so. Pullo looked to his master again, who gave his assent to continue. Fabius' piteous expression was ignored as Pullo used his filleting knife to cut away the skirt of his victim's tunic, to reveal his groin area. He knew that his master would enjoy watching what would follow.

As a self-satisfied Rufus Scorpus was about to nod his head one more time he was distracted by sounds and shouting coming from the front of the house.

"If it's the bitch causing a disturbance we'll strap her to the chair next."

But Claudia was still in her room, burying her tear-soaked face in her hands, praying to the Gods that Fabius would be okay. She prayed to the Gods to be merciful, for she knew that her husband wouldn't be.

Lucius Oppius entered the triclinium. One of Atilia's slaves had been travelling from the cottage to the market and she had witnessed Fabius being overpowered and abducted. She quickly ran back to the house and breathlessly told the centurion what had happened. Believing that he did not have enough time to call upon any legionaries from the camp he rode directly over to Scorpus' estate.

"How dare you enter my house in this manner? Do you not know who I am?" the official announced in a shrill voice, adjusting his toga afterwards, attempting to retain his dignity and authority.

"I know who you are. And if you know who I am you'll know that it would now be best to untie my legionary."

"I know who you are, Oppius. And I'll make sure that Caesar reprimands you, after Pullo here has finished teaching you a lesson."

"Don't worry, I'll be speaking to Caesar soon enough. Who do you think he will side with on the eve of a civil war, a centurion of the first rank or a second-rate bureaucrat with connections to Cato?"

"You're just another dumb, expendable soldier. And it'll be difficult for you to say anything to Caesar after my attendant here breaks your jaw. Pullo, if you would like to show our guest out."

The brawny enforcer wore a sneer cum smile on his face as he walked towards the stationary centurion, still carrying his knife.

Oppius caught his opponent by the wrist as he thrust the weapon towards him. The centurion then yanked the attendant towards him. The first head butt broke his nose, the second rendered him unconscious. When seeing the wound in Fabius' thigh Oppius picked up the butcher's knife on the tiled floor and plunged it into the prostrate sadist's leg.

Rufus Scorpus gave out a dry-throated yelp as the officer walked towards him. His attempted scream was abruptly cut short as Oppius clasped him by his scrawny neck and lifted him off the ground, his back to the wall. Piss soaked the official's toga and dripped down his leg.

"I'll show myself out. Both Fabius and Claudia will be accompanying me. If you ever attempt to harm either one of them again I'll bury my sword in your face. Understand?"

Scorpus nodded, repeatedly – emptying his bladder even more freely whilst doing so.

Later that evening Oppius met with Caesar and spoke about the incident. Caesar's reaction was to laugh. "I wouldn't even have minded if you made this Claudia a widow rather than divorcee." Caesar proceeded to write to the official, politely suggesting that for health reasons and in order to further his career Rufus should consider taking another wife.

14.

The merchant, Quintus Furius, appeared before Lucius Lentulus and explained how he had sold his wagon to three men – and how one of the men, he now realised, was Mark Antony. The merchant was hoping to earn twice, both from the sale of the wagon and also the sale of information. When his cousin and business partner superstitiously warned that the gods were likely to punish such treachery in the afterlife Quintus countered that he would rather be rewarded in this world than the next. Unfortunately, after Lentulus had extracted from the merchant all he knew, he merely proclaimed that Rome would honour his service and loyalty (though quite how Rome would do this the politician left unanswered). Rather than honours Quintus was keen for riches to be bestowed upon him instead.

Once Quintus had been dismissed Lentulus sent out messengers to a number of fellow optimate senators, explaining how Mark Antony, accompanied by two other soldiers, had escaped from the city in a wagon and were heading north, back to Caesar. There were a limited number of roads the party could take and he suggested that they muster together several forces - consisting of their lictors, gladiators and bodyguards – in order to capture Caesar's lieutenant, dead or alive.

Clouds marbled the night sky. The stars shone like polished gems on a silk gown. The three men breathed a sigh of relief, almost in unison. Antony held the reins whilst Roscius and Teucer sat in the back of the wagon. The soldiers had smuggled themselves out of the city. They were now travelling along a track, having come off a major road, leading north. Antony thought to himself how he had failed to secure peace. But he had little hope of doing so before coming to Rome. One didn't need to pay an augur to foresee that sooner or later Caesar or Pompey, or the optimates and populares, would come to blows. A small victory had perhaps been won already through the Senate curtailing the powers of the tribunate. Caesar could now claim to be acting in the people's interest, as well as his own, should he go to war.

"I could use some rest. Tertia gave me another sleepless evening last night," Roscius remarked to his friend, after yawning.

"Let's just hope that she didn't give you the pox, as well as a sleepless night," the archer replied, whilst sharpening an arrowhead.

"Well I'm itching to see her again," Roscius countered, rehashing an old joke. "But how did you get on last night? Want me to ask if Tertia has a mother, or grandmother, when we're next in Rome? I know how you like your women old."

"No, I like my women cheap. There's a difference," Teucer answered back, half-jokingly.

Roscius' hearty laughter was succeeded by the low rumble of horse hooves on the ground. Ten dim silhouettes appeared across the horizon behind them. The riders kicked the flanks of their horses. Antony flicked the reins and the two chestnut mares pulling the wagon broke into a fast trot. The cold wind spewed up dust on the track in front and behind them. The two legionaries briefly, vigorously, rubbed their hands to bring the feeling back into them. Teucer attached his bowstring and reached for his quiver of a dozen or so arrows. Roscius took stock of his weapons also, buckling on his sword and moving the blankets and jars of wine out of the way to ready his two pilums.

"Wait until they're upon us before attacking. Make your shots count," Mark Antony issued, shouting above the howl of the wind and tamp of the horses.

The enemy closed in. Roscius could see the breath of the horses mist up in front of their faces. Those that possessed javelins – and possessed the skill to throw the missiles whilst riding – began to retrieve them. Teucer knew that he could not allow any of the enemy to pass him and stop the wagon; if that happened then their time remaining upon the earth would be as short as one of Tertia's skirts.

The pursuers charged down the sloping grassland – out of formation and lacking a cohesive plan. Each man craved glory and adrenaline was taking over; they believed that they could easily best their enemies, given their numbers and weaponry.

Teucer and Roscius crouched down in the back of the wagon, not wishing to make themselves too large a target – but once the range was right they quickly sprung up and launched their attack. The archer first brought down the rider who seemed most capable, just as he brought his arm back to throw his javelin. Without pausing to admire the shot - that thudded dead-centre into horseman's chest – Teucer fired off another arrow and again it hit its mark. The wind whistled in harmony with the shafts. Roscius' first pilum skewered into the horse's neck. A high-pitched whinny rippled the air as the colt fell to the ground, crushing its rider. Another horse, distracted or terrified by the scene, lost its footing on a steep part of the slope and threw its rider too.

Antony flicked the whip again and drove on the team of mares. Out of the corner of his eye he saw an enemy pass him, with the aim to come in front of the wagon and slow his horses to a standstill. Before the rider could reach the track however Antony stood up and held the reins in one hand. With the other he drew his knife and threw it at his enemy, the blade slotting into his the base of his spine. Caesar's lieutenant part smiled and part snarled in satisfaction and flicked his whip once more.

His heart pounded to the rhythm of the galloping horses as Roscius roared - in anger and exertion – and threw his remaining pilum. The spear, its polished head briefly shimmering in the moonlight, struck an enemy in the sternum. The force of the shot knocked him off the back of his horse.

Teucer drew back the bowstring again, as the enemy in his sights riding alongside him drew out a throwing axe. Yet just as the archer was about to release his arrow the wagon rode over a ditch in the rode and the shaft fell off the bow and onto the floor. Teucer saw the rider bare his white teeth in a victorious smile. The legionary knew that he would not miss with the axe from such close range. Teucer sighed and closed his eyes in resignation; the darkness would be a good preparation for death.

Instead of feeling the force of an axe bury itself into his body however the archer heard a dull thud, succeeded by the sound of the horseman falling to the ground. He opened his eyes to see the enemy prostrate upon the track, with a jar of wine near to his head.

The remaining horsemen, now outnumbered, retreated.

"You're lucky that it wasn't a vintage, otherwise I might have been tempted to save the wine rather than yourself," Roscius remarked to his comrade, half-jokingly.

15.

Stars sleepily blinked in the night sky. Oppius stood outside by the carriage but he could hear the murmur of conversation and laughter from the villa, where Caesar was dining out for the evening. The centurion thought to himself how he would have raised an eye in scepticism, or confusion, should someone have told him six months ago that he would be planning to leave the army and get married again. Yet the chapter he was about to write himself into instilled a sense of quiet contentment; he was surprised at the lack of surprise he felt in regards to starting a new life, outside the legion. A warm glow came over him, distracting him from the cold, as he thought of Atilia. He enjoyed her company even more than her cooking. She was aware of his sins as a soldier, yet could forgive him for his dark and violent past. And if she could forgive him of his sins, then maybe he could forgive himself. But more so than dwelling on the past, he looked forward to the future – building a home with the woman he cherished. He looked forward also to meeting Atilia's young son, Cassius. He was determined not to make the same mistakes his father had made when he was growing up, although Oppius wryly conceded that he would probably make entirely new ones.

Although he had spent the day with Caesar, he had still to tell him of his intention to leave the army once they entered Italy.

Atilia had prompted him to do so, repeatedly. In order to temper her recent frustration with him Oppius had bought her a silver pendant, studded with a ruby (but it only staved off her frustration with him for a day; with the riches of Alexander he could perhaps buy her silence for a week, he thought). Partly the moment was never right for telling Caesar – and also he still dreaded letting his friend and commander down in what could prove his hour of need. Oppius had been with Caesar when he had received the message that the Senate had passed the ultimate decree, disbanded the tribunate and declared him an enemy of the state. Perhaps only Oppius and Joseph had noticed the brief gleam in his eye and flicker of a smile shortly afterwards. Caesar cited how the Senate were acting unlawfully in taking the powers of the tribunes – "the powers of the people" – away. But both Joseph and Oppius felt that this was more of a welcome excuse, than justification, for Caesar committing himself to war.

"My intention is to emancipate rather than conquer... Pompey and the optimates are the true tyrants, over legislating and over taxing Rome for self-serving reasons. And they have the gall to dress up their autocracy as being for the good of the people... The ultimate decree has not passed sentence on me, it has passed sentence on them..."

Joseph was unsure how much Caesar believed in his own arguments but his supporters – and the populares – would lap them up willingly. Like garden weeds, conflict always seems to find a way of sprouting up, the old servant wearily thought to himself.

Rather than reaching for his gladius though Caesar reached for his stylus the following day and wrote a number of letters (often while dictating other missives to his secretaries). Among others he composed letters to Cicero, Brutus, Marcus Phillipus (step-father to his great-nephew, Octavius), his wife Calpurnia and his political agent Marcus Balbus. The wily yet loyal Balbus would in turn write letters to key clients of Caesar, securing support and resources.

During the afternoon Oppius had accompanied Caesar to watch a group of gladiators spar (with an eye to recruiting some of them for a new ludus he was intending to build). Caesar wished to give off the appearance, both to his friends and opponents, that recent news had neither shocked nor alarmed him - that all was well and in hand. Although Oppius would sometimes catch his commander deep in thought, his brow creased in worry, for the most part Caesar appeared good humoured and untroubled.

"Are you not tempted to step into the arena again and show them how it's done?" Caesar remarked to Oppius, smiling.

"Twice was more than enough," the officer replied. Indeed once was more than enough, Oppius mused – briefly remembering his time as a gladiator, but not with any fondness. He preferred the battlefield to the arena. Although Oppius admired the skill and courage of the gladiators on show he was appalled by the jeering and bloodthirsty behaviour of the spectators.

"Perhaps this is how Pompey and I should settle our differences. It would save lives and we could make money on the gate receipts.

I'm not sure about how much of a spectacle it'd be however. Rather than swords, we're more likely to fence with walking sticks soon, such are our ages."

Caesar laughed briefly but then sadness crept into his expression as he recalled how he once great friend and ally was now his greatest enemy. His lines deepened in his face, like scars, as he thought of Julia too.

The table was a feast of colour and aromas (honey-glazed hams, cheeses, steaming fish, salads, radishes, poultry, fresh fruit). The host, one Gaius Voltedius (a wealthy merchant, who had made his fortune from selling on prisoners as slaves during Caesar's campaigns in Gaul), finally summoned up the courage to ask Caesar what had been on everyone's mind.

"So what will Caesar do next?"

The twelve dinner companions, who had been babbling on about all manner of things – from the disinclination of Gauls to wash to the latest translation of Plato – swiftly fell in to a silence, as if their venerated guest was the Delphic Oracle, about to deliver a prophecy. Pausing, so as to make sure he had everyone's attention and to increase the sense of drama, the proconsul amused himself by enigmatically remarking, "Caesar will be Caesar."

"And what of Pompey? What will he do?"

"Regretfully I do not know. Perhaps you should invite him around to dinner next to ask him. I understand that he has been stamping his feet quite a lot though. Whether this is to raise armies, or to merely keep warm in this cold weather, I'll let you decide."

The audience laughed, in sycophancy as much as amusement. Fearing he was not getting anywhere trying to draw Caesar out as to his future plans Voltedius asked his guest about his past glories.

"We will let the future look after itself then. But as to your history, what do you consider your greatest conquest?"

In a mood to entertain rather than inform – and suspecting that most people around the table would have difficulty telling one end of a pilum from the other – Caesar replied:

"My greatest conquest? Some might argue invading Britain, or defeating the Gauls at Alesia. But ultimately I would have to say that my greatest conquest was the wife of the optimate senator Tillius Galba. Especially when I consider that she was as frosty as the alps towards me during our first encounter."

Several guests drunkenly banged the table to applaud the joke, whilst others just roared with laughter - in amusement as much as sycophancy.

"What finally made her thaw out, so to speak?" Voltedius said.

"She saw the size of my – assets!"

16.

Snow flecked the air and powdered the ground. Oppius watched as Caesar gave his final thanks to his host at the front door to the house. He smiled and shook hands effusively with Voltedius. The centurion couldn't help but notice how Caesar hugged his host's adolescent daughter for longer than was perhaps appropriate. He also whispered something in her ear which made her laugh – and blush. Caesar ended by saying that he would try and return to catch the end of the dinner later that night, his schedule permitting. For all intents and purposes it appeared that the last thing on the proconsul's mind was an impending civil war.

Yet as soon as Caesar turned his back on the merchant and his family the gregarious smile fell from his face, like a plate smashing to the ground. He wore a storm upon his semblance. A thoughtfulness and determination shaped his brooding features. It was an expression that Oppius had oft witnessed previously, before a battle. Caesar nodded to Oppius and the centurion standing next to him, one Asinius Pollio, and they joined their commander as he climbed into the carriage. Asinius was a soldier and a scholar. Caesar enjoyed his company and valued him as an officer. The centurion was just as happy drilling legionaries as he was discussing literature with Marcus Fabius. The order was given to depart and the carriage, which was pulled by a team of mules borrowed from a nearby bakery, moved out and was quickly swallowed up by the night and snow.

Caesar changed into his red boots. He also put on his scarlet cloak, breastplate and sword. Not far from Voltedius' house the carriage was met by a small force of cavalry and infantry from the Thirteenth legion. They were soon on the road to Ariminium. Earlier that day Caesar had despatched a number of legionaries, dressed as civilians, to take a cache of weapons ahead and reconnoitre the town.

Oppius and Pollio were among the few who were party to Caesar's plan. Many believed that Caesar would delay any invasion until he had assembled all of his legions. They were wrong.

He was right. Laco, his face smeared in mud, observed the growing number of legionaries from the other side of the river. Caesar was looking to steal a march on the enemy immediately and Laco had predicted that he would make for Ariminium. Having surveyed the map he judged that the best ground for an ambush would be at the river crossing. Once Caesar's carriage was on his side he would send a small detachment of his men to bottleneck or cut off the forces behind their commander. With the rest of his men, dressed up as bandits, Laco would attack the carriage and assassinate Caesar. Surprise and swiftness would hopefully compensate for inferiority in numbers. Cut off the head and the body will die. Once the proconsul was slain he would sound a retreat.

The tangled forest was a blur as Oppius stared out of the carriage window. His breath fogged up in front of his face. He pulled the woollen blanket up over his chest to lock in more warmth. Asinius was asleep; Caesar's head was buried in his correspondence. As much as the centurion felt privileged to be by his commander's side at such an hour he found himself yearning even more to be with Atilia. His body never felt cold when next to hers. She was his friend and lover. He regretted not meeting her years ago. She could have been his first wife (indeed he sometimes even regretted not having married the Medusa, instead of his first wife). Oppius vowed however that Atilia would be his last wife. He wanted to make a home and family.

"You look preoccupied Lucius, as though you're in another place – or wish to be in another place," Caesar expressed with genuine concern. "Perhaps you are worried about your friends back in Rome. I'm sure they'll be fine. Antony has spent half a lifetime sneaking out of bedroom windows, from hearing husbands on the stairs. I've every confidence that he'll be able to sneak out of the city unnoticed."

Before Oppius had a chance to reply – and he wondered if this might prove the time to broach the subject of him resigning his commission – the driver of the carriage announced that they had reached the river.

17.

The Rubicon glowed with the dark beauty and sheen of a black pearl. Although half an army was assembled not a stone's throw away the scene was strangely quiet, eerie. The undulating sound of the river, along with the soughing wind, reverberated in the air. Caesar wondered whether the river was singing, or laughing, at him. Oppius stood next to his commander, awaiting the order. But the centurion barely recognised Caesar. His expression was coloured with anxiety - or fear even. The colour had drained from his face, taking with it something of his character also. For once it felt like Caesar was detached, as opposed to being in full possession of himself.

"I know that you must be uneasy about this campaign. I am too. They wanted this war though, remember that. I am not the attacker. I am defending – defending my person and my dignity. Know that I do not intend to harm any innocent in this conflict. Mildness and generosity must be our shield. Clemency, rather than cruelty, will win us this war. Yet keep your blade sharpened my friend. I would not trade you for a hundred of the enemy, much like Marius would not have traded your father. I remember when you first came to my attention, Lucius. I might have to ask you to offer up another legionary's prayer for luck. We will be outnumbered, but never outmatched. I fear neither Cato's oratory nor his martial prowess.

Pompey however may pose a different question, a question I will ultimately have to find an answer to. I hope Cicero and Brutus understand. I would prefer not to win this war at the expense of losing their friendship. Yet more than asking what the cost will be to me if I cross this river, what price will Rome pay if I fight - or surrender?"

Oppius, akin to Caesar, found himself staring into the calm waters, as if upon its surface an image – answer – might be found. Would the war be akin to the river and, starting out with a slow trickle, gain momentum to climax in violence and destruction as it reached its conclusion?

Caesar buried his head in his hands and for a moment Oppius thought that his commander might break down, or fall to his knees. But neither occurred. When Caesar removed his hands his jaw was fixed in grim determination - his countenance no longer haunted by doubts. He smiled at the valorous centurion, his eyes shining in the moonlight.

"I am in blood stepped so far that, should I wade no more, returning were as tedious as go o'er."

Oppius failed to recognise the phrase, taken as it was from a play which Caesar had recently read (and had forwarded on to his great-nephew, Octavius).

"Shall I give the order to cross the river?"

"Yes."

As Oppius marched off towards the anticipant Thirteenth legion Asinius Pollio approached his general, with the news that his three hundred cavalry were now mustered. Before he could speak however he heard Caesar, with his back to him, utter the following words:

"The die is cast."

The centurion would often replay Caesar's words back in his mind. Had he expressed them with regret, resignation or contentment? He could never decide.

Shortly after relaying orders to various centurions Oppius spotted Fabius. The legionary was walking somewhat gingerly and a dressing covered part of his face, but the light was still undimmed in his eyes.

"Get lost on the way from the infirmary? I thought I ordered you to rest up."

"I didn't want to miss history being made," Fabius replied. In truth the young legionary felt he owed both Oppius and Caesar a debt of gratitude – and serving with them on their present campaign was the least he could do.

"The only history being made is me not kicking a legionary's arse for disobeying an order." Oppius' slight reprimand was lessened even more by the fond expression on his face for seeing his friend.

"How was Caesar?" Fabius asked, out of a natural curiosity from having seen Oppius speak to him by the side of the river. Similarly, like Asinius Pollio, Fabius had a mind to write up an account one day of the campaign. What with the prospective cost of keeping a wife, he realised that he could make more money from prose than poetry.

"Caesar was Caesar."

18.

A force of twenty or so cavalry and twice that number of infantry ran ahead of the carriage as it drove over the bridge. Caesar wanted to be one of the first to cross the Rubicon, to lead the way. The carriage was now led by a team of the finest black Spanish geldings that money could buy. The proconsul breathed out in a sigh of relief – or disbelief – as he finally crossed over the border between Gaul and Italy. In the former he had been a king in all but name, but in the latter he was now an outlaw.

Flavius Laco breathed in and unconsciously held his breath as the legion moved ever closer to the tree line, either side of the road to Ariminium. The ambush would work. The force in advance of Caesar would not be strong enough. Caesar's pride, it could have been argued, had been the making of him. Now it would be his downfall, Laca posed to himself. He held his sword aloft and glanced to his left and right, assuring himself that he had the attention of his officers. They had their orders, as did the ranks of soldiers, mercenaries and gladiators below them. Laco finally breathed out, as the sword swished down, signalling the attack.

A devastating volley of arrows and spears whispered through the air. The enemy cavalry – and the men immediately surrounding Caesar's carriage - were targeted first. A hail of missiles rained down upon them in the dark, yet still the enemy remained unseen –

as though they were being attacked by the ghosts of the forest. Laco had forbidden his men to issue war cries, which further disorientated their prey. Death would strike in silence, in the darkness. The screeches of pain from horses and men alike formed a macabre duet, or high-pitched dirge. Decurions fell from their mounts, many dead before they hit the ground.

Laco unleashed his own small force of horsemen. They galloped out of the darkness and made straight for the mouth of the bridge. The first wave attacked the infantry making their way over into Italy, the second doused the bridge in oil and the third set the wooden structure alight. A wall of fire lit up the scene and would temporarily cut off reinforcements.

Arrows thudded into Oppius' scutum as he crouched down by the side of the carriage. He immediately realised that the enemy were too well trained and organised to be mere bandits. Their target would be Caesar. Despite the raucous clash of arms and howls of agony scything through the air, Oppius still made himself heard as he called out for the men to form shield walls and defensive formations. Their scutums started to resemble pin cushions, but it was better than their bodies resembling them.

Asinius had advised Caesar to remain in the carriage at first, despite or because of the swarm of arrows which drummed upon the roof and sides of the vehicle. Yet when it became apparent that a number of fire arrows had hit the carriage he shielded Caesar with his own body and made his way towards the small force of men forming around Lucius Oppius.

Flavius Laco led a pack of his infantry out into the killing zone. He spied Caesar's scarlet cloak in the night and wolfishly grinned to himself. For years the cloak had served as a beacon to his troops, to rally them; now it served to highlight his position to the enemy. He quickly scanned the battlefield. The fire raged on at the bridge. Although he could see legionaries diving into the river to reach the shore many would freeze or drown. They were brave, but foolhardy. The rest of the field was littered with enemy wounded and dead. The legionaries were bloodied, half-defeated. A centurion was marshalling a small body of men around his commander however. Laco grunted in begrudging professional respect, that the officer seemed to know his business, as he witnessed Oppius organise a shield wall in front of Caesar. But cut off the head and the body will fall, Laco thought as he plucked a javelin out of a dead decurion and closed in on the officer.

Oppius' attention and shield were facing towards the line of infantry moving towards him from the left. Laco was outflanking him and coming in from the right. Pompey's agent could not remember the last time he had missed from such a middling distance. In one quick movement he judged the weight of the javelin one last time in his hand and then launched the weapon at his unsuspecting enemy in a slight arc.

The spear punched through Fabius' shield – and chest – as the legionary put himself between the missile and his centurion. He had once saved his friend before in a similar manner, on a beach during the invasion of Britain. But that time, in saving Oppius,

272

Fabius had not damned himself. Oppius heard the noise and turned, catching the legionary as he fell in his direction. He gazed up to see the eyes, teeth and blade of his enemy shining brightly in the moonlight, marching purposefully towards him, his face contorted in frustration and fury.

A round gladiator's shield hung on Laco's forearm. He gripped his sword all the more tightly as he swung the weapon and it came crashing down upon the soldier's scutum. The force of the blow jarred his entire body but Oppius swung his gladius in reply. Swords thrashed against each other a dozen times in quick succession – but the gladiator was too good for the centurion. Laco back-slashed, knocking his opponent's shield away to leave him vulnerable. Before Oppius had time to adjust the enemy stabbed his shoulder, cutting through his armour as if it wasn't there. Oppius dropped his sword, stumbled backwards and fell onto the grass. Laco's eyes were ablaze - with both malice and the burning carriage reflected in them. Pompey's agent knew that he should now concentrate his energies in leading his men to murder Caesar, but his blood was up and he wanted to finish off the irksome officer.

Oppius wearily looked around him. Although still lying upon the ground he could blurrily see a line of enemy infantry coming towards him. They had run out of missiles and appeared from out of the tree line to finish off the Thirteenth at close quarters. They had the numbers and momentum to overcome the small force protecting Caesar, he miserably judged. The fire raged on across the other side of the field, cutting off any meaningful reinforcements. The men upon - and over - the bridge were in chaos. The war would end in its first engagement, an ambush. Perhaps that was a good thing, Oppius mused. More men Fabius' would be spared that way. The soldier's shield weighed heavy on his arm; as did his eyelids begin to weigh heavy. The night grew even blacker. Sounds grew dimmer.

Laco walked slowly towards the wounded officer, savouring the moment. As he raised his sword however, to plunge into his enemy's chest, pain bit him in the thigh from an arrow. He swore, cursing his own men for not following his orders; once the first wave of infantry commenced to engage the enemy his archers had been instructed to ready themselves with swords and attack their opponents.

Oppius' eyes opened fully again at seeing the arrow and its distinctive flights. He raised a corner of his mouth in a grim smile and believed that this night might yet see the dawn.

Mark Antony rode into back of the line of enemy infantry at an angle so as to cause as much disruption as possible. Teucer cursed himself for only being able to hit the bastard who stood over Oppius in the leg, although given the distance and fact that he was riding in the back of a wagon over rough ground it had been one of the finest shots he had ever made. Jars of wine first smashed into the enemy, before Roscius began to hack and slash his opponents with his sword.

Laco swore again, witnessing the scene of the line of his infantry breaking. He swore again too as Asinius Pollio, flanked by two capable looking legionaries, stood in between him and the wounded centurion. The tide had turned. The Thirteenth had been given the breathing space to not only form a greater defensive formation around Caesar but they were even sufficiently galvanised and confident to counter-attack. Laco began to witness his forces at the bridge lose their resolve and commence to retreat. Soon reinforcements would break through and he would be overrun. Pompey's champion swore once more and retreated, disappearing into the night and forest. Flavius Laco was brave, but not foolhardy.

The air was thick with the odour of sweat and tang of flesh. Oppius kept pressure on the wound. Despite having covered him with a couple of blankets Fabius still shivered. He coughed, spotting the blankets with blood. His breathing was short and shallow. The legionary's complexion was pale and waxy, as if his face had already been replaced with a death mask. The nausea of grief began to swell in the centurion's stomach and brain.

"Is Caesar safe?" Fabius asked, his voice reduced to a whisper. Sometimes his voice gurgled from the blood seeping into his lungs.

"Yes," Oppius replied, trying to speak and smile in as best a consoling manner as he could manage.

"I'm scared."

"It's okay to be scared."

His face grew paler. The hand which Oppius held grew colder. Fabius no longer had the strength to squeeze his hand back.

"I've never seen you scared."

Oppius wanted to answer that he was scared now, but sorrow already started to choke off his words. Tears welled in his eyes.

"Tell Claudia I genuinely loved her. It wasn't just a poet's fancy."

"You can tell her yourself, when you recover."

"That must be the first time that I've ever heard you tell a lie," Fabius said, the hint of a wry smile on his lips. He then coughed again. He motioned to speak once more but blood, rather than words, came out. Fabius sunk into unconsciousness and passed away shortly afterwards. Oppius buried his head in his hands, fell to his knees and - for the first time in a long time - wept.

Epilogue

Later that evening, closer to dawn rather than dead of night, Caesar summoned Oppius to his tent. Caesar dismissed all of his attendants, even Joseph. He asked his friend to take a seat and poured him out a large measure of wine. Since the attack Oppius had burned with anger - and sorrow. Even hearts of stone can crack. He was unable to find the words and strength to compose a letter to Titus. All he wanted to do was drink - to try and wash away the grief. His eyes were red with sleeplessness and tears.

"Pompey was responsible for the ambush this evening. How do I know this? I recognised the man who killed Fabius. He's Pompey's agent. My old friend has acted dishonourably, but I am not so angry or surprised. Honour is often the first casualty of war."

Oppius' face tightened a little, but otherwise his expression remained impassive. He wanted to be free of both Pompey and Caesar. He'd seen enough death and suffering for one lifetime, drawn his sword enough times. Caesar refilled his cup and continued to speak.

"His name is Flavius Laco. He was once a soldier in the Ninth legion. I first saw him, many years ago, in the arena – when he killed your father. I cannot tell you either way whether Laco baited his sword with poison, but that makes little difference I suspect.

My clemency might reach to Pompey, but know that it will not reach to his agent."

The centurion remained silent. He breathed in deeply, taking in Caesar's words. Blood, rather than tears, would now be spilled. Oppius would draw his sword one last time.

The following day Caesar granted his officer a special leave of absence to travel back to Ravenna. Oppius did not want to break things to Atilia in a letter - although he would have preferred a letter, to a conversation, in regards to informing Claudia about Fabius' death. His lover's face fleetingly shone with happiness, believing that Oppius had come back to her from having resigned his commission, but the soldier's sombre expression quickly put out the light in her eyes.

After telling Atilia about Fabius and the death of his father she consoled him. She made him dinner and caressed him as Oppius finally drifted off to sleep. The next morning Atilia pleaded with her lover to stay and not return to camp.

"How will getting yourself killed bring back Fabius or your father?" she argued, her cheeks streaked with tears. When she realised that his mind was made up to return she grew angry however. She wouldn't marry him unless he divorced the army, she asserted. He was choosing death over a new life. When she said that Fabius was dead because of him she regretted her words, but failed to apologise.

"Revenge won't bring you peace. Let the gods deal with this Laco... You cannot have me and your revenge."

Oppius' here realised, sadly, that his desire for revenge was greater than that of his desire for a new life. When she asked him one last time, as he stood at the door, why he was going back to the army the soldier grimly recalled Caesar's words the night before.

"I am in blood stepped so far that, should I wade no more, returning were as tedious as go o'er."

He said nothing in reply however and closed the door behind him. The cold draught was causing the fire to go out.

Oppius returned to camp, reporting for duty to his commander. After receiving his orders and being dismissed Caesar's elderly servant Joseph kindly mentioned how sorry he was to hear about the loss of one of his men – and that he would pray for the centurion. More than prayers however the officer felt like he needed a drink. He duly joined his comrades around the fire. Oppius, Roscius and Teucer drank deep into the night, remembering and toasting their friend, until the glow of the dawn swelled and bled into the night sky.

Sword of Rome: Pharsalus

1.

Dusk. The spongy clouds on the distant horizon seemed to be either soaking up the blood-red light or secreting it. Lucius Oppius was too tired or careworn to decide which it was. The stone-faced centurion had spent a large part of the late afternoon in fencing practise. Oppius had fought and bested his friend Roscius, the veteran legionary Crastinus and Mark Antony. Usually Oppius was prudent enough to allow Antony to win one or two of their bouts but a red mist descended, like the dusk, and passion overruled his reason. He saw the figure of his enemy Flavius Laco before him and attacked with speed and fury. Laco was a former legionary and gladiator, who now served as a bodyguard and agent to Pompey the Great. Laco had murdered Oppius' father many years ago, baiting his sword with poison during a fencing bout. Pompey's agent had also led a small force of mercenaries during an assassination attempt on Caesar, as he crossed the Rubicon. The attempt failed, but a life was still lost. During the attack the agent murdered Oppius' young comrade and friend, Marcus Fabius. Laco fought with such speed and power he would have also killed Oppius, having bested him in combat. But reinforcements arrived in time and Oppius was left wounded, rather than dead, after the fight.

"Do you have any orders for the men?" Roscius asked his officer.

"No. They know their drills and preparations by now," the centurion replied, staring up the slope at the enemy's camp, wondering if Laco was present.

Oppius had continued to serve Caesar after crossing the Rubicon, but his principle duty now was to avenge the death of his father and his friend. His mind's eye was fixed upon Laco. Nothing – and no one – else seemed to matter. Livia, his mother and Atilia all faded from view. In regards to Atilia he had been close to beginning a new life with her in Rome. But then Laco had killed Marcus. Atilia had argued that he was wedded to death more than life in choosing to remain in the army and at the time Oppius thought she did not understand him. But perhaps she did understand him, all too well, the soldier blackly thought.

"Some wine?" Already knowing the answer to his question Roscius commenced to pour his friend a cup of undiluted acetum. Oppius took the cup in silence and gulped down half its contents.

"Anything else?"

"Yes. Leave the jug," Oppius replied.

Roscius looked as if he were about to say something to his centurion and friend, but then he thought better of it and walked away, gently shaking his lowered head.

Oppius soon drained the cup but the wine failed to wash away the doubts he had, which nagged at him more than his ex-wife. He would be unable to defeat Laco in a single combat. Laco would again prove too quick, too powerful – despite all of his extra training and conditioning. The centurion recalled his meeting with Baculus, a former gladiator whom Oppius had visited in order to find out more about his opponent. Oppius had himself fought and defeated Baculus in the arena, but had spared his life. The soldier had visited the old warrior at his farm. The veteran gladiator shared some vintage Massic and some candid thoughts:

"I respect you Lucius, but I do not envy you for this task you've set yourself... I was good, but he was the best. Laco instinctively knew what you were going to do even before you had thought of it... And he is equally adept upon a battlefield as he is within an arena... He's never lost a fight... I've seen him kill with a sword, spear, axe, trident, knife and his bare hands... I once saw him gouge out the eye of a wounded opponent and then stuff it into the dying man's mouth, more so to entertain himself than the crowd... You could argue that you have a chance because age might be catching up with him, but his experience will compensate for any physical deterioration... Your friend, Marcus, would not wish you to die yourself, in an attempt to avenge his death... When you spared my life in the arena I was grateful to the gods and yourself. I took your advice. I kill time rather than people now. I bought this farm and have lived a quiet, contented existence. I carry a shovel rather than sword. I'm responsible for things growing rather than dying and I don't take orders from anyone, except of course my wife."

The crimson sky dulled to a dark purple, then black. For a time the firmament appeared mottled, like a bruise. Campfires began to sprout up across the contoured plains. A gust of wind kicked up some dust. Oppius squinted. Time and sorrow lined his face. The sun finally fell off the edge of the world and beneath the sound of the howling wind Oppius found himself echoing Baculus' words.

"You can't beat him."

The fire spat and crackled as the fat from the leg of pork dripped onto it.

"How is he?" Teucer asked Roscius, whilst scraping a sharpening stone against his arrowheads. The archer was a Briton but Caesar, having witnessed his skill with a bow, had allowed him to be recruited to the Tenth legion.

"Oppius is Oppius," the stolid legionary replied, shrugging his shoulders and frowning. After Fabius' death the centurion had distanced himself from his friends. He drank heavily, but alone in his tent. Oppius had also recently spent long periods away from the legion. Balbus, Caesar's chief political agent and intelligence officer, had recruited Oppius to his staff. His mission had been to locate and kill Laco, who had been ordered by Pompey to threaten or buy off key supporters of Caesar in Macedonia. Unfortunately Laco had always been one step ahead of the centurion. Roscius in particular had noticed and mourned the change in his friend since Fabius' death. He was worried that Oppius had descended so far into the underworld of despondency and revenge that, should he somehow find and defeat his enemy, he still would not be able to return and wholly be himself again.

"Do you think the Gods will be kind to him? Oppius has to first survive a battle and then he will need to find Laco – and defeat him."

"The gods are the gods. They can be even more changeable – and miserable – than the British weather. Even with the gods on his side Oppius may still not be able to defeat Laco. He has already bested him once. Oppius' desire for revenge may also make him lose, rather than gain, his focus during combat. Revenge has blinded him to many things since we crossed the Rubicon."

Roscius here briefly thought of how Atilia was a good woman, but Oppius had burned, rather than built, any bridges there. He also remembered a line of poetry, that Fabius had composed: *When you kill someone, a little piece of you dies inside.*" Perhaps they had all killed too many men and were in danger of losing themselves, the soldier mused.

"Well if the gods put that bastard Laco in my sights tomorrow I'll take the shot, for Oppius and Fabius."

"I'd be willing to offer up a prayer for that," Roscius replied, raising his wine cup.

"In the meantime though, offer up some of that wine. I don't mind dying in battle, but I'll be damned if I'm going to die of thirst."

2.

Flecks of gold had sparkled over the sapphire-green Enipeus during the day, but the evening had seemingly poured ink into the river. 'Tis now as black as Styx, the sage statesman ominously thought to himself. Marcus Tullius Cicero, gaunt from fatigue and grief, stood on the riverbank. The night air was balmy but still a chill ran down the statesman's spine as he imagined how the Enipeus might run red with the blood of Romans tomorrow – as the Tiber had done during the previous civil war and the reign of Sulla. Would tomorrow's battle finally bring an end to the conflict? A last victory – peace – would not be worth the costs of the war though, Cicero darkly ruminated.

The crackle of a fire, the scraping of a sword being sharpened and the cheers and curses of soldiers playing dice could occasionally be heard in the background but for the most part the army camp's atmosphere was eerily quiet, like a funeral. Cicero had suggested to the leading commanders of their forces that they spend the evening spreading encouragement and confidence among their soldiers. But most were ensconced in their tents, either spending time with their mistresses or thinking about the assets they would strip from their enemies once they had claimed victory and returned to Rome.

One officer had been conscious, however, of spending time with his cohort that night. Marcus Brutus had the build of a soldier, yet the mind of a statesman. Although Brutus did not and could not fraternise with his men like Mark Antony the legionaries still liked and respected their aristocratic commander. Unlike many of the senior officers Brutus possessed a noble, rather than haughty, air. Ironically he had learned the value of getting to know his soldiers from his now enemy, Caesar. Brutus visited campfire after campfire throughout the evening. He had argued how important their cause of fighting for the Republic was. But far more than for their cause, or for Pompey, the soldiers fighting under his command would be fighting for Brutus, their standard and each other come the battle. The officer brought both wine and words to cheer up his legionaries.

"After the battle, you too may consider yourself veterans. For this battle will be worth ten others... Victory is neither impossible nor improbable. The ravages of time, taxes, bad Greek food – these are all inevitable. But it is not written in stone that Caesar shall remain undefeated. Remember Dyrrachium and our enemy's reverses there."

It was towards the end of his rounds when Brutus spotted his friend by the river. Cicero liked the young aristocrat. Brutus was a student of philosophy – and more importantly a keen reader of his own writings. He had a good head and a good heart, Cicero believed. How much had the two been at odds when the civil war had broken out? Brutus fought for the Republic but he was under the command of Pompey, the man who had been responsible for the death of his father. Yet Caesar, his enemy, had all but been a father to him during the years that he had been his mother's lover.

The venerable old statesman peered up at the night sky and fancied that the twinkling stars were the eyes of the gods, blinking in disbelief and dismay at the folly upon the world below.

"A denarius for your thoughts," Brutus remarked.

"I would that I could sell, or give away for gratis, some of the thoughts which haunt me at present." Cicero attempted to smile in a consoling fashion after he spoke, either for his benefit or his companion's.

"Well allow me to insert the thought into your head that you should not go and try to be a hero tomorrow. You're far more talented and useful with a stylus, as opposed to a sword."

"You're not alone in your concern. My secretary Tiro has bought and trained an especially prudent horse that will turn tail and run in the opposite direction at the first sign of trouble. But who knows what will happen? My horse and I may surprise everyone – including ourselves. Everyone has the capacity for bravery and cowardice, love and hate. There is still a part of me that believes Caesar has the capacity to extend another invitation to Pompey to discuss terms for peace. And there is still a part of me that believes Pompey would accept his old ally's invitation."

"Let us hope that by this time tomorrow this civil war will be over," Brutus expressed. Neither his head nor his heart seemed fully married to his optimistic words however.

Should the war somehow end tomorrow then a reign of tyranny, by either Caesar or Pompey, would likely commence, Cicero grimly thought.

"Aye, where there is life there is hope. But this war, Brutus, has taught me that war is an evil. Occasionally it is a necessary evil, but nonetheless it is an evil. The victims far outnumber the victors. The patient is seldom healthier after the bloodletting."

The philosophical statesman paused as the sight of a shooting star caught his attention. Brutus saw it also and the two men auspiciously glanced at each other and raised their eyebrows.

"Now I'm not usually given over to superstition – thank the gods! – but that could well have been an omen. Whether it was an omen for good or ill, for Caesar or Pompey, I know not however," Cicero remarked.

"Do you think that Caesar witnessed it? What would he think?"

"I know not that either I'm afraid. I'm starting to brim with Socratic ignorance, or wisdom, it seems. I warrant I do know what the augurs will think though, should they have observed the phenomenon."

"What?"

"They'll be thinking that they can double their rates, in light of people being desperate to know what the cosmic omen means for them."

Brutus wryly smiled at his friend's cynical, but fair, comment. He hoped that Cicero and his horse would indeed duly stay out of trouble during any battle. Rome would an orphan be should somehow "the Father of his Country", as Cicero was once titled, be lost to them. Cicero, remembering how he still had to finish off a letter to his friend Atticus, excused himself. The two men, who once would have perhaps considered themselves teacher and student, warmly clasped hands and bid each other goodnight. As Ciccro walked back to his tent he fleetingly, conceitedly, pictured the shooting star again and thought how perhaps it signified the death of a god. He shook the fancy from his mind though and dwelt upon the far graver scenario of the many men – good Romans – who soon might die in battle. And all for the sake of the pride of two men, who thought themselves gods.

3.

Numerous braziers glowed around the chamber. Maps, lists from quartermasters and correspondence were splayed out across the table. The war council of senators and centurions had recently departed. The smell of the copious amount of wine they had drunk still hung in the air.

Pompey was tempted to call for an attendant to give him another massage and ease his backache. His knees cracked again. His eyes were rimmed with tiredness and sleeplessness. As well as Caesar, Pompey mused upon how he was battling old age. The latter was a far more formidable opponent however – and would ultimately be victorious. The veteran commander took the weight off his feet and invited his agent to take a seat too. Pompey noted how age was even catching up with Flavius Laco. The hair around his temples had turned grey; he was now in possession of the colouring, as well as the cunning and savagery, of a wolf.

"I have received intelligence that Lucius Oppius is back by Caesar's side again. By all accounts he is still as determined as ever to hunt you down. He's still eaten up with feelings of grief and vengeance. He may seek you out on the battlefield."

"This prey is happy for the hunter to corner him. I can then put him out of his misery," Laco coldly remarked, baring his sharp yellow teeth in a sneer.

"By the end of tomorrow I will have hopefully put everyone out of their misery. Romans will no longer fight Romans. Our venerable senators can return to Rome and squabble over various properties and valuables owned by Caesar and his supporters. They also intend to punish anyone who remained neutral during the conflict, for good measure. The legions can go home and spend their money on wine or whores, or if they're lucky enough both. This battle will decide the war. Yes, we have reason to be confident my old friend," Pompey stated, trying to convince himself as much as Laco. He was unhappy however. During the meeting a number senators such as Scipio and Afranius had questioned his willingness to give battle to his old ally. The snakes even hinted that he was fearful of facing his opponent. They argued how they had the numbers to crush their enemy. They wanted to taste glory. Pompey had countered that they should retain the higher ground. There was no real need to give up their advantage and attack. Logistics, rather than bombast, win campaigns. Caesar was running out of food, despite his reports to the contrary. Starvation and disease could halve their ranks within a month or two. Pompey wondered what Caesar would do in his position. During their time as allies they often had dinner together and discussed military strategy and tactics. They would analyse the campaigns of Alexander and Hannibal. Julia (Pompey's wife and Caesar's daughter) would chide them for talking too much about war, yet she would also correct them if ever they got their facts wrong about history. Pompey mused how the two men had a certain pride and ambition in common – but so too they shared a genuine love and admiration for Julia. She had brought them together. Julia's ghost haunted him still in so many ways.

"What will you do when you defeat Caesar? You cannot show him the same mercy he has shown to others. It will be too dangerous to leave him alive. Yet you must be careful. You must avoid having the blood on your hands. Even Caesar's memory will command support from the people and some of the army."

"Cato would have me put Caesar on trial, with Cato himself acting as the advocate for the prosecution. Caesar would doubtless look to Cicero to defend him. But I agree, he must travel back to Rome in a box, rather than chains. I must appear blameless in regards to the manner of his death though. I will duly show Caesar love, but after I execute him. I will praise him as a great Roman and worthy opponent. I can have Cicero write the speech. I may even arrange for a series of games, to honour his memory. The first man of Rome can be gracious towards the second, once dead. I will of course expropriate part of his estate to finance any events," Pompey said, watering down his wine a little. He could not drink like he used to. He just hoped that he could still command and fight like the Pompey of old.

"Caesar will not easily be captured though. He will probably retreat, rather than surrender. But where can he run to?"

"He will make for Egypt, to try and raise support and an army there. How do I know? Because that's what I would do."

4.

The ever considerate Tiro silently entered Cicero's tent. He placed a blanket around his master's shoulders and wordlessly departed. His master continued to write and read over his letter.

Dear Atticus,

Please forgive me should you already be aware of some of what I will report below. Indeed you may already be aware of it because I have been the one to speak of things previously. But in framing and explaining the events to you it may help frame things in my own mind.

Caesar crossing the Rubicon is as good a place as any to start to discuss this civil war. If we are to believe Caesar (and we perhaps have more cause to trust an augur or tax collector) then he still had his doubts then. He confided to one of his officers that, "Even now we could turn back; but once we cross that tiny bridge, then everything will depend on armed force."

From the very start he had the backing of his legions, perhaps because of his doubts rather than in spite of them. He addressed them directly, listing the slanders and injustices his self-interested enemies had heaped upon him. He spoke of his regret at how Pompey, his former ally, had succumbed to envy at his achievements. His enemies had poured poison into his ally's ears and recruited him as a mouthpiece for their lies. Caesar declared that he was going to war in the name of the people – as the Senate had revoked the rights and veto of the tribunate. Caesar promised the soldiers that he would give them their freedom and rights back. More importantly he promised his army a rise in pay and plots of land. He also vowed that he would gain the support of Italy through love, rather than fear. "Let us see if in this way we can willingly win the support of all and gain a permanent victory, since through their cruelty others have been unable to escape hatred or make their victory lasting. This is a new way of conquest, we grow strong through pity and generosity," he announced.

And so, accompanied solely by the Thirteenth legion, Caesar not only invaded Italy but he even managed to conquer through clemency. News travelled ahead of him of his peaceful invasion and towns opened their gates to him. People talk of Caesar's divine fortune, by more so he has made his own luck over the years. During this time the optimates tried to paint him as a monster, but this image was quickly whitewashed over by his mercy (and propaganda).

The enemy wasn't even at the gates and Pompey made the decision to leave Rome – like rats scurrying to leave a sinking ship. History may deem this choice a fateful decision. The optimates in the Senate believed that they embodied Rome, so if they abandoned Rome they were taking it with them. But Rome is Rome, or rather the people embody Rome (for good and ill). Caesar, who partly grew up in the subura, understands this only *too well. We first taxed the people in the name of providing security for them – and then departed without thanks or an apology. Should it have come as such a surprise that most of Rome embraced Caesar's tyranny? His rule filled a power vacuum and prevented something far less appealing – anarchy.*

Yet Caesar did not have it all his own way. He lost Labienus to us, although he took the setback in his stride and even generously forwarded on the defector's baggage. Pompey and the Senate also slipped through his fingers in Brundisium. As you know he also failed to recruit me, to help legitimise his coup. I partly admire the man – but hate his cause. This is in contrast to my republican brothers, who I hold in contempt for the most part but agree with ideologically. Caesar even visited me personally. We spoke of his dictatorship in a remarkably civilised way. He was polite and reasonable – even when I refused to support him. We then had a pleasant evening talking about Plato and Herodotus. He showed me some of his poetry, like a student looking to please a teacher. I had to remind myself however that here was a man who was also looking to rewrite the constitution and had rewritten our borders with Gaul in the blood of its peoples. Caesar devours, but he is never satisfied. At one moment he can be Odysseus, but at the next he can be the Cyclops. He is both man and monster.

It took him little time to maul and devour Pompey's forces in Spain. He remarked how he went to face an army without a leader – and then would face a leader without an army. Caesar is a better prophet than poet. During this time Pompey argued that he would ultimately retake Rome, he just needed the time and men. "If Sulla did it, why can't I?" he postured. But Pompey might not prove to be Sulla I fear, in this respect. I even worry that Pompey is no longer even Pompey, but rather a shadow of the man he once was. This might explain why the two armies performed such a dance of shadows for so long, refusing to give battle. But yet as you may have heard when we did finally step out of the shadows we fought well. Yet Pompey could have turned the victory at Dyrrachium into a rout. The enemy could have been cornered and slain, but instead it was allowed to escape and lick its wounds. I will not inflict a quote from Caesar's poetry on you my friend, but I will repeat what he was purported to have said to his men after the engagement. "Today the enemy could have won, if they had a commander who was a winner." Remarkably Caesar even turned defeat to his advantage and bolstered morale.

I have recently come from a meeting of senior senators and officers. For so long Pompey has remained constant and prudent, looking to stave rather than fight his enemy. But even I have wondered though if Pompey is being too prudent, or something less than prudent. Caesar has repeatedly offered to give battle, but Pompey has refused. Granted we may have half the enemy's experience, but we have twice his numbers. Senators and centurions alike are baying for Caesar's blood. Yet this evening the criticisms and goading of Pompey seem to have stung him too much. He was accused of acting like Agamemnon – looking to delay the war in order to hold onto power and play the king. We will be the ones to offer battle tomorrow. Caesar will not refuse.

How will the battle play out? My ignorance of military matters is more than just of a Socratic nature my friend. I am only sure that the ferryman will profit from the outcome, though not even Crassus himself could furnish us with enough coins to cover the eyes of all that will fall in the fight. Civil war is anything but civil.

My apologies should you have heard my reluctant praise of Caesar – and my reluctant criticisms of Pompey – before.

I have, over the years, sometimes ended a number of my letters to you with the phrase that "where there is life there is hope". I dread however that by nightfall tomorrow there will be decidedly less hope, for there will be fewer lives to act as vessels for it. The fields of Pharsalus are about to become fields of blood.

Cicero.

5.

"When, or *if* I am starting to consider, Pompey ever decides to give battle then I would like you to command our forces on the left. You have proved both capable and loyal over the years. You deserve the honour," Caesar remarked.

Mark Antony's barrel chest expanded even further with pride. Caesar's famous lieutenant (famed for his prowess as a lover and soldier) was in the best condition of his life. Caesar considered that even the sculptures that Antony had recently commissioned, which would remind people of his supposed bloodline from Hercules, might not do his current physique justice.

"I'm grateful for such an honour. I will not let you down. Should Caesar so order it, I'll serve up Pompey's head on a plate."

Caesar was pleased with Antony's martial passion, but he shook his head.

"I desire no man's head upon a plate my friend, especially not Pompey's. Sparing his life will ultimately do our cause more good. I also intend to spare Cato's life once I catch up with him, just to annoy the cantankerous old sot some more."

Caesar smiled at his own comment but his features still seemed soaked in weariness. Caesar's legionaries still saw him at his best – dynamic, determined and good humoured – but his private attendant Joseph had increasingly witnessed the commander being plagued by doubts and anxieties. They buzzed around him, like flies around a corpse.

"Aye, showing him mercy would be the last thing that Cato would ever want to forgive you for. I hope you spare his wine cellar too though. I understand he has some vintages that are as old as his grudges."

"Indeed. Far more than Cato or Pompey however I want you to make sure that Brutus is sought out and spared after any battle."

"You still favour him, after he betrayed you?" Antony replied, outwardly incredulous and inwardly envious. Caesar had always spoken fondly of Brutus and the lieutenant viewed him as a potential rival to inherit Caesar's influence and estate. Caesar also spoke fondly of his great nephew Octavius, but Antony felt he had little to fear from a sickly boy who sat around in a sun hat all day reading philosophy.

"Yes, he is worth a thousand of those who poisoned his mind against me. His honesty and industry will be of value to Rome once this war is over. I am of course also terrified of upsetting his mother. We may no longer be lovers but I have no desire to earn Servilia's enmity."

Shortly after this exchange Caesar dismissed his officer. Once out of sight the general sighed and slumped into the nearest chair. He felt light-headed and worried that he might suffer another bout of the falling sickness. He hated feeling weak, mortal. Joseph, Caesar's aged Jewish attendant, entered yet the commander did not possess the energy or inclination to alter his defeated air. Julius looked up at his old servant with an almost grief-stricken expression on his face. It reminded Joseph of how Caesar looked after his father passed away. For a time the youth often looked at the attendant pleadingly, as if it might be in his power to provide a remedy and take the pain away.

"You look as old as I feel," Caesar wryly posited, looking up at the kind but wizened face above him. "Perhaps I should have allowed you to remain in Rome."

"You shouldn't fret about that. Should I have spent these past months back home my wife would have aged me even more." There was a croakiness in his voice but a gleam of humour in the old man's glassy eyes.

"I sometimes think that you regret your wedding day."

"I do not regret my wedding day, or my wedding night. But as to the question do I regret my marriage? I am reluctant to answer, just in case the wind carries the answer back to my better half."

"I would Pompey answer my offer to commence peace talks, or give battle. If his army refuses to draw its sword tomorrow then we must pack up our tents again and forage for food and re-supply elsewhere. Rations are starting to grow scarce again. An army marches on its stomach – and it seems that Pompey's strategy is to starve us. Our army could suffer a death by a thousand cuts, without the enemy having even to draw its sword. It's not the most honourable way to wage war, but it could prove effective."

Joseph was aware of the army's increasing difficulty it had in feeding itself but he had faith in Caesar that he would solve the problem. Caesar had remedied the problem initially by immediately marching upon Pompey's supply depots in Oricum and Apollonia once landing in Macedonia. After the army's reverse at Dyrrachium Caesar also told his senior officers that a bloodletting was what the patient needed – and he sacked the town of Gomphi. Pillaging, rape and drinking ensued. Although Caesar was still keen to show clemency towards his fellow Romans, barbarians were a different matter. Morale was raised and faith in their commander was restored. Gomphi would also serve as an example for any other town that would side with Pompey or refuse Caesar supplies.

Caesar sighed again, his body seemingly shrivelling up as he exhaled. He closed his eyes, either in pain or in prayer. Perhaps both.

"I sometimes wonder, Joseph, will this war truly bring about peace and progress? Or am I on a fool's errand?"

"We are all on a fool's errand in some respect. It's just that some fools get to complete their errands. The gods, yours or mine, created man for amusement. The trick is to learn to laugh along with the joke."

6.

Tongues of flame still flicked up from Oppius' campfire, tasting the night air. He sat outside his tent, his face half illuminated in the fire's light. He couldn't sleep. He had one last order to give to Roscius too. Whilst waiting for the legionary Oppius remembered his father. Unless his mood had been softened by wine, he was a stern and distant figure (when he wasn't absent altogether on campaigns). One afternoon, when his father either hadn't had any wine or had drunk too much, he returned to the house and punished his son for not having practised his letters for the day (instead Oppius had been practising, or playing, sword fighting). After the beating he had sat his teary-eyed son down and explained himself.

"I'm hard on you boy because I don't want you to end up like me. I want you to use your brains, not brawn, to get on in life. And to get on you need to learn your letters. Even if the gods will it, my fate doesn't have to be your fate."

A wistful then grim smile briefly shaped the centurion's expression as he thought how he had not only followed his father's path in becoming a soldier but he might also share his fate in being slain by his killer. *You can't beat him.*

Roscius arrived. Oppius greeted his friend not, but rather relayed his request straightaway.

"Should Pompey give battle tomorrow then I want you to command the men after the fighting starts. My mission tomorrow is different to that of yours."

A pause hung in the air. The tough-looking legionary breathed heavily and appeared awkward, nervous. His heart beat like a drum sounding out an approaching battle. In all the time that they had known each other Roscius had never refused an order, or request, from his friend.

"You're my commanding officer – and far more you're my friend. It's as both as those things though that I'd ask you not to give me such an order. The men need *you* to lead them, not me."

Oppius rose to his feet – and raised his voice. If it had been anyone else the centurion might have struck the legionary for defying him.

"I have to do what I have to do. You know that. Until the bastard is dead I feel like I won't ever be able to start my life again. I owe it to my father and Marcus. If we lose the battle tomorrow, but Laco falls, then it's still a good day for me."

Spittle flecked the legionary's face. Oppius had spoken in both anger and dismay. He wore a storm on his brow. He involuntary made a fist; his other hand clasped his gladius. At seeing his friend stare down at his hands though Oppius immediately relaxed them. The two friends had never come to blows before or seldom had a crossed word. He wanted to apologise – but more so he needed to make his case and have Roscius take command so that he could hunt down his enemy.

"You owe a duty to the living as well as the dead. I'm worried about you," Roscius said, his features creased in concern rather than anger.

"I don't need your sympathy. I just need your support."

"I've seen you cut down twenty barbarians as if you were scything weeds, I've seen you fight wounded, drunk and in the dark. You were even willing to take on a whole army yourself when you grabbed the standard and jumped into the sea. But even taking all that into account Laco may be one fight too many. Even Tiro Casca said he was the best he'd ever seen. Laco wasn't born, but rather the underworld spat him out."

"Then that's even more reason to send him back to where he came from," Oppius replied, his voice flat with malice. "You need to decide whether you're for me or against me. I'm going to do what I have to do whether you agree with my reasons or not."

"It's because I'm for you that I'm against you in this decision. If I lose your friendship over this it's because I'm trying to stop you losing your life."

The centurion shook his head, either in disbelief at his friend's lack of loyalty or understanding – or in refusal at the consideration that Laco would defeat him.

"I have to do this," Oppius remarked quietly, but unwaveringly, as much to himself as to his long time comrade.

"But you don't have to do this alone. Do you think I don't want Pompey's agent dead for what he did to young Marcus? Do you think me and Teucer haven't mourned him or aren't angry? I want to put a javelin through his neck as much as you want to fillet him with a sword. But between Laco and us stands an army twice the size as ours. By all means lose your temper – but don't lose your reason!"

Another pause hung in the air. Oppius was expecting his friend to also add, "You can't beat him."

Instead of continuing to argue however both men caught the sound of a drinking song, from some nearby legionaries, reverberate through the evening air. For many it might prove to be their last. Oppius and Roscius had heard many a slurred revel before; many a time they'd been the ones slurring. The two old soldiers and old friends relaxed their expressions. Half-smile was met by half-smile.

"Rome is at war with itself. The world scarce needs us to fight too," Roscius said, clasping his comrade on the shoulder.

"Aye, let's not finish this conversation. I would you help me finish my last jug of wine though. I can't think of anyone who I'd rather share it with," Oppius warmly replied.

And so the two soldiers shared a jug of wine and a song, hoping that it wouldn't be their last – but acting as if it would be.

7.

The stars had glistened last night, but the heavens now had competition from a man-made spectacle as the sunlight glinted off thousands upon thousands of helmets, shields, spear tips and swords. Pompey had offered to give battle. Caesar had accepted. That morning he had planned to break camp to make for the town of Scotossa, in order to re-supply. But he quickly changed tack and started to plan for a victory.

"Our spirits are ready for battle. We shall not easily find another chance," the commander exclaimed. For fighting in such an historic battle they would gain immortality, Caesar promised his soldiers. Teucer whispered to Roscius that he would rather Caesar gave them their back pay to enjoy in this life.

The dry, hot air was thick with the smell of sweat and horseshit. For some – many of Caesar's veterans – the scenario of two large armies forming up to give battle was a sight for sore eyes. They were home. For others however, on both sides, the metallic light seared their eyes, stabbing fear into their souls. Many felt sick. Many were sick. Palms were wiped upon tunics. Snorts of anticipation came from men and horses alike.

Caesar commanded twenty-two thousand legionaries and a thousand cavalry. He sat astride his large charger in his distinctive red cape. Although he would stand out and be prey to enemy archers or cavalry, he knew that his red cloak could act as a rallying point and inspire his soldiers. Caesar positioned himself on the right of his army, alongside the Tenth legion. He looked on – calm, imperious – as Pompey's cavalry and archers continued to amass in front of him. The Enipeus prevented Pompey outflanking him upon the right, so Pompey's aim would be to muster additional forces upon his left and outflank him there – and eventually come round to attack his legions from the rear. It was a simple, yet potentially effective plan. But Caesar gave the hint of a smile and thought to himself that Pompey was just a pounder after all, lacking originality and subtlety.

Earlier in the morning Caesar had derided the opposing commander and his army even more, as he briefed his senior officers and centurions. Caesar quoted Lucullus, who Pompey had replaced in the war against Mirthridates (he also reminded his staff that it had been Crassus, rather than Pompey, who had defeated the bulk of the slave army, commanded by Spartacus).

"Pompey is but a carrion bird. Rather than take a prey himself, he can but live off the kills of others... Remember, although Pompey claims to fight for Rome he does not fight with Rome. Rather than Romans you can take heart today that you will be fighting a bastardized force of barbarians. Our enemy will consist of Gauls, Thracians, Macedonians, Thessalians and other contingents who we have bested before... Pompey has a plan. But Caesar has a plan too."

Sweat ran down the lines in Pompey's face. Through the shimmering heat and the dust kicked up by his forty thousand infantry and seven thousand cavalry he thought he spied Julius' bright red cloak. Pompey toyed with the idea of ordering his archers and cavalry to target the opposing commander, but by focusing on Caesar they could take their eyes off the rest of the battle. Besides, many would be targeting Caesar independent of any direct order.

Pompey looked on with satisfaction as to the left of him Labienus was acting with authority and competence in organising his cavalry – and then the archers behind them. To his right he witnessed his long lines of infantry, ten ranks deep – as opposed to Caesar's forces, three or four ranks deep. The sword and hammer of his superior numbers of horse and legionaries would cut and pound the enemy down. By the end of the day Julius Caesar would be but a footnote to the story of Pompey the Great in the annals of history.

"Without his laurel wreath you'd see how bald Caesar is. Now, without Labienus as his second in command, you will see how beatable Caesar is," Titus Labienus had exclaimed to his circle of cavalry officers the evening before. He sneered, his expression becoming even more pinched, as he caught sight of Caesar's cloak in the distance. Labienus had served as legate to Caesar throughout the wars in Gaul. Although he had served his commander loyally – and with distinction – during the campaign (he had particularly shown his mettle and brilliance at the battle of Alesia) Labienus increasingly felt embittered towards Caesar for not being given credit for a number of victories. He often felt second favourite to Mark Antony and believed he was being snubbed – and his name was being written out of history – in regards to Caesar's account of the Gallic wars.

Labienes' resentment increased all the more when Caesar seemingly acted with indifference towards his defection to Pompey's camp when the civil war started. He had hoped that the act would prove a turning point in the war, inspiring other officers to abandon Caesar's illegitimate cause. Yet only a section of German and Gallic horsemen followed him. And Caesar was able to partly spin the incident – and win respect and approval – by forwarding on the legate's baggage without a word of condemnation. Now those same centurions who Labienus had hoped to win the support of were baying for his blood. After Dyrrachium, Labienus tortured and executed a number of prisoners. Caesar made a point of telling his forces that Pompey had not given the order to kill the prisoners, but rather Labienus alone was culpable.

He cursed Caesar underneath his breath once more. Julius had made it clear that he would show no mercy to him if captured, which signalled to the rest of his officers that they too could punish Labienus with or without prejudice. As sure as if he were wearing a long red cloak he would be a target. Yet any spectre of retribution would end once Caesar was defeated. Labienus also promised himself that he would write his own history of the Gallic wars when he returned to Rome, to counteract the propaganda of Caesar – for history is written by the victor.

"This could be the day that you make a name for yourself Domitius," Mark Antony remarked to his lieutenant, raising his voice over the sounds of soldiers rumbling forward and officers bellowing orders.

Domitius Enobarbus' horse, irritated by flies, shook his head as if replying to the commander's comment. Antony's lieutenant was solidly built and pleasant – yet also somewhat non-descript looking. He was born to a wealthy and respected family but he gave himself an education rather than aristocratic airs. Enobarbus nodded in agreement with his friend, but inwardly he was in agreement with his horse. The young officer was content to remain in the shadows. "Names" had a habit of turning up on proscription lists during and after Rome's civil wars.

Enobarbus hoped however that Mark Antony would continue to make a name for himself as a result of the battle and further come out from Caesar's shadow. It was not just because Antony had saved the soldier's life at Alesia that Enobarbus felt he owed the commander his loyalty. Despite his flaws (some of which the lieutenant believed he could help diminish) Antony was a great soldier and leader. He possessed a noble bearing, but also a common touch. He could and did drink with anyone and, even though heavily in debt, Antony was generous and gregarious. The only thing that could hold him back from eventually being the First Man of Rome was himself. Although he claimed to be descended from Hercules Antony behaved far more like a son of Bacchus or Priapus.

"But it could also be the day that we make a grave for ourselves my friend, so keep your eyes open," Antony added. "Although the river is currently preventing the enemy from outflanking us make sure that we stretch out the line during the fighting so they cannot come around us at any point. If we get out of this I'll not just buy you a drink Domitius, I'll buy you a vineyard."

"And what would you like, after the battle?"

"Well Caesar recently mentioned that I should find a good woman to stand beside me. But, as you know, I much prefer a good woman under me."

Enobarbus' sable mare now whinnied, laughing in unison with its rider.

His expression appeared as emotionless as the face upon the statue of his ancestor, which stood sentinel-like back in Rome. Lucius Junius Brutus had too fought against tyranny – vanquishing the cruel monarch Tarquin the Proud – and had founded the Republic.

Behind his impervious looking expression however Marcus Brutus' mind raced, as he sought to recall a phrase or quotation from his extensive reading that could act as a guide or sum up his situation. Yet even philosophy failed to provide him with the wisdom and consolation to deal with his warring soul.

Brutus sighed also, gazing upon the virginal-faced soldiers as they shuffled forward and formed ranks. They were lambs led by donkeys. Scipio and Afrinius had won their commands of the centre and right wings of the army through influence rather than merit. They had bought their commissions and that morning instead of discussing the forthcoming battle they had bickered over who should inherit Caesar's title of Pontifex Maximus after his defeat. At least Pompey had been wise enough to arrange for Labienus to lead the main cavalry attack, which would slice through Caesar's line and cause havoc from the rear. Pompey also had devised a stratagem to hopefully blunt the edge of Caesar's hardened infantry.

Although Brutus was in command of a cohort at the centre of the army and it appeared that Caesar was positioning himself on the right wing of his force he still envisioned the scenario of the two men meeting upon the battlefield. How would he react? Brutus stoically told himself that he would cut Julius down, as Lucius Brutus would have done should he have encountered Tarquin the Proud during a battle for the Republic all those centuries ago. As Cato would do now. Duty and honour should be sovereign over one's personal feelings; they had been before, when Brutus chose to side with Pompey over Caesar at the outbreak of the civil war. Brutus' personal feelings punched through again though, with all the power of a cavalry charge. His stony features cracked. Guilt pierced his soul, like a dagger, knowing that Julius would spare his life should he have the opportunity to cut Brutus down.

Why did you have to go so far? Brutus asked the question, in a tone of pity rather than anger, as if Julius was standing before him. He answered his own question by recalling the fable of the frog and the scorpion. Once day a scorpion approached a frog and asked it if he could carry him on his back to get to the other side of the river. The frog however was wary and replied how the scorpion might sting him whilst doing so. The scorpion replied that he would not do such a thing for then he would drown as well. The frog accepted the scorpion's reasoning and duly carried him on his back across the river. At the halfway point however the frog felt a sting in his back. With his dying breath the frog asked the question why the scorpion had stung him, as they both would now perish. The scorpion replied that he could not help himself – it was in his nature.

Brutus squinted in the stinging sunlight and wanly smiled, remembering how it had been Caesar who had first told him the fable.

"Hopefully this will be the battle to end all battles," the young legionary remarked, with both hope and fear in his voice, as he re-adjusted his helmet again. A small red welt marked his chin from where he had cut himself. Such was his youth that he was little practised in the art of shaving. So too his hands had shook with nerves, as he thought about the impending battle.

"Hah, there's no such thing lad. They'll always be another battle of some sort, as sure as night follows day," Roscius posited. "And don't go thinking about what may happen after the fighting. Concentrate on what's happening now. Remember to keep your shield up but when we get to close quarters watch for the enemy going for your shins. Do as I say boy and you might just avoid ending up in the underworld by the end of the day."

Roscius thought that if the fighting got too hot, or he received a nasty wound, then the fresh-faced recruit might wish himself in the underworld instead anyway. Yet if he could survive the day then, although he may not look forward to the next battle, he would not be so frightened by it.

"And stay away from anyone as ugly looking as Roscius," Teucer joked, in all seriousness.

"Or as old as the whore Teucer visited the other week. They will doubtless be a veteran – and they've stayed alive this long for a reason. Keep your sword and shield between you and the enemy. The Tenth don't fall from wounds in the back."

"If you can survive the first five battles then you will survive the next fifty," Teucer added, recalling the advice they had given to Marcus Fabius all those years ago.

You can't beat him.

Oppius rehearsed in his head the feints, angles, offensive and defensive tactics he would employ should he encounter his enemy. He didn't know how or why but Oppius believed he would finally come face to face with Laco by the close of day. He felt the two ivory handled daggers by his side. He had practised throwing them every day for the past year, picturing Pompey's agent as the target whilst doing so. Part of the centurion wished to best his enemy in a fair fight however – and twist the sword as it slid between Laco's ribs. See the pain in his eyes. Caesar had promised his officer that his famed clemency would not include sparing Pompey's agent. Yet Oppius had asked his commander that he be allowed to face Laco in single combat still. Like Hector the soldier was destined to fight his Achilles, even if he was destined to be defeated by him too.

8.

His face was as weather-beaten as an old village stone statue. Gaius Crastinus, Primus Pilus (First Spear, centurion of the first rank), reached up and clasped his commander's forearm in a Roman handshake.

"Today, general, I shall earn your gratitude whether I live or die," Crastinus determinedly remarked. The veteran soldier had served Caesar throughout the Gallic wars, having commanded his men with distinction at the battle of Alesia.

"It's I – and this army – who need to be worthy of you today my own friend. You earned my gratitude the first time that you drew your sword for me Gaius."

Crastinus merely nodded in reply and then closed his eyes, in prayer. The centurion would offer himself up to the gods of the underworld, pledging his soul to ensure victory against the enemy. Along with one hundred and twenty of his men Crastinus would lead an attack against Pompey's lines and draw first blood. That morning, he called his legionaries or "myrmidons" as he titled them. Some saw their forlorn hope as suicidal; some deemed their inclusion an honour. All would do their duty though. They had followed their officer at Alesia – and against the Helvetii, repelling a force three times their number to prevent their opponents from crossing a river. They would follow him now.

"Follow me, my old comrades, and give your general true service. Only this battle remains; when it's over he will regain his dignity and we our freedom," Crastinus announced, stabbing the air with his polished sword.

With another nod of his head the valorous unit formed ranks and marched slowly but purposefully towards a section of opposing infantry. Small puffs of dust were kicked up in time to the sound of the ground murmuring. The low, melancholy noise was akin to a dirge, Domitius Enobarbus thought to himself. Thousands upon thousands of heads swivelled, on both sides, as the lone (brave, mad) unit stepped out to face the enemy. Shields were raised – and jaws dropped.

Pompey could scarce believe what he was witnessing. He recalled the scenes of Caesar's veterans under siege, how they had lived off roots and uncooked meat; Pompey had deemed them more like beasts than men then. Now he thought them possessed.

The officer in charge of the men facing the oncoming enemy was partly confounded, partly awestruck. He either forgot or dismissed the idea of his legionaries launching their javelins. His men need not waste their pila on such an insignificant force. The mass of his infantry would soon swallow them up and spit them out easily enough. Perhaps the men were advancing in order to offer their surrender, he conjectured.

The young officer, the son of an influential senator, recognised the enemy's intention soon enough however as their centurion gave the order to charge once close enough and upon a slight slope on the battlefield. Their faces were contorted with rage, charging on and roaring on as one man. Pompey's forces winced slightly and then pointed their pila upwards as if the oncoming force was a unit of cavalry and the horses would see the shiny spear points and cease the attack. Yet the spear tips were swatted aside with contempt and Crastinus' veterans made short work of the enemy's front rank, like a fire burning up oil. It was as though a hornet's nest had been released among the inexperienced cohort. Caesar's men roared on still, as Pompey's men screamed. Crastinus was at the vanguard of the attack, a plough cutting a furrow through virgin soil. He used his shield as a battering ram and both the point and edge of his sword tasted blood. Blood dripped from his knuckles too, from punching the enemy at close quarters. The "myrmidons" followed their centurion's voice and the wake he made as he continued to create havoc. Some of Pompey's men pressed forward towards the murderous centurion, whilst others looked to escape him and his bloodthirsty legionaries.

Crastinus drove them onwards, issuing orders and inspiring his men – until the sound of his booming voice was abruptly cut short as a sword was thrust through his mouth. The war cry turned into a gurgle, a death rattle. The breath was consequently taken away from Crastinus' men too. Flavius Laco pulled the sword out of his enemy's mouth, the blade scraping against bone and teeth, and counter-attacked. In a savage display of skill and brutality he quickly killed a half a dozen men and turned the tide of the advance.

Few were now focusing their attention however on the progress –
or lack of – of Crastinus' forlorn hope.

9.

Pompey had spat out a curse at observing the chaos and casualties that the forlorn hope had created. He envisioned the effect the opening foray would have – on both sides. Pompey quickly determined that he would not be put on the back foot by Caesar. It was time to unleash his first offensive for the day – and his first offensive would prove decisive, he hoped. The cavalry attack would be of such power and potency that not even the three hundred of Sparta could stand against it, Pompey believed. His seven thousand horsemen would smash through Caesar's right wing and then roll up the rest of his army like a blanket. The charge would be remembered and celebrated for decades to come. It would save the Republic. He gave the order for the trumpets to sound out to attack.

Caesar nodded in approval at the success of Crastinus' advance attack. It would raise morale – and it distracted the enemy from focusing on the key part of the battlefield. Through the dust and hot, shimmering air he saw Labienus take his place at the head of the huge mass of cavalry. Julius gave a hint of a smile again, imagining how his former legate would be now thinking how he was about to wipe the smile off his face. Caesar then glanced at his own force of cavalry amassing in a cloud of dust to his right.

During the past couple of weeks, whilst both armies were camped upon the wheat fields of Pharsalus, there had been a number of minor skirmishes between the opposing cavalries and Caesar's men had fared well. They would be outnumbered, but not outclassed.

Hundreds upon hundreds of archers and slingers had also formed up behind Pompey's cavalry and for a few moments Caesar suffered some pangs of anxiety believing that his opposing commander might be able to see behind his own cavalry and the right wing of his infantry.

A welcome cool breeze wafted over the ranks of soldiers who were squatting behind Caesar's right wing. More men continued to form up behind them. The reverse slope helped to conceal their growing numbers.

Oppius recalled Caesar's words as he by rode by his men earlier on in the day. Again he explained how he had not instigated the war.

"My soldiers, I call on you, every last man, to witness the earnestness with which I have sought peace up until now. It has never been my desire to expose my troops to bloodshed, nor to deprive the state of this army or that of which stands across the plains from us today. But I have been given no choice."

Caesar's actions had spoken louder than his words over the past couple of years however and Oppius doubted his "earnestness". Caesar had soldiering and conquest in his blood. The centurion thought how Caesar was either the greatest actor, or leader, of his time. Perhaps the two roles were one and the same. Yet Oppius would still fight for him. And as well as taking time to address as many legions as possible Caesar took time out to speak to the centurion personally.

"I need you to be my standard bearer one last time Lucius. The men will look to you to hold the line. And I must look to you to advance after you have done so. The Tenth will at first be the anvil, upon which Labienus will strike. Yet you must then counter-strike and be the hammer. Pompey's forces are filled with barbarians and mercenaries. His cavalry will be littered by young aristocrats and sons of merchants too. Those fine young dancers won't endure the steel shining in their eyes. They'll fly to save their handsome faces. Labienus is a capable commander but his men won't have the stomach for the fight – and they'll rout. Once you have bested the cavalry offensive do not expend any energy finishing off the defeated but rather look to use your momentum to attack the enemy's left wing. I will give you what support I can. Pompey will be posted there. Laco will be close by. I need you to draw your sword one final time my friend and fight for Rome, the Tenth and Caesar."

Oppius would draw his sword again, but he would not be fighting for Rome, the Tenth or Caesar this time. As the soldier had grown older the world had grown smaller. He would be fighting for Roscius and Teucer – and the memory of his father and Marcus.

Rather than carrying the burden of command, Oppius carried around with him the burdens of guilt and revenge.

His head felt like an oven inside his sun-baked helmet. He could hear the distant whinnying of the assembling enemy cavalry. A presentiment swelled up in his stomach again – and he had learned to trust his gut instincts – that this would somehow be his last battle. He had arranged through Balbus, Caesar's secretary and chief political agent, that should he die his estate would be conferred upon his mother. Oppius had also recently composed a couple of letters and apportioned part of his estate to Roscius and Teucer. The letters, entrusted to Balbus to pass on to his friends, contained an apology for his behaviour towards them since crossing the Rubicon. They also contained a couple of lines of poetry, which Marcus Fabius had once composed.

Should he have known the whereabouts of Livia then he would have written to her too – and enclosed funds. If she went through gold – and shoes – like his former wife then she might be in need of the money (despite having stolen part of the contents of a treasure chest after the battle of Alesia all those years ago). And what of his first wife? The news of his death would be the gift that would keep on giving for her, Oppius wryly – and somewhat unfairly – considered.

For all of the recent torment of his grief and anger the centurion felt strangely at peace for once. He recalled Roscius' comment about the afterlife and smiled to himself. "As long as there will be women and wine there, what is there to worry about?" Lucius

Oppius doubted whether he could consider himself a good man. He had been a good soldier though. Unfortunately the two roles were not always one and the same. A shard of sorrow here sowed itself into the sense of peace, finality, he was feeling. In some ways he already felt dead to the world.

The trumpets, sounding the order for Labienus to attack, suddenly brought the centurion back to the land of the living.

10.

The ears of many a horse twitched at hearing the trumpets sound – and many a horse scraped their hooves upon the sun-baked ground in anticipation. Labienus kicked the side of his lithe, sweat-stained Spanish colt and led the seven thousand horsemen off. A trot soon turned into a canter, a canter turned into a gallop. War cries were spat up into the air in as many languages as there were colours of horses. The ground soon shook, to the thrum of beating hearts (on both sides). The ranks of archers, who had formed up on the left wing behind the cavalry, fired over the horsemen's heads. But many of the missiles missed their mark – and some even landed in the backs of their comrades from a lack of accuracy or strength from a few of the hungover bowmen.

From the opposite side of the battlefield Caesar's thousand or so horsemen set off too, gaining momentum and showing that they would not be cowed by the larger force. Again the two extensive lines of infantry snaking across the plains were spectators rather than participants in the battle. Mark Antony craned his head to get a better view of the action taking place at the opposing wing of his army but all he could see was an indistinct mass shrouded in a cloud of dust. Indistinct cheers also littered the air and left him no wiser as to what was happening. A part of Antony wished to be at the heart of the fighting, leading the cavalry against Labienus. Yet

Caesar had stated how Antony would be of greater value commanding the left wing of the army, as much as he would have liked him at the head of his cavalry too.

"But even you can't be in two places at once my friend," Caesar had remarked.

"I'm not so sure about that. I recently told the husband of my mistress that I was attending a dinner party, when I was really with his wife," the rakish officer replied.

Antony shook such thoughts from his head however and again concentrated on the enemy in front of him.

Labienus drew his sword and shouted orders over the tamp of hooves to his officers. His blood was up, his thoughts shaping his visage into a snarl. Caesar would finally appreciate his greatness, to his profound cost. Once he had destroyed the enemy's right wing he would then drive Mark Antony into the Enipeus – and he would drown under the weight of his self-importance and depravity, Labienus thought to himself.

A mass of men and horses slammed into each other, a bloody mesh. A cacophony of sounds reverberated east and west and echoed up to the heavens: clangs, grunts, curses, wails of agony, the sound of horses being winded and cut. Men hacked, sliced and clubbed each other, fighting for their lives rather than respective causes. Casualties fell, or half fell, from their gore-splattered mounts. Horses buckled as they stepped upon blood strewn corpses.

For a time Caesar's forces matched their foes but the sheer weight of numbers soon began to tell. Caesar ordered a number of his light infantry to help bolster his cavalry, but refrained from committing too many troops. Believing the bulk of Caesar's cavalry to be at worst contained – and at best doomed to defeat already – Labienus instigated the second stage of his offensive and ordered his contingents of Gallic and German horsemen to separate themselves from the melee and attack the right flank and rear of Caesar's infantry.

Pompey looked on with satisfaction as he watched Labienus gather half his forces to move on to engage the right flank of Caesar's infantry, as Marcus Petreius was left to command the other half. His battle plan was working. The years appeared to fall from Pompey's round, aged countenance as a gleam of triumph began to form in his features. The light in his eyes was not dissimilar to that of when he had been the "Young Butcher".

Trumpets now sounded upon Caesar's side and Pompey expected his old friend to launch the last throw of the dice. His lines of infantry would attack. But the trumpets sounded out a different order.

The reserve troops, mostly veterans from Caesar's Tenth legion, appeared from over the reverse slope on the battlefield. They quickly formed rank, springing up from the ground like a force from Hades, at such an angle that Labienus was no longer able to outflank Caesar's right wing. Indeed, although the number of cavalry still outnumbered the infantry forces, Labienus and his horsemen felt like they had been led into a trap, ambush. But still their momentum carried them forward – onto the tips of their enemies' spears. This manoeuvre and ruse by Caesar had not been foreseen by Pompey – and there was nothing in the plan to counter its impact.

Oppius bellowed out an order to advance (he also instructed Teucer to start picking off any capable looking officers who could rally the enemy). The legionaries had been briefed beforehand not to employ their pila as missiles – but rather to jab their spears into the faces of the men and horses, as they moved into close quarters with Pompey's cavalry.

Carnage ensued. The wheat plains of Pharsalus increasingly resembled a charnel house. Oppius was akin to a woodsman, cutting a path through a forest. He fought like a man possessed. Every scream of pain, or each time he silenced an enemy, was a small victory which brought him closer to facing Laco. Like Crastinus he was at the vanguard of the fighting and just when it seemed like he might be overreaching himself, or he was hemmed in, Roscius would appear at his shoulder or an arrow from Teucer's bow would fell an opponent. The men around the centurion fed off his small victories too. The smell of blood, death, was as welcome and intoxicating as acetum for some. Whereas weight of numbers had won Pompey's cavalry its first victory, experience now triumphed as the hardened mettle of Caesar's famed Tenth's legion yielded not.

Screams curdled the air as faces were sliced and skewered. Blood spat, oozed and wept from eye sockets. Horses threw their riders. Further chaos reigned as the rear ranks of Pompey's cavalry crushed the forward ranks, further pushing them towards the brutal legionaries. The momentum of Pompey's charge was not only halted, but soon reversed. Whereas Caesar's veterans fought for each other, almost as one man, Pompey's horsemen (filled with mercenaries and young officers) soon considered it was every man for himself and broke ranks to retreat, riding away in the opposite direction to the fighting. Whether his intention was to rally his troops, or whether he felt the cold chill of defeat run down his spine, Labienus disengaged and pursued his comrades.

A sense of defeat grew contagious as Oppius and his fellow centurions led the veterans onwards to engage with the other half of Pompey's cavalry, led by Marcus Petreius; witnessing their comrades retreat from the battle only spurred them on to do so too as the Tenth commenced to scythe through their ranks.

Observing how the tide was turning in his favour Caesar gave the order for the rest of his army to engage the enemy. The trumpets sounded once more.

11.

The order was given for the front two ranks of Caesar's infantry to advance. Their sweat-glazed countenances were soon scrunched up in determination and malice. Many were battle hardened veterans who had fought – and triumphed – on the shores of Britannia and plains of Gaul. Caesar briefly wondered how Antony and Sulla (who commanded the centre of his army) would fare in their commands, but then thought how it would likely be that the centurions and veterans would lead their commanders on. Over the years his veterans had been called many things – animals, barbarians, butchers. They had fought, fucked and drunk their way across a continent and back. Even Caesar had remarked that his army was composed of the scum of the earth – but yet there had been a pride and fondness in his tone.

Marcus Brutus tightened his grip on his gladius. The sounds of the skirmishing cavalry to his left faded into the background. Two ranks marched towards a force of ten. Was it bravery or folly? They would impact on their shield wall like a wave crashing against a cliff face. Or so he hoped. Some of his men, or rather more accurately some of the boys, shuffled their feet nervously around him. They licked their dry lips and wiped the sweat (or in a few cases the tears) from their faces.

The order was given for Caesar's infantry to charge - their war cries and curses painting the blue sky even bluer. Yet Pompey's legions remained stationary in their shield wall. Caesar's eyes widened in surprise and then narrowed with alarm. Should his legionaries continue to race towards the enemy, with Pompey's lines not meeting them half way, they would be breathless by the time they engaged them.

Pompey drew a breath, daring to hope that the unorthodox plan would work. The tactic had originated from Gaius Triarius, a naval officer. By having the enemy run twice the distance expected, Pompey hoped that they would be twice as fatigued – and he would blunt the edge of Caesar's initial attack. Should the plan work then Pompey would re-write history so as to take credit for its success, he determined. And it would work. Caesar could not and did not have the time to alter his orders, the commander judged.

But Caesar did not need to adjust his orders. Such was the experience of his troops – and Caesar's philosophy of having his officers and veterans act on their own authority – his lines of infantry slowed to a halt.

Pompey the Great's sigh dissolved into the soughing breeze.

Caesar sighed with relief.

In the same way that Caesar's legions instinctively cut off their offensive as one they regained their breath and shape, before advancing again unison. They marched and charged once again and, once in optimum range, the veterans opened up their bodies whilst running and launched their pila. A shower of spears rained over Pompey's stationary lines. Men fell, injured or dead. Orders were given for Pompey's troops to launch their own volley of spears but their aim lacked accuracy and power. Before they could fully re-group Caesar's veterans were upon them. The momentum of the charge immediately pushed the front ranks backwards. Swords crashed down on shields, or slid between them. Brutus was not the only soldier to fight back against the initial reverse. He swam against the stream and rallied his men in the line to do so too. The noise was deafening and disorientating. Shields butted against each other and swords stabbed forward relentlessly. The tang of blood – and a mood of attrition – started to stain the air as the opposing shield walls fought over every inch of ground.

The remnants of the cavalry had been routed. Oppius and the seasoned soldiers of the Tenth legion now faced the ranks of Pompey's archers and slingers. Shields were raised and many of the veterans clustered together forming testudos. They swiftly closed in on their enemies, nullifying their ability to utilise their slings and bows. The opposition from the slingers in particular melted like snow. The archers – many of them mercenaries from Crete and Syria – drew their short swords but those that didn't retreat were cut down.

"Not even the Gauls routed quicker than this," Teucer breathlessly remarked to Roscius with a grin as he retrieved a couple of arrows from a corpse.

"It's not over yet," the begrimed legionary replied, as he took in the shield walls contending with each other. Pompey's First legion appeared to be pushing Caesar's right wing back. They were veterans too, with greater reserves of men.

"But it soon will be," a strong and confident voice called out. Caesar drew his horse to a halt. "Oppius, Pompey's cavalry and archers are half way to Athens, or Hades. His left wing is now more exposed than a harlot's breast. Take the Tenth and wrap yourself around its flank and rear. Squeeze the head of the serpent and the life will go out of the rest of its body. I'll provide what reserves I can spare you and commit our remaining ranks to engage the rest of Pompey's line."

"Yes, Caesar," Oppius replied. The centurion had only just sheathed his sword, but he withdrew it again.

"And don't go getting yourself killed. Even with my renowned clemency, I could never forgive myself if you didn't last the day."

Before Oppius could reply Caesar kicked the flank of his charger and rode back to his reserves to give the order to attack. If his two ranks of infantry could create a stalemate against Pompey's ten, then perhaps his remaining troops could tip the balance. Caesar thought again of Oppius though, knowing how crucial his offensive would be. If he could rout the First legion, Pompey's finest soldiers, then the rest would follow.

"Lucius, win me this battle," the commander whispered under his breath. If some considered Caesar a god, then the god was now praying.

But Lucius Oppius was little concerned about winning a battle. He just wanted to find and kill one man – and then his war would be over.

12.

Age and anxiety crept back into Pompey's features. He watched Caesar's red cloak billow in the wind as he rode back to his lines. No doubt he had just given orders for the Tenth legion, which had defeated his cavalry and ranks of archers, to attack his exposed left flank and rear. No doubt he would also be ordering his final reserves to support the two ranks of infantry which were contending with his ten. Pompey's left wing, the First legion, needed to hold, however, else all would be lost.

"Laco, Caesar will attack our left flank. Quickly muster what reserves you can and make sure that you hold the line. Not one step back. Kill anyone who tries to retreat, to make an example of them. Also, I have a suspicion that it is your friend Oppius commanding the opposing force. Kill him too."

Antony had dismounted and joined the melee. His large cavalry sword crushed shields and collar bones alike. He rallied the legionaries around him, promising them that the enemy's resolve would soon break. Yet he watched his own ranks thinning – and feared that his lines could break. Pompey's forces would gush through like water through a breached dam and cover the entire plain. He prayed for Caesar to send in his final reserves to support the offensive. The next throw of the dice was the only throw he had left.

Antony stamped down on the gladius attempting to stab his shin. He roared as he then thrust the point of his sword through his enemy's battered shield and into his chest. The enemy soldier slumped to the ground but his place in the shield wall was soon filled by another legionary, using his scutum to push Antony back and jabbing his rusty gladius forward as if his life depended on it (which it did).

The fighting was relentless and Antony possessed few reserves to rotate the front rank. His arms and shoulders ached, as if he had been Hercules battling the Nemean lion and Cerberus. A sudden surge from the enemy pushed him back and he fell to the ground, tripping over a fallen comrade behind him. He opened his eyes to find two combatants above him, each ready to finish off the enemy commander. They grinned toothily. The smiles were wiped off their faces though as Domitius Enobarbus launched himself at both men and knocked them to the ground. He immediately slit the throat of one and wrestled with the other. Yet, as if they were battling the Hydra, two more enemy soldiers appeared above him. Antony raised his shield and sword but he also then closed his eyes – readying himself for the ferryman.

But his prayers were answered. A brace of javelins skewered the soldiers over the commander. Antony felt the ground shake beneath his back as Caesar's reserves charged towards the frontline.

Oppius stood at the head of the Tenth. The legion had wheeled around to engage the First legion's flank. Laco had called for those who still possessed javelins to target the centurion, once he came into range. Two spears arced towards him at the same time. The first struck his raised shield but the second flew low. The razor sharp head of the javelin sliced through his thigh. Oppius let out a curse and winced in pain. His leg was soon awash with blood. As a young legionary applied a make-shift field dressing the centurion called out the order to attack. A volley of spears was followed up by the veterans drawing their swords and charging. The rear ranks of the legion wheeled around further and attacked Pompey's left wing from behind. A fresh wave of curses, clangs and screams erupted on the battlefield. Caesar's men made more noise – and more kills.

The first to flee were the foreign auxiliaries. The raw recruits, following the example of the young aristocratic officers, soon looked to retreat too. Flavius Laco attempted to rally his comrades – and he killed a couple of soldiers looking to escape past him – but the dam had burst.

Pompey took some consolation from his decision to order his son to remain back at the camp, rather than give in to his request to fight on the frontline. At least he would be safe. He then cursed Cato underneath his breath. The influential senator had been behind the campaign to give battle, rather than stave Caesar's army and decimate his forces that way. As a result of Cato's efforts to undermine him he had ordered the ever-complaining stoic to take charge of the supply depot in Apollonia. Cicero had half-jokingly suggested that he could be trusted to hold the keys to the grain stores, but not the wine cellar. He regretted not having posted Cato on the frontline for the battle, to reap what he had sown.

The retreat would soon grow into a rout. He had never tasted defeat before. He felt physically sick. Pompey wordlessly turned his horse around and galloped back to camp, his army disintegrating around him.

Mark Antony mounted his horse and urged the reserve forces on to finish off the enemy. Dead soldiers can't re-group, he thought to himself. Some looked to be retreating back to their camp. Some were trying to escape by swimming across the Enipeus. Rats leaving a sinking ship.

The veterans of Pompey's First legion fought on bravely, but in vain. There were shield lines contesting the ground still but also individual soldiers fought each other. The remnants of Caesar's cavalry rode on, mowing down retreating legionaries. Chaos and carnage still swept across the plains like the clouds of dust being kicked up.

Oppius walked gingerly on. Heat, fatigue and his wound sapped his strength but still the centurion moved forward, squinting in the sunlight as he scanned the battlefield, searching for Laco. But Laco had found him first. His arm was drenched in blood from where he had buried the blade of his gladius into an enemy's stomach. Pompey's agent was aware that the battle was lost, but they could still win the war – regroup and counter-attack. Laco also determined that he would gain the small victory of killing Caesar's talismanic centurion. He wouldn't just blunt, he would break the "Sword of Rome," (the title that the people had given Oppius whilst he fought as a gladiator – as Caesar's champion).

Laco raised his gladius and pointed it at the centurion, blood dripping from the blade. The two men walked towards each other, or rather Oppius limped on. A brace of legionaries confronted Laco but he despatched them quickly. He slashed the face of one and ended his high-pitched screams by stabbing him in the neck. The second was floored from the former gladiator kicking his opponent's shield. Laco put his foot upon the prostrate soldier's throat and slowly plunged his sword into his victim's sternum. Laco watched his body writhe and then stop moving, taking in the sight with the coldness and curiosity of a scientist.

The two men stopped before fully closing in on each other. They stood ten yards apart. Laco glanced down at the blood-soaked dressing on the centurion's leg and grinned, wolfishly. Oppius had been plagued by doubts in regards to his ability to defeat Laco, but given his wound the improbable had now become the impossible. He could barely stand. Yet he would stand, rather than retreat.

"This'll be more like putting down a wounded animal, than a contest," Laco exclaimed, clearing his throat and spitting out a clump of phlegm.

"Did you bait the sword when you fought my father?" Oppius replied, his voice devoid of emotion – but his heart brimming with it.

"Ha! Is that what's been eating you up? You'll soon have an answer to your question, as you can ask your father yourself when you meet him in the afterlife."

Oppius' body tensed up in hatred – and his injured leg erupted in pain, giving way. The soldier sank to one knee and nearly lost consciousness.

"I'd feel sorry for you Oppius, if I was capable of pity. You must know that you can't beat me."

Blood trickled down his leg. His face was ashen. The centurion closed his eyes. Darkness smothered him, like a shroud. His inward eye pictured his father and Marcus Fabius. Oppius' eyes suddenly snapped back open though and, digging his sword in the ground for support, he rose to his feet.

"I know. *I* can't beat you. But we can," the soldier replied, grinning wolfishly back. Oppius' eyes darted either side of Laco. He wanted the sadist to see his end, before meeting it. Roscius and Teucer stood ten yards either side of their enemy. As Laco turned to take in Roscius, holding a javelin aloft, Teucer let loose his arrow and it buried itself into his left ribs. Laco spat out a curse and convulsed in pain. No sooner did he fall to his knees than Roscius plunged his pilum into Laco's thigh.

Pompey's agent spat out several other curses in between seething in agony. Oppius limped slowly towards him, offering a solemn smile and nod of thanks to his two friends. But then the soldier bent down so that he was an inch away from his antagonist's face.

"You can't beat us," Oppius calmly remarked, before thrusting his sword up through Laco's chin and out the top of his head.

13.

The dry heat felt even more oppressive. A dejected Pompey had returned to camp. He sat, alone, in his tent having dismissed all his attendants and staff officers. Pharsalus had been his first real failure in battle as a commander. Unfortunately Pharsalus had also been his most crucial battle in regards to the fate of himself and that of Rome. He downed another cup of wine, but it couldn't wash away the bitter taste of defeat. He felt nauseous, bile sticking in his throat. In his mind he blamed everyone for the tragedy (Cato, Metellus, Labienus and even Laco), except himself. Could he still re-group and counter-attack? Or he could venture east – where he still possessed wealth and allies – and raise another army. His dejection overshadowed any rays of hope he could muster, however. Tears welled in Pompey's tired eyes as he thought again how much his life – and the world – would have been different if Julia were still alive.

A loyal young officer, Marcus Favonius, entered the chamber. Pompey lowered his gaze so the soldier could not see the tears in his eyes.

"General, the enemy are attacking the camp already. You must leave."

The day, Rome, was Caesar's. At least he had sent his son Gnaeus away, as soon as he had returned from the battlefield. At least things could not get any worse. And he was still Pompey the Great. "Don't lose your head," he said out loud, either to Favonius or himself. Pompey rose to his feet and, with a handful of loyal supporters, he arranged his escape. Firstly Favonius and Pompey's secretary, Philip, removed Pompey's insignia and distinctive cloak. They quickly then made their way to the rear of the camp, before Caesar's troops could surround Pompey's headquarters completely, and rode northwards towards the town of Larisa.

"I blame Cato," the melancholy commander repeatedly muttered underneath his breath, like a mantra.

Teucer cleaned and then stitched up his centurion's wound. Oppius barely registered the pain as he watched the dust trails in the distance and heard the cheers as Caesar's forces breached the enemy's camp. He winced, but not in pain, as the putrid smell of death festered in the air. Flies buzzed around eviscerated corpses and birds circled overhead, eyeing the prospective feast. The dead appeared to outnumber the living.

Oppius shook his head either at the piteous sight or in disbelief that Caesar had won the battle (or, indeed, had won the war). Yet this triumph felt different, even more sombre. Too many Romans had died, on both sides. Spears jutted out of the side of boy-soldiers. Clumps of flesh, fingers and limbs littered the plains. A number of wounded legionaries limped around, seeking out the enemy dead and dying. A few may well have been assessing if any needed medical attention, but for the most part the soldiers were looking to relieve Pompey's men of any valuables they might have in their possession – spoils of war. They were no better than vultures. Part of him wanted to offer up a prayer for the fallen, but the sights before him shook any faith he might have had in the gods.

Caesar dismounted and stood next to his officer, pensively taking in the same haunting scene.

"Next to a battle lost, the greatest misery is that of a battle gained," Caesar remarked with genuine sorrow.

Oppius merely nodded. The thousands of silenced voices in view spoke for him.

There had been times when Caesar had acted triumphantly, or indifferently, in response to some battles. But not today, the centurion judged.

"Neither I nor Rome will want to be reminded of the events of today. I will honour Crastinus, but I will not glorify this victory in my commentaries or dispatches. But tell me a little of your commentary upon the battle Lucius. Did you find Laco and win your own personal war?"

Again Oppius nodded in reply. Caesar clasped his officer upon the shoulder.

"I'm pleased. You must now no longer allow Laco or your father to cast a shadow over your life. Caesar will of course, however, continue to cast a shadow over you. We still have work to do, but this war is largely won. We have broken the back of our enemy. He shall not stand again. No doubt the likes of Cato will look to resist still but we have just bested Agamemnon. Besting Nestor shouldn't prove too much trouble. You have served Caesar well and, should you have a wish that is within my power, I shall grant it to you Lucius."

Oppius nodded once more, unable to muster the energy or enthusiasm to desire anything – that was in Caesar's power. Only the gods could bring back his father and Marcus Fabius. But the soldier had too much blood on his hands to expect his prayers to be answered.

"There are few men in this world I trust more. You consider honour to be more than just a word Lucius. The war may be won but it is perhaps because of, rather than in spite of, this fact that those close to me might be vulnerable. Do you know of my great nephew, Octavius?"

Epilogue

Caesar's forces plundered Pompey's camp. The republican army, both officers and common soldiers, were scattered to the four winds. Caesar made sure to secure the road to Larisa quickly to prevent any of the enemy from joining up with its commander. The following morning the remnants of Pompey's army laid down their weapons at Caesar's feet, surrendered and joined the ranks of their former opponent's forces.

One of the first orders the commander gave after the fighting ceased was to arrange for special funeral rites and a tomb to honour Crastinus.

That evening Caesar donned a toga, as opposed to a breastplate, for the first time in a long time. A burden had been lifted. He ate well, knowing that his legions were being fed well too. He also regained his sexual appetite and took one of Antony's mistresses to bed, explaining to her that Antony had but been a dress rehearsal for the main performance. Perhaps one day Antony would take one of his former mistresses as a lover, Caesar mused, and his lieutenant would make the same comment.

Brutus surrendered the next day. His body was still caked with dust and blood. As he stood before his enemy Brutus felt a mixture of shame and resentment. Caesar, still wearing his pristine white toga, warmly embraced the nobleman. A part of Brutus desired to draw his dagger and do what Pompey the Great and forty thousand men couldn't do – defeat Caesar and preserve the Republic. Yet Brutus found himself embracing his enemy – friend – back. Caesar had won the war; he would give him the opportunity to win the peace too. "Just as long as he wants to be consul, rather than king," Brutus remarked to Cicero later in the evening.

Cicero too was shown clemency – and Caesar invited him to dinner. Winning over the statesman's sympathy and support was worth more than wining over any of Pompey's legions he considered.

"We are both keen students of History, Cicero, but let us look to the future, together, rather than dwell upon the blood-stained past... Some people compare me to Gracchus, or Sulla. But I am neither. Caesar must be Caesar... This civil war reaches back further to when I crossed the Rubicon, we both know that. Rome has been divided for decades. Like you my aim is to bring harmony to the classes."

Cicero was tempted to cynically and satirically reply that, due to his ears still ringing from the battle, it might be difficult to hear such harmony – should it occur. But the philosopher was too tired to argue and was willing to give Caesar the benefit of his many doubts, for now.

Dawn. The tufts of cloud on the horizon were ringed with light. The three soldiers could not tell whether the sight augured a sunny day or impending storm. Oppius, Roscius and Teucer had never known an army camp to be so quiet. Sleep, like wine, was a balm.

The favour that Oppius asked of Caesar was not for himself, but for his friend. Teucer wished to be granted a discharge in order to return to his homeland. Caesar reluctantly agreed. He didn't wish to lose the archer, but Caesar kept his word in order not to lose the loyalty of his centurion. Pharsalus had been one battle too many. The Briton told his officer how he wanted to visit his tribe again – to honour his father's wish and lead it. He wanted something to live for, or even die for. Rome wasn't it. When Roscius asked why the Briton wanted to go back home he wryly replied that, "I miss my country's weather and cuisine. The question is though my friend, will you miss me?"

"Well not quite as much as the hundreds of aged whores across the peninsula will, but yes."

"I shall miss your bow Teucer. I may have to start practising again with the thing myself, to make up for your loss," Oppius remarked, half joking and half in earnest.

"Well the harder you practise the luckier you get."

"I'll also miss your jokes. Well, some of them," the centurion said, his face breaking out into a rare smile.

"And in return I'll miss your orders. Well, some of them."

The three friends laughed. They had shared so much over the years, but so much remained unsaid during their farewells. They were soldiers, not garrulous politicians.

Teucer mounted his horse. His saddlebag clinked from the gold coins that both Caesar and Oppius had gifted him. The sun began to melt the clouds on the horizon. Perhaps the storm would abate, for now.

"Safe journey my friend," the centurion said whilst reaching up and clasping the Briton's forearm in a Roman handshake.

"Keep safe too."

"I'm not sure if I'll have any choice. I'll soon be playing wet nurse to Caesar's great nephew. The only danger I'll be in is through dying of boredom."

"We'll see. You never know, guarding the boy may turn out to be quite eventful."

"Aye, maybe," Oppius replied, thinking how the young Octavius was, after all, a Caesar. And a Caesar must be a Caesar.

End Note

Since the release of *Augustus: Son of Rome* I have received a number of letters asking about when the follow-up will be published. The reply has been "not yet". I fear that the reply may remain "not yet" for some time, due to other commitments. I hope that the *Sword of Rome* series will provide some compensation though in the form of a prequel, as opposed to sequel. For those of you who have read the series without having first read *Augustus: Son of Rome* you may be interested to know that the characters of Oppius, Roscius, Tiro Casca and Julius Caesar all feature heavily throughout *Augustus: Son of Rome* too.

Should you be interested in some further reading then I can recommend the works of Adrian Goldsworthy, particularly his biography of Julius Caesar and also *In The Name Of Rome*. The works of Cicero, Suetonius and Plutarch are classics for good reasons too. If interested in reading more historical fiction on Rome then I can recommend Conn Iggulden, Steven Saylor, Simon Scarrow and Robert Harris.

Perhaps no book can do true justice to describe the events of the battle of Alesia but I hope that what you have just read has given you a taster of its significance, both in terms of Caesar's career and also as a feat of arms. It may be considered Caesar's finest hour as a general - and Rome's Rorke's Drift. Should you be interested in reading more about Caesar and the campaign I can recommend the works of Adrian Goldsworthy, most notably his biography of Caesar and the relevant chapters of *In The Name of Rome*.

For the most part I like to think I have remained true to the spirit and facts of the real history behind *Sword of Rome: Gladiator*. However, I have perhaps been a bit unfair and used dramatic licence in my portrait of Cato in this book. To redress the balance I can recommend reading Plutarch's *Life of Cato* (indeed it would be remiss of me not to recommend reading the whole of Plutarch). *Rome's Last Citizen* by Rob Goodman & Jimmy Soni may also be of interest. Should you be interested in reading more about gladiators then Philip Matyszak's *Gladiator: The Roman Fighter's Manual* is a fun and fact-laden starting place (it also provides a list of further reading at the back).

For those readers familiar with the events leading up to Caesar's crossing of the Rubicon I apologise for conflating and re-writing history, but it's the prerogative of the novelist to make things up. For those readers spurred on to learn more about the era then I can recommend the following books: *Rubicon*, by Tom Holland; *Rome's Last Citizen*, by Robert Goodman & Jimmy Soni; *Caesar*, by Adrian Goldsworthy. Should you be interested in reading more fiction then I can recommend the novels of Conn Iggulden and Steven Saylor. Even more so though I would urge you, for both the entertainment and educational value, to read the works of Plutarch, Suetonius and Cicero should you wish to get to grips with the events and great figures of the period. The poem included in chapter 7 is 'The Waggon of Life' by Alexander Pushkin.

Some of you may well have noticed a number of historical nods to the battle of Waterloo in *Sword of Rome: Pharsalus*. I partly inserted them for their general resonance but I also wanted to highlight how, in some ways, Pharsalus was Caesar's Waterloo. Although I could have continued the story to take in the death of Pompey and Caesar's campaign in Egypt I thought it fitting that I should sheath, so to speak, the *Sword of Rome* series here.

Sword of Rome: *Pharsalus* is a work of fiction. Although based upon historical sources there are numerous occasions in the book where I altered the chronology of the battle, as well as just made stuff up. I hope however that there has been enough good history and/or fiction in the story for you to want to read more about the battle or the life and campaigns of Caesar. If so I can recommend the works of Adrian Goldsworthy, as well as Christian Meier's biography of Caesar. The works of Cicero, Plutarch and Suetonius also served as sources of information and inspiration whilst writing the *Sword of Rome* series. You may also be interested in reading *Augustus*: *Son of Rome*, a novel which features the characters of Lucius Oppius and Roscius.

Please note that the *Sword of Rome* series is a work of fiction rather than history and contains deliberate – and unwitting – errors in regards to historical accuracy.

I have thoroughly enjoyed writing the *Sword of Rome* novellas - partly because of the responses I have received from a variety of readers saying how much they have enjoyed them too. Please do get in touch should you wish to write to me about the *Sword of Rome* books (or the *Raffles* series, or the novel *Warsaw*). I'd be particularly interested to hear your thoughts in regards *Augustus: Son of Caesar*, should you have read its predecessor. Your comments are appreciated and I will duly reply to any relevant mail.

I can be reached via richard@endeavourpress.com @rforemanauthor on twitter or through richardforemanauthor.com

Richard Foreman.